Web Style Guide
3rd edition

Web Style Guide
Basic Design Principles for Creating Web Sites
3rd edition

Patrick J. Lynch
Yale University

Sarah Horton
Dartmouth College

Yale University Press
New Haven & London

Designed by Sarah Horton.
Original artwork and photographs by Patrick J. Lynch.
Illustrations by Patrick J. Lynch and Sarah Horton.
Set in Goudy and Myriad type by Sarah Horton.
Printed in the United States of America by Courier, Kendallville in Kendallville,
Indiana.

See Illustration Credits for URLS and copyright information for web site images.

Library of Congress
Cataloging-in-Publication Data
Lynch, Patrick J., 1953–
     Web style guide : basic design principles for creating web sites /
     Patrick J. Lynch, Sarah Horton ; foreword by Peter Morville. — 3rd ed.
     p.   cm.
     Includes bibliographical references and index.
     ISBN 978-0-300-13737-8 (paperbound : alk. paper)
     1. Web sites—Design. I. Horton, Sarah, 1962– II. Title.
TK5105.888.L96 2008
006.7—dc22   2008020139

A catalogue record for this book is available from the British Library.

This paper meets the requirements of ANSI/NISO z39.48-1992 (Permanence
of Paper).

10 9 8 7 6 5 4 3 2 1

www.webstyleguide.com

For Susan, Devorah, Alex and Tyler
PL

For my son (sun), Nico
SH

Contents

Foreword   *ix*
Preface to the Third Edition   *xi*
1   Process   1
2   Universal Usability   51
3   Information Architecture   71
4   Interface Design   95
5   Site Structure   121
6   Page Structure   151
7   Page Design   171
8   Typography   205
9   Editorial Style   231
10   Forms and Applications   249
11   Graphics   267
12   Multimedia   301
Abbreviations   315
References   317
Illustration Credits   327
Index   329

Foreword

Once upon a time, there was a pig named Wilbur. What? Did you expect a line on design or a word about the web? Or would you prefer a simile, a figurative yet sincere invocation of kinship with *The Elements of Style* by William Strunk and E. B. White?

It's true, this book has style. And it covers all the elements from css and typography to HTML and the structure of prose. But, if we focus too narrowly on the conjunction and the comma, we may lose sight of the composition.

So let's return to the runt who becomes "some pig" thanks to the writing in *Charlotte's Web*. Wilbur and his spider friend, Charlotte, teach us about loyalty and friendship in a way that touches all readers, young and old.

In similar fashion, *Web Style Guide* delivers value and meaning to seemingly disparate audiences, from the student prodigy who would be webmaster to the grizzled veteran information architect who's been there and organized that.

For the beginner, this book teaches the fundamentals of interface design, information architecture, and usability without unnecessary complexity or jargon. It's the clearest, most practical guide to Web design you'll find.

Experts will savor this book differently. In an age of specialization, we often get stuck in a rut. *Web Style Guide* invites us once again to see the whole and to learn the latest techniques from related disciplines and communities of practice.

But this book is more than a manual. It speaks not only to what we do but why. Patrick Lynch and Sarah Horton inspire us to strive for universal usability. And because not everyone can enjoy the beautiful images and typography of the printed work, the authors walk the talk by sharing an accessible version of *Web Style Guide* online, for free.

After all, concern for people lies at the heart of design. We lift ourselves up by helping others. As Charlotte explained to Wilbur at the end of her story, "I wove my webs for you because I liked you." Isn't that our story, too?
—Peter Morville

Preface to the Third Edition

We have come a long way—*Web Style Guide* and the World Wide Web. The first version of *Web Style Guide* was a web site called the Yale C/AIM Web Style Guide posted in 1993, just as the world outside computing and academia began to notice the new medium and the Internet in general. The early web was sorely lacking in aesthetics but exploding with potential. *Web Style Guide* provided much-needed guidance on structure and design based on several decades' worth of experience with print, hypermedia, and multimedia design and authoring.

In 1997 we updated the *Web Style Guide* site to reflect the maturing design trends and changes in web technology. In the web a novel landscape opened up, like a new continent rising from the sea, ready for explorers and builders. People from the arts, publishing, and dozens of computing disciplines poured in, enriching the web and pushing out the boundaries of what might be possible while bringing the wealth of centuries of media and design culture along with them. The web changed to accommodate these new settlers, whose expectations for what could be achieved in the web environment often outstripped its capabilities. This was a time of significant progress in visual design and interface sophistication, but at the cost of standardization and accessibility.

In 1999 we produced the first print edition of *Web Style Guide*. The web site had gained a significant following as more and more organizations turned to the web as their primary means of communication. People with little or no background in design were assigned the responsibility for web site development, and they looked to *Web Style Guide* for calm, reassuring, and practical guidance. For many, the slim and straightforward *Web Style Guide* was a welcome relief from the esoteric, hyperactive, and voluminous books that lined the shelves in the Web Design section of their bookstores.

Since its inception as a web site in 1993 and into this third edition, *Web Style Guide* has presented solid design advice based on classic design principles, acknowledging the possibilities and limitations of current web technology while trying not to let the media confetti overwhelm good sense and an information-oriented aesthetic. Thanks to enormous advances in HTML, Cascading Style Sheets, and the "web standards" philosophy for building sites, this edition does not contain sections on cross-platform issues or special techniques for making web sites accessible to people with disabilities. Given where we are with web technology, we can finally concentrate on good design and content, knowing that we have the tools on hand to make the web a friendlier, more efficient, and more productive place to read and work.

In this third edition of *Web Style Guide*, and the nineteenth year of the World Wide Web, we celebrate how far we've come and how much we can do to make the web accessible to and usable by everyone.

IN ADDITION TO ALL THOSE who contributed to the first two editions of *Web Style Guide* and whom we acknowledge in our earlier prefaces, we thank Jean Thomson Black, Laura Jones Dooley, Matthew Laird, Christina Coffin, James Johnson, and Aldo Cupo at Yale University Press for their hard work and guidance in producing this third edition. We are particularly grateful to Peter Morville for his foreword.

I extend heartfelt thanks to my friends and my colleagues at Yale University for their support over the years—I could not have done this without them: David Bolinsky, Roger Despres, Frank Gallo, Carmine Granucci, Sean Jackson, Carl Jaffe, Janet Jeddry, Chris Kielt, Jane Livingston, Philip Long, Andy Newman, Kimberly Pasko, John Paton, Noble Proctor, Stacy Ruwe, Phillip Simon, Virginia Simon, and Victor Velt. In particular, I thank Carl Jaffe for over twenty years of generous friendship and wise counsel. Much of Carl's wisdom and insight appears on these pages. I also thank my coauthor and dear friend Sarah Horton for her enduring commitment to this enterprise, and for her efforts in making the web more accessible to everyone.

Without family, none of this would have meaning. For her unfailing love, support, and generosity of spirit, I thank the wisest woman I know, Susan Grajek. For their love, support, and no small amount of advice now that they know much of the 'Net better than I do: Devorah Lynch, Alex Wack, and Tyler Wack.

—PL

First and foremost, I thank my coauthor, Patrick Lynch. I am indebted to Pat for his unfailing support and confidence throughout my professional career. He is an amazing mentor, an inspiring artist, and the very best of friends. I would not be where I am today if I had not been taken in by Pat and the other great and talented people (especially Carl Jaffe and Phillip Simon) at the then Yale Center for Advanced Instructional Media.

Dartmouth College has also been instrumental in this endeavor by providing me with the context and encouragement to practice and refine the methods and techniques laid out in this book. I am grateful for the support and inspiration of my friends, colleagues, and mentors: Rick Adams, Malcolm Brown, Dave Bucciero, Sheila Culbert, Joe Doucet, Alan German, Karen Gocsik, Martin Grant, Tim Hozier, Brian Hughes, Ellen Kanner, Barbara Knauff, Joe Mehling, Rita Murdoch, Mike Murray, Mark O'Neil, Marie Stebbins, Ellen Waite-Franzen, and Susan Warner.

And finally, my deepest thanks to my guys: Malcolm, for always lighting the home fires, and Nico, for keeping them burning bright.

—SH

It didn't take long for the commercial Web's pioneers to learn that the slogan "If you build it, they will come" was a hollow joke: You have to build it well, thoughtfully and ambitiously and inventively, and then you have to keep rethinking it and rebuilding it, if you have any hope of attracting a crowd.

—Scott Rosenberg, Salon.com

CHAPTER 1

Process

The first step in designing any web site is to define your goals. Without a clearly stated mission and objectives, the project will drift, bog down, or continue past an appropriate endpoint. Careful planning and a clear purpose are the keys to success in building web sites, particularly when you are working as part of a development team.

Planning a web site is a two-part process: first you gather your development team, analyze your needs and goals, and work through the development process outlined here to refine your plans. Next you create a project charter document that details what you intend to do and why, what technology and content you'll need, how long the process will take, what you will spend to do it, and how you will assess the results of your efforts. The project charter document is crucial to creating a successful site: it is both the blueprint for your process and the touchstone you'll use to keep the project focused on the agreed-on goals and deliverables.

THE SITE DEVELOPMENT TEAM

The strategic importance and project budget for your web efforts will largely determine the size and skill depth of your web site development team. Even for a smaller project, however, you'll need to cover the core team disciplines. In most small to medium projects one person may handle multiple tasks or someone with specialized expertise (graphic design, for instance) is hired for specific assignments. Many managers who are assigned the responsibility of creating a web site don't have the luxury of picking specialist team members. Inventory the skills and aptitudes in the team you assemble, and consider careful outsourcing to supply any expertise your team lacks.

The core skill sets needed in a web site development team are:

- Strategy and planning
- Project management
- Information architecture and user interface design

- Graphic design for the web
- Web technology
- Site production

In larger web projects each role may be filled by a separate person, although in more specialized skill areas those contributors are not likely to be full-time team members for the duration of the project.

WEB TEAM ROLES AND RESPONSIBILITIES

Core web team roles and extended secondary team roles in larger web projects are:

- Project stakeholder or sponsor
- Web project manager
  - Account executive
  - Quality assurance tester
- Usability lead
- Information architect
- Art director
  - Web graphic designer
  - Interactive designer (Flash, JavaScript, Ajax)
  - Media specialist (photography, illustration, audiovisual, Flash)
- Web technology lead
  - Web application programmer (.Net, Java, PHP/Perl, Ruby)
  - Web page engineer (XHTML, CSS, JavaScript, Ajax)
  - Database administrator
  - Web systems expert or webmaster
- Site production lead
  - HTML page coder
- Site editor
  - Site copywriter
  - Content domain expert (content coordination, research)

Project stakeholder or sponsor

The project sponsor or stakeholder is the person or group responsible for initiating the web site project. In most instances the sponsor is the client or customer for the web site development work, but in smaller in-house department projects the sponsoring manager and the web project manager may be the same person. The sponsor provides the overall strategic vision and purpose for the site development project, approves the contract or work plan, is responsible for the budget and project schedule, and provides the resources to support the work of the site development team.

The sponsor is the client the team works to please, but sponsors have critical work to perform as part of the overall site development team. Sponsors act as a liaison to the rest of the sponsoring organization, provide critical domain expertise, coordinate with the larger goals of the sponsoring organization, and deliver site content and domain expertise to the project. As such, it is critical that sponsors and other stakeholders understand their responsibilities to the web team: late delivery of web site content is the most common cause of blown schedules in web development projects. Sponsors also are typically responsible for third-party or external content contracts, other media licensing negotiations, and coordination with other marketing, information technology, and communications efforts at the sponsoring organization or company.

Web project manager

The web project manager coordinates and communicates the day-to-day tactical implementation of the web site project, acting within the constraints of the project charters and goals, project budget, development schedule, and quality objectives laid out in the planning stages. The project manager is the team member ultimately responsible for keeping the overall team activities focused on the site strategic objectives and agreed deliverables, and he or she continually monitors the scope of the project activities to ensure that the team stays "on time and on budget." The project manager acts as the primary contact between the web team and the sponsor and manages the overall communication among creative, technical, and production elements of the web site team. In larger web projects the project manager is not normally part of the hands-on production team, but in smaller in-house projects the sponsor, design lead, or technical lead may also act as the project manager for the site team. Project managers create and maintain the project planning and strategy documents, budget spreadsheets, project schedules and Gantt charts, meeting notes, billing records, and other project documentation that details the team's activities (fig. 1.1).

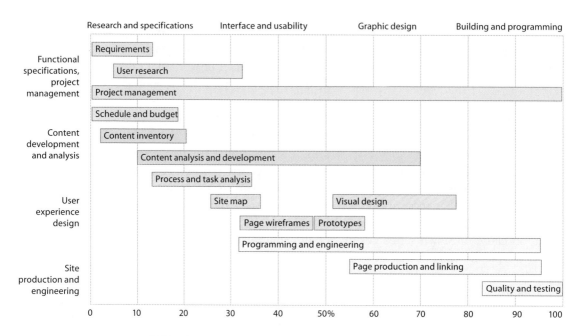

	Research and specifications	Interface and usability	Graphic design	Building and programming

Functional specifications, project management
- Requirements
- User research
- Project management
- Schedule and budget

Content development and analysis
- Content inventory
- Content analysis and development
- Process and task analysis

User experience design
- Site map
- Visual design
- Page wireframes
- Prototypes
- Programming and engineering

Site production and engineering
- Page production and linking
- Quality and testing

0 10 20 30 40 50% 60 70 80 90 100

FIGURE 1.1

Gantt charts are commonly used to keep track of project phases and team responsibilities.

Usability lead

The usability lead's role is to shape the overall user experience. The usability lead works closely with the information architect—in fact, the same individual often fills both information architect and usability roles. As the primary user advocate on the development team, the usability lead has responsibility for user testing, user research and persona development, and universal usability standards for the site project. In the initial stages of design, the usability lead is responsible for running interviews, field studies, and usability tests and for producing personas and scenarios to inform project requirements. Once designs are conceptualized in the form of diagrams, wireframes, and prototypes, the usability lead tests the designs with users and gathers feedback for the site designers and developers. In the final stages of a project, the usability lead evaluates the effectiveness of designs through additional field studies and user testing and ensures that universal usability goals are met. The usability lead is also responsible for evaluating the success of the project (Does the site accomplish the goals? Are users successful and satisfied with the design?) and for measuring project outcomes (Are more users visiting the site? Is the site producing more revenue?).

Information architect

The site information architect organizes and categorizes web site structure and content. The information architect is most active early in the design and planning phases of the project, developing content categorization schemes, consistent site terminology, content structure across the site, and site architecture diagrams that explain the overall site planning to both the sponsor and the web team members. Information architects also work closely with the site designers to craft page "wireframes," the diagrammatic page grids that show how various areas of the page will be used to support site identity, navigation, and page content. Page wireframes form the crucial link between the overall site architecture and what the user sees on each page of the web site, determining how easily a user can find the site's content and features and shaping the user's overall experience. Information architects often have a background in library science, using controlled vocabularies, carefully designed content and navigation nomenclature, and search techniques to help users find relevant content. The primary deliverables from the information architect are usually charts and diagrams: site architecture overviews, page wireframes, and user interaction explanations. These visual representations of the site planning process are crucial to communicating site structure and user experience to both sponsors and other web team members, particularly the back-end technical developers who support the interactive elements of the site. Wireframes in particular are used by the usability lead to test design concepts with users (fig. 1.2).

Art director

The art director's primary responsibility is the overall look and feel for the web site, establishing the site typography, visual interface design, color palette standards, page layout details, and the particulars of how the graphics, photography, illustration, and audiovisual media elements of the site come together to form an integrated whole. As the web has matured over the past decade, many graphic design professionals have become specialists in designing for interactive media for computer screens and are well versed in user interface design, web navigation, and site architecture. In smaller projects an experienced web art director often assumes the information architecture and usability roles in addition to directing the visual design of a site. In the site development and planning stages the art director creates or supervises the creation of increasingly complex design sketches to illustrate the evolv-

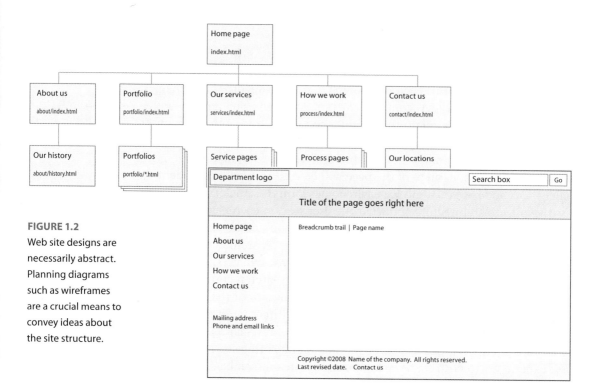

FIGURE 1.2
Web site designs are necessarily abstract. Planning diagrams such as wireframes are a crucial means to convey ideas about the site structure.

ing design proposals to the project sponsor and web team. As designs are approved the art director supervises the conversion of these design sketches into the detailed specifications of graphics and typography that the page engineers will need to create HTML (HyperText Markup Language) page templates (fig. 1.3). In larger organizations the art director is usually the person responsible for assuring that the new web design work is consistent with any established corporate identity and user interface standards.

Web technology lead
The web technology lead must have a broad grasp of web publishing environments, development languages and web development frameworks, web database options, and network technology. The technology lead acts as the bridge, translator, and plain-English communicator between the technologists and the creative and project management elements of the team.

As part of the site planning process the technology lead creates the general blueprints for the collection of technologies that will support the

chosen web site technology framework, including content management, RSS (Really Simple Syndication) or other XML (Extensible Markup Language) content formats, database integration and support, custom web programming, and integration with other applications or databases that supply content or interactive features to the web site. The technology lead provides the primary data-processing architecture for the project, determining the technical specifications for the overall web development framework, assessing the developing strategy and goals, and matching those needs to appropriate technology solutions. In larger projects the web technology lead typically manages teams of programmers, network or server engineers, database administrators, software quality assurance testers, and other information technology professionals that support the production and design teams.

FIGURE 1.3
Wireframes inevitably look boxy, but the final visual designs don't need to be.

Site production lead

Early in the design stage the site production lead is responsible for converting initial web site page mockups, designs, and wireframes into HTML pages. Once the site has been planned and the design and information architecture plans have been completed, the site production lead manages the work of building the site's pages, either directly in "plain" HTML or within a web content management system (CMS) or using web site production software such as Adobe Dreamweaver. In coordination with the site technical team, the site production lead is typically responsible for creating the master page tem-

WEB TEAMS

The well-known information architect and web user interface expert Jesse James Garrett created "The Nine Pillars of Successful Web Teams," a concise graphic description of the core roles in site development (see below). The disciplines and site development stages proceed from left to right in a logical progression from strategic planning to implementation and visual design (www.adaptivepath.com/ideas/essays/archives/000242.php).

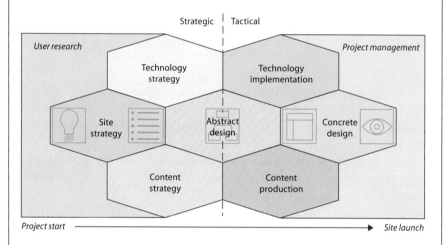

We've taken Garrett's diagram and added a more explicit time dimension and emphasis on the early and continuing role of project management throughout the process of web site development. We also emphasize the importance of getting broad participation and input in the user research and strategic planning stages of your project. The more you hear from stakeholders and potential users, the better your planning and design will be. Early in the process your designs and plans ought to change almost daily, as the iterative tasks of design, user research, and stakeholder input help you refine and improve your ideas. Design iteration is essential in developing the ordered complexity of a large web site.

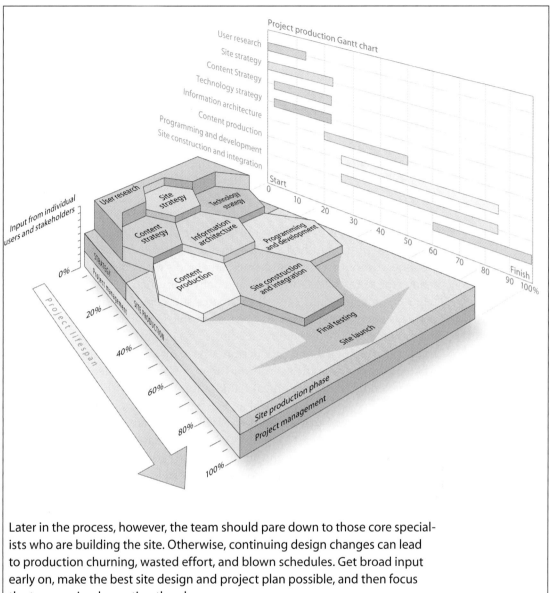

Later in the process, however, the team should pare down to those core specialists who are building the site. Otherwise, continuing design changes can lead to production churning, wasted effort, and blown schedules. Get broad input early on, make the best site design and project plan possible, and then focus the team on implementing the plan.

plates in xhtml (Extensible HyperText Markup Language) and Cascading Style Sheets (css), validating page code, and assembling the work of the information architects and site graphic designers into finished page templates ready to be filled with content. If a cms is used to deliver the finished content, the html/css page templates must be converted into the required format. In larger projects the site production lead usually manages a staff of web designers who fill pages with content, integrating finished text, graphics, and audiovisual elements on each page and linking pages to the larger web site and (usually) to other web pages on the Internet. In many web teams the site production lead also manages the work of site editors and copywriters.

Site editor
The site editor has overall responsibility for the written content and editorial quality of the finished site. He or she creates the editorial tone for the web site, determines style guidelines, and works with clients and content domain experts to collect, organize, and deliver finished text to the production team. In smaller teams the editor creates site copy, interviews domain experts to create content, and may be responsible for creating news and feature material for the site. Experienced editors also play an increasingly important role in the technical and production aspects of site content, ensuring that written content from the sponsoring organization is provided on time, in the specified editorial and technical markup format, and with sufficient quality to meet site goals. This technical aspect of content formatting is particularly important in sites where the content is ultimately delivered through a cms, in xml, or from dynamic links to a content database.

Because most search engine optimization (seo) efforts are based on careful, consistent use of keyword language and heading markup, the web editor is also the team member most likely to lead the day-to-day efforts to make the site as search-friendly as possible. Keeping the site optimized for both local search engine visibility (using your own local search tools within your site) and keeping public sites maximally visible to general Internet search engines like Google and Yahoo! are crucial strategic components of making the new content accessible and findable for your audience.

Unlike the other site development roles described above, the site editor's role is a long-term job, bridging the transition from a site development *project* into an ongoing web publication *process* that maintains the web site after launch and keeps the content fresh and relevant to your audience. If the project manager is the focal point of the early stages of creating your site, then the site editor should gradually assume the leadership role in the stages just before, during, and after the site launch. This transition of responsibilities ensures that the site won't become an orphan after the project team leaves the launch party and moves on to new assignments.

INITIAL PLANNING

Web sites are developed by groups of people to meet the needs of other groups of people. Unfortunately, web projects are often approached as a "technology problem," and projects can get colored from the beginning by enthusiasms for particular web techniques (Flash, blogs, podcasts, Ajax), not by human or business needs that emerge from engaging users in the development process. *People* are the key to successful web projects at every stage of development.

Although the people who will visit and use your site will determine whether your project is a success, ironically, those users are the people least likely to be present and involved when your site is designed and built. Remember that the site development team should always function as an active, committed advocate for the users and their needs. Experienced committee warriors may be skeptical here: These are fine sentiments, but can you really do this in the face of management pressures, budget limitations, and divergent stakeholder interests? Well, yes, you can—because you have no other choice if your web project is to succeed. If you listen only to management directives, keep the process sealed tightly within your development team, and dictate to supposed users what the team imagines is best for them, be prepared for failure. Involve real users, listen and respond to what they say, test your designs with a spectrum of users of different ages, abilities, and interests, and be prepared to change and evolve your cherished ideas in response to user feedback, and your project will be a success.

Thoroughly understand and communicate your top three goals

A short statement identifying two or three goals should be the foundation of your web site design. The statement should include specific strategies around which the web site will be designed, how long the site design, construction, and evaluation periods will be, and specific quantitative and qualitative measures of how the site's success will be evaluated. This initial statement will form the basis for your project plan (see *Developing a Project Charter*, below). Building a web site is an ongoing process, not a onetime project with

A LIST OF REMINDERS
—With apologies to E. B. White

Place yourself in the background Start and end with the users' interests in mind. If your site doesn't provide useful things to the audience, nothing else matters. Design your web site with universal usability principles.

Work from a suitable design Avoid the perils of the "ready, fire, aim" syndrome. The crucial part of the project is the planning. Know *what* you're doing, *why* you're doing it, and for *whom* you're doing it before anyone touches HTML or Photoshop.

Do not overwrite Small is good. A concise, high-quality site is much better than a big contraption full of broken links. Produce the minimum necessary to achieve an excellent result.

Prefer the standard to the offbeat Web conventions are your friends. Always favor the tried and true, and save your creativity for the hard stuff: interesting content and features.

Be clear Craft your page titles and content carefully, and make sure that the page title is consistent with your major headings.

Do the visuals last Early visual design discussions can ruin any chance of a rational planning process. Louis Sullivan was right: form follows function.

Revise and rewrite *Design iteration* in the early stages of the project is good. In planning, keep the team open to new ideas, feedback from existing and potential users, and the interests of your project stakeholders. However, *development iteration*—where you tear down and revise things late in the process—can ruin quality control, budgets, and schedules.

Be consistent Consistency is the golden rule of interface design. Be consistent with the general conventions of the web, of your home institution if you have one, and within your site.

Do not affect a breezy manner Avoid gimmicky technology fads. "We should use Ajax" is not a technology strategy, unless you know exactly *why and how* Ajax might benefit your site and help you achieve your strategic goals. Never use pointless Flash animations to "make the site more interesting." To make your site more interesting, add substantive content or features.

Degrade gracefully Apply universal usability principles in your site development and careful quality controls in your web applications. Provide a carefully designed "404" error page with helpful search and links if the user hits a broken link on your site.

Do not explain too much Be concise, and be generous with headers, subheads, and lists, so the user can scan your content easily.

Make sure the user knows who is speaking Good communication is always a person-to-person transaction. Use the active voice at all times, so the user knows who is speaking. Make it easy to find your mailing address and other contact information.

static content. Long-term editorial management and technical maintenance must be covered in your budget and production plans. Without this perspective your electronic publication will suffer the same fate as many corporate communications initiatives—an enthusiastic start without lasting accomplishments.

Know your audience

Identify the potential audience for your web site so that you can structure the site design to meet their needs and expectations. The knowledge, background, interests, and needs of users will vary from tentative novices who need a carefully structured introduction to expert users who may chafe at anything that seems to patronize them or delay their access to information. A well-designed system should accommodate a range of skills and interests. For example, if the goal of your web site is to deliver internal corporate information, human resources documents, or other information formerly published in paper manuals, your audience will range from those who will visit the site many times every day to those who refer only occasionally to the site.

Web analytics as a planning tool

One of the great things about the web as a communications medium is that it can provide a rich stream of data on how your site is used, what people are looking for, and how users typically traverse the various parts of your site. If you are redesigning an existing site, take a close look at the web server logs from the server that hosts the site and work with your webmaster to develop reports on how the site is currently used and on trends of use over time. In addition to providing gross traffic volume on your site and your most popular pages, web logs can give you detailed information on where your current users come from, what sites they visited before coming to yours, what search terms brought them to your web site, what kind of network connection they use, what size their computer screen is, and which operating system and web browser they use. If the data from your existing web hosting arrangement isn't adequate or is poorly formatted for analysis by your team, consider using tools such as Google Analytics to generate easy-to-read reports on your current site traffic as you plan the revised site.

Don't overlook search analytics in your data reviews. If your local enterprise or intranet uses a search engine such as Ultraseek Enterprise Search, Google Search Appliance, or other enterprise search tool, you have access to rich data on what people were searching for when they came to your site. Look closely at the most popular search terms for your site, and match those terms against your current site navigation links to be sure that popular content items are easily accessible. If people are entering search terms for things that you think should be obvious on your site, your navigation interface probably needs an overhaul. The conventional wisdom in web design is that about half of web users prefer to search for keywords, while the other half prefer to browse through pages and lists of links. Your search analytics reports are a powerful feedback tool for assuring that your new design meets the needs of both searchers and browsers.

Design critiques

Each member of a site development team will bring different goals, preferences, and skills to the project. Once the team has reached agreement on the mission and goals of the project, you'll need to establish consensus on the overall design approach for the web site. The object at this stage is to identify potential successful models in other web sites and to begin to see the design problem from the site user's point of view.

Unfortunately, production teams rarely include members of the target audience for the web site. And it is often difficult for team members who are not already experienced site designers to articulate their specific preferences, except in reference to existing sites. Group critiques are a great way to explore what makes a web site successful, because everyone on the team sees each site from a user's point of view. Have each team member bring a list of several favorite sites to the critique, and ask them to introduce these sites and comment on the successful elements of each design. In this way you will learn one another's design sensibilities and begin to build consensus on the experience that your audience will have when they visit the finished site.

Content inventory

Once you have an idea of your web site's mission and general structure, you can begin to assess the content you will need to realize your plans. Building an inventory or database of existing and needed content will force you to take a hard look at your existing content resources and to make a detailed outline of your needs. Once you know where you are short on content you can concentrate on those deficits and avoid wasting time on areas with existing resources that are ready to use. A clear grasp of your needs will also help you develop a realistic schedule and budget. *Content development is the hardest, most time-consuming, and most consistently underestimated part of any web site development project.* In many instances your team will be looking to the sponsor to provide content or domain experts. Be sure your sponsor or client understands the responsibilities and takes the content delivery deadlines seriously. Starting early with a firm content development plan will help ensure that you won't be caught later with a well-structured but empty web site.

TYPES OF WEB SITES AND DOCUMENTS

STATIC VERSUS DYNAMIC WEB PAGES

Static web pages

Static web pages don't change content or layout with every request to the web server. They change only when a web author manually updates them with a text editor or web editing tool like Adobe Dreamweaver. The vast majority of web sites use static pages, and the technique is highly cost-effective for publishing web information that doesn't change substantially over months or even years. Many web content management systems also use static publishing to deliver web content. In the CMS the pages are created and modified in a dynamic database-driven web-editing interface but are then written out to the web server ("published") as ordinary static pages. Static pages are simple, secure, less prone to technology errors and breakdown, and easily visible by search engines.

Dynamic web pages

Dynamic web pages can adapt their content or appearance depending on the user's interactions, changes in data supplied by an application, or as an evolution over time, as on a news web site. Using client-side scripting techniques (XML, Ajax techniques, Flash ActionScript), content can be changed quickly on the user's computer without new page requests to the web server. Most dynamic web content, however, is assembled on the web server using server-side scripting languages (ASP, JSP, Perl, PHP, Python). Both client- and server-side approaches are used in multifaceted web sites with constantly changing content and complex interactive features. Dynamic web pages offer enormous flexibility, but the process of delivering a uniquely assembled mix of content with every page request requires a rapid, high-end web server, and even the most capable server can bog down under many requests for dynamic web pages in a short time. Unless they are carefully optimized, dynamic web content delivery systems are often much less visible to search engines than static pages. Always ask about search visibility when considering the merits of a dynamic web content system.

WEB CONTENT MANAGEMENT

Enterprise web content management systems

Web content management systems enable large numbers of nontechnical content contributors to update and create new web pages with ease within the context of large, enterprise-wide web sites that may contain thousands or even millions of pages of content. These systems offer some variation on these three core features:

- Editorial workflow, an approval process, and access management for individual web authors

- Site management of pages, directories, content contributor accounts, and general system operations
- An interactive user interface, usually browser-based, that doesn't require technical knowledge of the web, HTML, or CSS to create web content

In a typical CMS-driven web site, the web editing workflow is as follows:

1. A domain expert, local department staffer, or writer adds, updates, or otherwise modifies the content of a page, using a web browser to access the CMS features and perform editing and site management functions;
2. The finished content is routed by a series of notifications to the designated approver for content in that area of the larger web site;
3. The approver reviews the new content and either releases it for publication or sends it back for revision; and
4. The CMS assembles the approved content for publication and, on larger web sites, is typically published to a "live" server on the Internet at specified intervals during the day. Most CMS products can also handle instant site updates if needed.

The text, graphic, and site management tools in a CMS are designed to allow users with little or no knowledge of HTML or CSS to create and manage sophisticated web content. Most large corporate, enterprise, and university sites are now managed with a CMS in a decentralized editorial environment where hundreds of individual authors, content approvers, editors, and media contributors create most of the content for the enterprise's sites.

Most enterprise CMS products use a database to store web content. Text and media files (graphics, photos, podcasts, videos) are often stored as XML to facilitate reuse and enable flexible presentation options, permitting content to be updated simultaneously on a variety of web pages. CMS products use templates to provide a consistent user interface, enterprise identity branding, and typographic presentation throughout the site. CMS templates increasingly are complex XSLT (Extensible Style Language Transformation) files that modify and transform XML content into web pages for viewing in conventional web browsers, in special formats for visually impaired readers, on mobile devices like cell phones, and in convenient print formats.

Blogs

Owing to their ease of use and the ready availability of supporting software, web logs, or blogs, are the most popular, inexpensive, and widespread form of web content management. Blog software such as Blogger, Roller, or WordPress allows nontechnical users to combine text, graphics, and digital media files easily into interactive web pages.

A blog is actually a simple CMS, typically designed to support three core features:

- Easy publication of text, graphics, and multimedia content on the web
- Built-in tools that enable blog readers to post comments (an optional feature)
- Built-in RSS features that allow subscribers to see when a blog site has been updated (fig. 1.4)

The typical blog content genre is an online diary of life events (personal blogs) or short commentary on particular subject (politics, technology, specialized topics), but blog software can easily be adapted to support collaborative work within social groups or internal and external enterprise communications. For example, many universities have adopted blog software as a simple CMS that allows nontechnical faculty and administrators to quickly post notices, emergency announcements, and other timely material.

For a small (ten-to-twenty-page), special-purpose, small business, or department web site, a blog-based site may be all you need to get up and running quickly with a set of friendly, nontechnical editing tools and (usually) such built-in features as calendars, automated category and navigation controls, and automatic RSS feeds. If the blog metaphor of posted-content-plus-reader-comments doesn't suit your purpose, turn off the comments features and you have a friendly web site development and editing tool plus a lightweight CMS in one inexpensive package.

Wikis

A wiki is a specialized form of content-managed web site designed to support the easy collaborative creation of web pages by groups of users. Wikis differ from blogs and other CMS options in that wikis allow *all users* to change the content of the wiki pages, not just to post comments about the content. Wikis such as the well-known Wikipedia online encyclopedia can be pub-

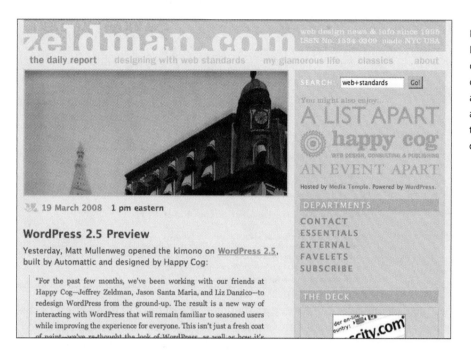

FIGURE 1.4
Blog sites generally
offer individual
commentary on
a particular topic
and give readers
the opportunity to
comment.

licly accessible and edited by any user, but wiki software can also be used
to support more private collaboration projects, where only members of the
group can see and edit the wiki content. Popular commercial wiki tools like
PBwiki, MediaWiki (used by Wikipedia), and JotSpot offer search, browsing,
and editing features, as well as account management and security features to
limit access to selected users. In wikis the changes to content are typically
visible instantly after changes are made, and the workflow model is "open,"
without a formal approval process for new content changes and additions.
This open model allows fast progress and updates by many contributors, but
may not be suitable for projects that handle sensitive or controversial material that is visible to the reading public on your enterprise intranet or the
larger World Wide Web audience (fig. 1.5).

RSS

Really Simple Syndication is a great way to generate a set of "headlines" and
web links that can appear many places at once on the Internet or your local
enterprise intranet. RSS is a family of XML-based feed formats that can automatically provide an updated set of headlines, web links, or short content

FIGURE 1.5

If blogs are about publishing and commentary, wikis are about group collaboration. In a blog the readers comment on an author's work. In a wiki, the collaborative group *is* the author.

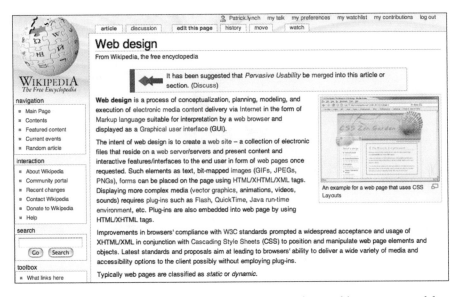

snippets to many forms of Internet media. RSS can be read by a variety of display software, including many email programs, major web browsers (Firefox, Internet Explorer, Opera, Safari), specialized RSS aggregator software like Surfpack or FeedDemon, and web portal sites such as iGoogle, MyYahoo!, and other customizable corporate and Internet portals. Most blog software can generate RSS feeds to notify users of updated content, and there are many special-purpose RSS feed authoring programs on the market. Once the RSS feed file is created by a blog or generated by desktop RSS software and placed on a web server, the feed can be addressed with a conventional URL (uniform resource locator) just like a web page (http://whatever-site.com/my-rss-feed.xml). Every time you update the RSS feed file your users see the new headlines in their email, web browser, or portal page (fig. 1.6).

THE EVOLUTION OF WEB TOOLS

As the web has matured and become a mainstream tool within enterprises, more capable web-based tools and collaborative genres have emerged that can augment, or even replace, a conventional web site. The following two examples of web publishing alternatives show the different routes that application designers are taking to publish content and work collaboratively on the web. The probable evolution of web publishing is away from such HTML authoring tools as Adobe Dreamweaver and CMS packages that han-

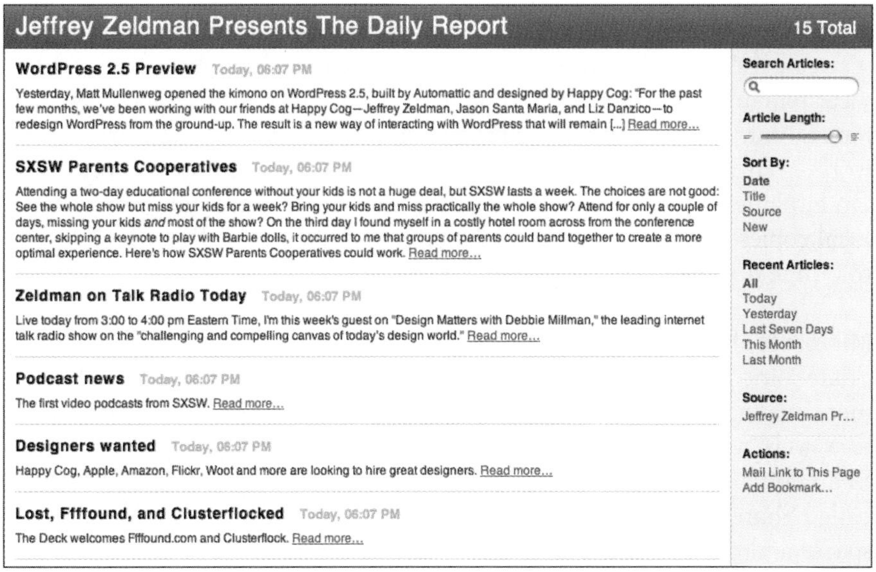

| Jeffrey Zeldman Presents The Daily Report | 15 Total |

WordPress 2.5 Preview Today, 06:07 PM

Yesterday, Matt Mullenweg opened the kimono on WordPress 2.5, built by Automattic and designed by Happy Cog: "For the past few months, we've been working with our friends at Happy Cog—Jeffrey Zeldman, Jason Santa Maria, and Liz Danzico—to redesign WordPress from the ground-up. The result is a new way of interacting with WordPress that will remain [...] Read more...

SXSW Parents Cooperatives Today, 06:07 PM

Attending a two-day educational conference without your kids is not a huge deal, but SXSW lasts a week. The choices are not good: See the whole show but miss your kids for a week? Bring your kids and miss practically the whole show? Attend for only a couple of days, missing your kids *and* most of the show? On the third day I found myself in a costly hotel room across from the conference center, skipping a keynote to play with Barbie dolls, it occurred to me that groups of parents could band together to create a more optimal experience. Here's how SXSW Parents Cooperatives could work. Read more...

Zeldman on Talk Radio Today Today, 06:07 PM

Live today from 3:00 to 4:00 pm Eastern Time, I'm this week's guest on "Design Matters with Debbie Millman," the leading internet talk radio show on the "challenging and compelling canvas of today's design world." Read more...

Podcast news Today, 06:07 PM

The first video podcasts from SXSW. Read more...

Designers wanted Today, 06:07 PM

Happy Cog, Apple, Amazon, Flickr, Woot and more are looking to hire great designers. Read more...

Lost, Ffffound, and Clusterflocked Today, 06:07 PM

The Deck welcomes Ffffound.com and Clusterflock. Read more...

Search Articles:

Article Length:

Sort By:
Date
Title
Source
New

Recent Articles:
All
Today
Yesterday
Last Seven Days
This Month
Last Month

Source:
Jeffrey Zeldman Pr...

Actions:
Mail Link to This Page
Add Bookmark...

FIGURE 1.6

A typical RSS display of new articles.

dle only web publishing and toward full-featured software platforms that not only enable easy content publishing on the web but deliver attractive, ready-to-use collaborative tools and document sharing for web development teams. Google Docs extends the desktop application metaphor to web-based shared documents, using web storage and access control much as a shared local network drive might have been used to support collaborations in the past. Microsoft's SharePoint is widely used in enterprises to create complex portal-like collaborative work environments that offer document libraries, web content publishing, and sophisticated web applications in addition to basic collaborative services for workgroups.

Google Docs

With web-based word processing, spreadsheet, and presentation tools, Google Docs allows workgroups to collaborate on documents that participants can access from any computer that is connected to the Internet. Google documents can be edited by multiple users in real time, allowing rapid collaborative content creation. Documents can be created in Google Docs or imported from other common document formats. The shared documents reside on Google's servers and are automatically saved and backed up within the Google server system.

Although Google Docs offers a remarkable range of web-based content services, the overall security and privacy of Google's applications and services remain in question, particularly for sensitive enterprise documents, financial information, and other private content. Like other network-centric work environments, Google Docs is dependent on a network connection. On airplane flights, train trips, or other mobile situations, you can work on local copies of your files stored on your laptop, but you will not have access to online documents until you can connect to the Internet (fig. 1.7).

Microsoft SharePoint

SharePoint is a portal-like web-based collaboration, publishing, and document management system from Microsoft that can provide a comprehensive web workgroup environment, particularly within large enterprises. SharePoint can be used to host sophisticated web sites and web applications, called SharePoint sites or "SharePoint portals," which provide shared workspaces and documents, as well as specialized applications such as wikis and blogs and RSS support, all from within a web browser. SharePoint sites also include such features as process workflows, to-do lists, group announcements, email-based alerts, and discussion boards. User access to SharePoint collaborative sites is usually handled through Microsoft Active Directory Services and thus offers a secure environment for corporate, medical, or other collaborations involving sensitive private data.

Although SharePoint has many attractive features, many of the more complex interactive elements are fully functional only within the combination of the Windows operating system and the Internet Explorer (IE) web browser. As with Google Docs, access to collaborative features and stored documents requires access to the Internet. The newest version of SharePoint, Microsoft Office SharePoint Server (MOSS), is much less dependent on proprietary Windows Active-x technology and the IE web browser, but SharePoint still offers a limited experience for Firefox or other Windows browser users or for users of Apple Macintosh or Linux computers. If you can live with its operating system limitations, SharePoint can handle most internal web publishing needs within an enterprise.

LEVERAGING WEB-BASED SERVICES

The web offers a remarkable range of free (or nearly free) content hosting and sharing services that can be useful to both individuals and small en-

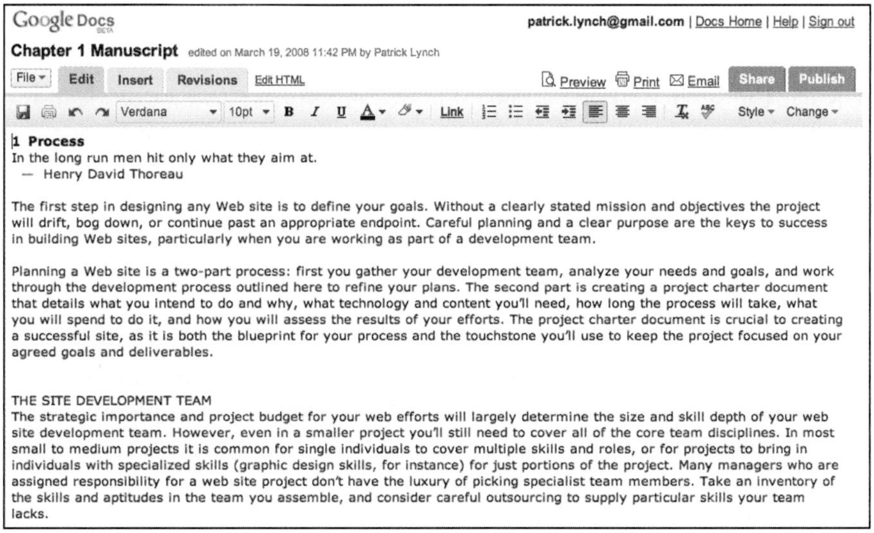

FIGURE 1.7
An example of basic word processing in Google Docs.

terprises with limited resources. The Google Docs web-based software service is just one of dozens of web-centric publishing tools offered by Google, Yahoo!, Microsoft, Flickr, FaceBook, MySpace, YouTube, Apple's iTunes (for podcasts), and other companies. Even if you are working within a larger enterprise that offers basic content services like email, web hosting, or web content management, you may find that the free or low-cost services of these popular web sites are good adjuncts to your primary web site or make useful collaborative tools to support small projects. For example, if you have a lot of visual information to post on the web to support a project, it's hard to find local enterprise tools that are as capable or user-friendly as Flickr or Picasa for image sharing. More specialized web tools such as SurveyMonkey's free or inexpensive survey tools are now widely used within companies, universities, government agencies, and other large enterprises.

Many companies have recognized that high-traffic web portals like YouTube and FaceBook aren't just great communications tools for individuals but are also influential mass communications media and have begun to establish a managed corporate online presence and regular press releases within these highly public sites. It makes sense to establish an enterprise presence where your customers and audience are, particularly for services and e-commerce sites aimed at younger users.

Any web-based software service entails risk to enterprise security, information privacy, and even intellectual property rights of material posted through the service. If you work in a large enterprise, be sure to clear any potential use of these web-based tools with your information security office or legal department to be sure that your rights and data are protected and that no legally protected personal financial, health, or proprietary company information is exposed to unacceptable risks.

THE SITE DEVELOPMENT PROCESS

Every significant web project poses unique challenges, but the overall process of developing a complex web site generally follows six major stages that you should think through before crafting your final project planning and proposal documents:

1 Site definition and planning
2 Information architecture
3 Site design
4 Site construction
5 Site marketing
6 Tracking, evaluation, and maintenance

Developing a large web site is a process that may have far-reaching budgetary, personnel, and public relations consequences for an organization, both during the development of the site and long after its deployment. Too many web sites begin life as ad hoc efforts, created by small interest groups working in isolation from their peers elsewhere in the organization and without fully considering the site's goals within the context of the organization's overall mission. The result of poorly planned, hasty development efforts often is an "orphan site," starved of resources and attention.

As you consider the development process outlined below, note that the construction of the pages that make up the web site is one of the last things that takes place in a well-designed project. Consider each step in the process and its impact on your developing project charter plan (see *Developing a Project Charter*, below). Think before you act, and make sure you have the organizational backing, budget, and personnel resources you'll need to make the project a success (fig. 1.8).

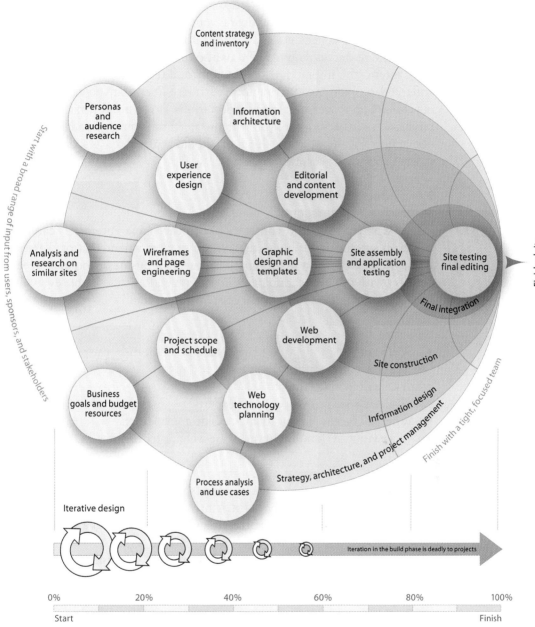

Content strategy
and inventory

Personas
and
audience
research

Information
architecture

User
experience
design

Editorial
and content
development

Analysis and
research on
similar sites

Wireframes
and page
engineering

Graphic
design and
templates

Site assembly
and application
testing

Site testing
final editing

Project scope
and schedule

Web
development

Business
goals and budget
resources

Web
technology
planning

Process analysis
and use cases

Start with a broad range of input from users, sponsors, and stakeholders

Finished site

Final integration

Site construction

Information design

Finish with a tight, focused team

Strategy, architecture, and project management

Iterative design

Iteration in the build phase is deadly to projects

0%   20%   40%   60%   80%   100%

Start   Finish

SITE DEFINITION AND PLANNING

This initial stage is where you define your goals and objectives for the web site and begin to collect and analyze the information you'll need to justify the budget and resources required. This is also the time to define the scope of the site content, the interactive functionality and technology support required, and the depth and breadth of information resources that you will need to fill out the site and meet your users' expectations. If you are contracting out the production of the web site, you will also need to interview and select a site design firm. Ideally, your site designers should be involved as soon as possible in the planning discussions.

Site production checklist

Not every site will require detailed consideration of every item on the lists below. Web teams within corporations or other large enterprises can often count on substantial in-house technology support when creating web sites. If you are on your own as an individual or small business, you may need to contract with various technology and design vendors to assemble everything you'll need to create a substantial content site or small e-commerce site.

Production

- Will your site production team be composed of in-house people, outside contractors, or a mix of the two?
- Who will manage the process?
- Who are your primary content experts?
- Who will be the liaison to any outside contractors?
- Who will function long-term as the webmaster or site editor?

Technology

- What operating systems and browsers should your site support?
  - Windows, Macintosh, UNIX, Linux
  - Firefox, Internet Explorer, Safari, Opera; minimum version supported
- What is the network bandwidth of the average site visitor?
  - Internal audience or largely external audience
  - Ethernet or high-speed connections typical of corporate offices
  - ISDN, or DSL medium-speed connections typical of suburban homes
  - Modem connections for rural audiences

- Will the site have dynamic HTML and advanced features?
  - JavaScript required
  - Java applets required
  - Third-party browser plug-ins required
  - Special features of the Linux, UNIX, or Microsoft IIS server environments required
  - Special security or confidentiality features required
- How will users reach support personnel?
  - Email messages from users
  - Chat rooms, forums, help desks, or phone support
- Does the site require database support?
  - User logins required to enter any site areas
  - Questionnaires required
  - Search and retrieval from databases needed
- Will the site have audiovisual content?
  - Video or audio productions

Web server support
- Will the site reside on an in-house web server or be outsourced to an Internet service provider for web hosting?
  - Disk space limitations, site traffic limitations, extra costs
  - Adequate capacity to meet site traffic demands
  - Twenty-four-hour, seven-day-a-week support and maintenance
  - Statistics on users and site traffic
  - Server log analysis: in-house or outsourced
  - Search engine suitable for your content
  - CGI, programming, database middleware support
  - Database support or coordination with in-house staff

Budgeting
- What are staffing costs?
  - Short-term development staff
  - Long-term editorial and support staff (site editor or webmaster)
  - Ongoing server and technical support
  - Database maintenance and support
  - New content development and updating

- What hardware and software are needed for in-house development team members?
- What are staff training costs?
  - Web use, database, web marketing, web design
- What are the outsourcing fees?
  - Site design and development
  - Technical consulting
  - Database development
  - Site marketing

Appoint a site editor to become the "process manager"

Every successful new web site makes a transition from a development project to an ongoing editorial process that keeps the site alive and fresh over time. You'll need a *project manager* to get your new site launched, but you'll also need to hand the site over to a *process manager* (read: "editor") after the site is launched. A site that is "everyone's responsibility" can quickly become an orphan. For current content and consistent editorial, graphic design, and management policies you'll need one person to act as the editor of the overall web site. The site editor's duties will vary according to how you choose to maintain your site. Some editors do all the work of maintaining site content, relieving their coworkers of the need to deal directly with web page editing. Other editors coordinate and edit the work of many contributors who work directly on the site pages, aided by a maintenance plan that specifies who is responsible for the content of each section of the site. When multiple people contribute to site maintenance, the site editor may choose to edit pages after they are created and posted to avoid becoming a bottleneck in the communications process. However, high-profile public pages or pages that contain important information should be vetted by the editor before posting. A site editor will also typically bear the primary responsibility for keeping the site content as visible as possible in local enterprise or general Internet search engines. Broken links and scrambled content organization schemes can harm your search engine rankings and make your content harder for users to locate. The site editor is also the logical person to handle the collection and analysis of web site analytics and to produce periodic reports on the usage of the site.

In addition to ensuring editorial quality, a site editor must also make certain that the content of the site reflects the policies of the enterprise, is consistent with local appropriate use policies, and does not contain material that violates copyright laws. Many people who post pictures, cartoons, audiovisual files, or written material copied from other sites on their own sites do not understand copyrights and the legal risks in using copyrighted materials inappropriately. A site editor is often an institution's first line of defense against an expensive lawsuit over the misuse of protected material.

INFORMATION ARCHITECTURE

At this stage you need to detail the content and organization of the web site. The team should inventory all existing content, describe what new content is required, and define the organizational structure of the site. Once a content architecture has been sketched out, you should build small prototypes of parts of the site to test what it feels like to move around within the design. Site prototypes are useful for two reasons. First, they are the best way to test site navigation and develop the user interface. The prototypes should incorporate enough pages to assess accurately what it's like to move from menus to content pages. These prototypes can be used to test the information architecture with users. Second, creating a prototype allows the graphic designers to develop relations between how the site looks and how the navigation interface supports the information design. The key to good prototyping is flexibility early on: the site prototypes should not be so complex or elaborate that the team becomes too invested in one design at the expense of exploring better alternatives.

Typical results or contract deliverables at the end of this stage include:

- Detailed site design specification
- Detailed description of site content
  - Site maps, thumbnails, outlines, tables of contents
- User-tested wireframes and prototypes demonstrating site architecture
- Multiple graphic design and interface design sketches
- Detailed technical support specification
  - Browser technology supported
  - Connection speed supported
  - Web server and server resources
- Proposals to create programming or technology to support specific features of the site
- A schedule for implementing the site design and construction

SITE DESIGN

At this stage the project acquires its look and feel, as the page grid, page design, and overall graphic design standards are created and approved. Now the illustrations, photography, and other graphic or audiovisual content for the site need to be commissioned and created. Research, writing, organizing, assembling, and editing the site's text content is also performed at this stage. Any programming, database design and data entry, and search engine design should be well under way by now. The goal is to produce all the content components and functional programming and have them ready for the final production stage: the construction of the actual web site pages.

Typical products or deliverables at the end of this stage include:

Content components, detailed organization and assembly
- Text, edited and proofread
- Graphic design specifications for all page types
  - Finished interface graphics for page templates
  - Header and footer graphics, logos, buttons, backgrounds
- Detailed page comps or finished examples of key pages
  - Site graphic standards manual for large, complex sites
- Interface design and master page grid templates completed
  - Finished HTML template pages
- Illustrations
- Photography

Functional and logic components
- JavaScript scripts, Java applets designed
- Database tables and programming, interaction prototypes completed
- Search engine designed and tested

Templates

Whether you develop your site on your own or hire a professional web developer, you should develop page templates for your new web site. It's much easier to add new pages when you can start from a page that already contains basic navigation and site graphics. If you have a team working on page development, you will want to share templates, along with standards on how to handle page text and content graphics. Popular web site development software packages such as Adobe Dreamweaver offer powerful templates and standard reusable libraries of site graphics and HTML that make it easy to create new pages and maintain consistency in your site.

Accessibility
In most large enterprises, providing universal access to web pages is long-established institutional policy, and in many instances it is required by state or federal regulations. It is critical, therefore, that you validate your designs and page templates and the content of your site throughout the development process to ensure that your pages are accessible to all users. Use the guidelines and techniques developed and maintained by the Web Accessibility Initiative (WAI) as a measure against which to test the accessibility of your pages.

SITE CONSTRUCTION
Only at this mature stage of the project are the bulk of the site's web pages constructed and filled out with content. By waiting until you have a detailed

site architecture, mature content components, fully tested wireframes and prototypes, and a polished page design specification you will minimize the content churning, redundant development efforts, and wasted energy that inevitably result from rushing to create pages too soon. Of course, you will always learn new things about your overall design as the prototype matures into the full-blown web site. Be prepared to refine your designs as you and your users navigate through the growing web site and discover both weak spots and opportunities to improve navigation or content.

Once the site has been constructed, with all pages completed and all database and programming components linked, it is ready for user testing. Testing should be done primarily by people outside your site development team who are willing to supply informed criticism and report programming bugs, note typographic errors, and critique the overall design and effectiveness of the site. Fresh users will inevitably notice things that you and your development team have overlooked. Only after the site has been thoroughly tested and refined should you begin to publicize the URL of the site to a larger audience.

Typical products or deliverables at the end of this stage should include:

- Finished HTML for all web pages, all page content in place
- Finished navigation link structure
- All programming in place and linked to pages, ready for user testing
- All database components in place and linked to site pages
- All graphic design, illustration, and photography in place
- Final proofreading of all site content
- Detailed testing of database and programming functionality
- Testing and verification of database reporting features
- Testing of site user support procedures, answering email, etc.
- Archives of all site content components, HTML code, programming code, and any other site development materials

Maintainable code

Most businesses or departments in larger enterprises will contract with a web development group to create the initial site design and to build all the pages in the first version of the web site. They then assume responsibility for the site, doing some or all of the daily maintenance and updating content as needed to keep the site current.

Often not until the practicalities of site maintenance arise do customers realize the importance of understanding the details of how the web developer generated the HTML and other code that makes up the web site. Although all HTML and CSS markup is much the same to web browsing software, how the HTML and CSS is formatted and what web authoring tool the developer used can make a huge difference in how the code looks to a human reader.

Consider the two code examples below:

Example 1
```
<table summary="HR Committee Schedule, FY 2008">
    <tr>
        <th>Meeting Dates 2008</th>
        <th>Agenda Item Submission Deadline</th>
    </tr>
    <tr>
        <td>Monday, Oct 6, 2008</td>
        <td>Friday, Oct 3, 2008</td>
    </tr>
</table>
```

Example 2
```
<table summary="HR Committee Schedule, FY 2008"> <tr> <th>Meeting
    Dates 2008</th> <th>Agenda Item Submission Deadline</th> </tr>
    <tr> <td>Monday, Oct 6, 2008</td> <td>Friday, Oct 3, 2008</td>
    </tr> </table>
```

Which example do you find easier to understand? These code examples are exactly equivalent to a web browser, but most people would find Example 1 significantly easier to read and understand. If you contract with a developer to build your site, it is important to understand how the developer writes code, what state the code will be in when the site is delivered, and whether the software used by the developer is compatible with what you will be using to maintain the site after delivery. Some web development software produces HTML code that is nearly impossible for a human to read without significant (and expensive) reformatting. Other programs (such as Adobe Dreamweaver) produce HTML code that is easy for web programmers to read, which can make a huge difference if you decide to change web developers or if you decide to edit HTML directly when maintaining your site.

If you hire someone to create your web site or components of your site, such as database or dynamic elements, be sure to ask what tools they will use to write the HTML and any other code. Ask to see examples of code written for other clients. Have your technology lead examine the code to be sure the developer inserts explanatory comments and dividers for legibility in the code. Be sure to find out whether there will be problems or conflicts if you use your favorite tools to edit the code the developer produces. Make sure the developer understands what editing tools you prefer to use and develops the code for maximum compatibility with your maintenance tools.

HTML and CSS code validation

Also ask for representative sites the developer has created, and choose pages to test for code validity, using the free online tools available from the W3C (see below). Many perfectly functional pages will fail W3C validity tests either for relatively minor code mistakes or for complex links to database or application URLs that use problematic characters like ampersands (&). Ignore minor failures in the code validation, since they are unlikely to cause major functional problems. But if representative pages come back from testing with long lists of HTML code problems and CSS mistakes, beware of that developer's work, and thoroughly discuss and put in writing your expectations around code validation as part of any contract.

HTML and CSS code validation tools from the W3C:

- HTML validation: validator.w3.org
- CSS validation: jigsaw.w3.org/css-validator

Today's web pages are much more complex than pages in the past, and many new mobile and other devices can now display web pages. Search visibility is crucial to successful web sites, and web accessibility is a legal requirement with a growing set of case law behind it. Using carefully validated HTML and CSS code is one of your best strategies for getting maximum flexibility and value from your web development dollars. Be extremely wary of a web developer who tells you, "Validation isn't important."

SITE MARKETING

Your web site should be an integral part of all marketing campaigns and corporate communications programs, and the URL for your site should appear on every piece of correspondence and marketing collateral your organization generates.

If your web site is aimed primarily at local audiences you must look beyond getting listed in standard web indexes, such as Yahoo! and Google, and publicize your URL where local residents or businesses will encounter it. Local libraries, newspapers, and schools are often the key to publicizing a new web site within a specific locale.

You may also find opportunities to cross-promote your site with affiliated businesses, professional organizations, broadcast or print media, visitor or local information agencies, real estate and relocation services, Internet access providers, and local city or town directory sites. Your organization could also feature local nonprofit charitable or school events on your web site. The cost in server space is usually trivial, and highly publicized local events featuring a web page hosted within your site will boost local awareness of your web presence. Site sponsorship might also interest local broadcast media as an interesting story angle.

Your home page URL should appear in all:

- Print advertisements
- Radio and television advertisements
- Lobby kiosks in high-traffic areas of your enterprise or in local libraries, schools, or other suitable venues
- Direct mail campaigns
- Business cards
- Stationery
- Bills and statements
- Product manuals and product packaging
- Response cards and warrantee cards
- Publications and promotional materials
- Press releases
- Posters and billboards

TRACKING, EVALUATION, AND MAINTENANCE

Your web server software can record an abundance of information about visitors to your site. Even the simplest site logs track how many people (unique visitors) saw your site over a given time, how many pages were requested for viewing, and many other variables. By analyzing the server logs for your web site you can develop quantitative data on the success of your site. The logs will tell you which pages were the most popular and what brands and versions of web browser people used to view your site. Server logs can also give you information on the geographic location of your site users. Detailed logs are the key to quantifying the success of a web site. Your webmaster should archive all site logs for long-term analysis and should be prepared to add or change the information categories being logged as your needs and interests change.

A number of popular software packages are designed to produce easily readable site traffic reports, complete with data graphics and charts to aid in data analysis. As a service to customers, site hosting companies often offer reports from popular site analysis programs like Google Analytics for no additional charge. Before contracting with an Internet service provider for site hosting services, always ask about site analysis services. If your ISP (Internet service provider) or corporate web site does not offer a good site traffic analysis package, ask whether the webmaster can give you access to a monthly server log of your account. Basic versions of traffic analysis programs like WebTrends are inexpensive and you can run them on a personal computer if you can gain access to the raw web server log from your ISP or corporate webmaster (fig. 1.9).

Maintaining the site

Don't abandon your site once the production "goes live" and the launch parties are over. The aesthetic and functional aspects of a large web site need constant attention and grooming, particularly if a group of individuals shares responsibility for updating content. Your site editor will need to be responsible for coordinating and vetting the new content stream, maintaining the graphic and editorial standards, and ensuring that the programming and linkages of all pages remain intact and functional. Links on the web are perishable, and you'll need to check periodically that links to pages outside your immediate site are still working. Don't let your site go stale by starving it of resources just as you begin to develop an audience—if you disappoint

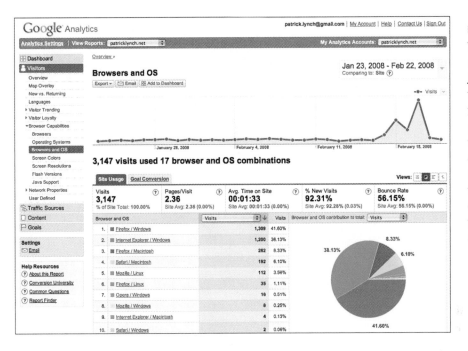

FIGURE 1.9
Web statistics are much more than just raw measures of traffic. They can tell you what content people looked at, where your visitors are coming from, and provide a rich set of technical information on what technology your typical readers are using.

them by not following through, it will be doubly difficult to attract your audience back to the site.

Backups and site archives

The site editor should be sure that the web site is regularly backed up onto a secure and reliable storage medium to ensure that a catastrophic hardware failure in your web server does not wipe out your web site. Most web servers maintained by IT professionals or commercial web service providers are backed up at least once a day. If you don't know what your backup schedule is, ask your webmaster or web hosting provider. Human error is the most common reason you may need quick access to a backup copy of your web site. Unfortunately, it's easy to overwrite an old file (or a whole directory of files) accidentally over a newer version on the web server, to delete something important in error, or to wipe out someone else's work by mistake when updating a web site. A recent backup (ideally no more than twenty-four hours old) can often be a lifesaver.

If your site is successful, it will quickly become an important record of your enterprise's work, your accomplishments, and a valuable record of the

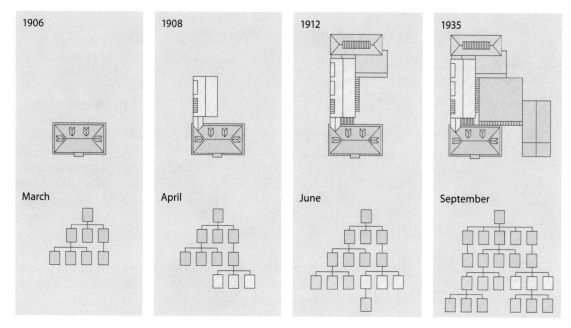

1906	1908	1912	1935
March	April	June	September

"state of things" as the site evolves over time (fig. 1.10). Unfortunately, too little attention is paid to this aspect of web sites, and we are collectively losing huge pieces of our history because no one thinks about preserving permanent records of a web site. Unless your web site is prohibitively large, your web site editor should arrange to collect and store the files of the site periodically or contract with your web service provider to set aside a backup version at regular intervals as a long-term archive. We take for granted the "paper trail" of history left by conventional business and work practices. Without a plan for preserving our digital works, our collective history may vanish without a trace.

DEVELOPING A PROJECT CHARTER

The project charter is the planning team's concise statement of core goals, values, and intent in order to provide the ultimate policy direction for everything that comes next. Designing a substantial web site is costly and time-consuming. When you're up to your neck in the daily challenges of building the site, it can be easy to forget why you are doing what you are doing and to lose sight of your original priorities, not knowing whether the decisions you are making firmly support the overall objectives. A well-written project charter is a powerful daily tool for judging the effectiveness of a development effort. It becomes a compass to keep the team firmly pointed at the goals established when you started the journey. A good project charter becomes a daily reference point for settling disputes, avoiding "scope creep," judging the potential utility of new ideas as they arise, measuring progress, and keeping the development team focused on the end-result.

At minimum, a project charter should define the content scope, budget, schedule, and technical aspects of the web site. The best project charters are short and to the point, often outlines or bulleted lists of the major design or technical features planned. The finished project charter should contain the goals statement from the planning phase, as well as the structural details of the site.

Goals and strategies

- What is the mission of your organization?
- How will creating this web site support your mission?
- What are the two or three most important goals for the site?
- Who is the primary audience for the web site?
- What do you want the audience to think or do after having visited your site?
- What web-related strategies will you use to achieve those goals?
- How will you measure the success of your site?
- How will you adequately maintain the finished site?

Production issues

- What is the budget for the site?
- What is the production schedule for the site, including intermediate milestones and dates?
- Who are the people or vendors on the development team and what are their responsibilities?
- How many pages will the site contain? What is the maximum acceptable count under this budget and schedule?
- What special technical or functional requirements are needed?
- Who will be responsible for the ongoing support once the site is launched?

These are big questions, and the broad conceptual issues are too often dismissed as committees push toward starting the "real work" of designing and building a web site. However, if you cannot confidently answer all of these questions, then no amount of design or production effort will guarantee a useful result.

Avoiding scope creep

The project charter defines the scope of your project: what you need to do, the budget, and the development schedule. Scope creep is the most prevalent cause of web project failures. In badly planned projects, scope creep is the gradual but inexorable process by which previously unplanned features are added, content and features are padded to mollify each stakeholder group, major changes in content or site structure during site construction are made, and more content or interactive functionality than you originally agreed to create is stuffed in. No single overcommitment is fatal, but the slow, steady accumulation of additions and changes is often enough to blow budgets, ruin schedules, and bury what might have been an elegant original plan under megabytes of muddle.

One excellent way to keep a tight rein on the overall scope of the site content is to specify a maximum page count in the project charter. Although a page count is hardly infallible as a guide (after all, web pages can be arbitrarily long), it serves as a constant reminder to everyone involved of the project's intended scope. If the page count goes up, make it a rule to revisit the budget implications automatically—the cold realities of budgets and schedules will often cool the enthusiasm to stuff in "just one more page." A good way to keep a lid on scope creep is to treat the page count as a "zero sum game." If someone wants to add pages, it's up to them to nominate other pages to remove or to obtain a corresponding increase in the budget and schedule to account for the increased work involved.

Changes and refinements can be a good thing, as long as everyone is realistic about the impact of potential changes on the budget and schedule of a project. Any substantial change to the planned content, design, or technical aspects of a site must be tightly coupled with a revision of the budget and schedule of the project. People are often reluctant to discuss budgets or deadlines frankly and will often agree to substantial changes or additions to a development plan rather than face an awkward conversation with a client or fellow team member. But this acquiescence merely postpones the inevitable damage of not dealing with scope changes rationally.

The firm integration of schedule, budget, and scope is the only way to keep a web project from becoming unhinged from the real constraints of time, money, and the ultimate quality of the result. A little bravery and honesty up front can save you much grief later. Make the plan carefully, and then stick to it.

SHAPING THE FINAL PROJECT CHARTER

The project charter is the document that formally authorizes a project to begin. In projects bid out to external contractors this information is generally contained within a request for proposal (RFP) document, but a project charter should exist for every web project, even small in-house web sites.

Statement of work or deliverables

The project charter should begin with a concise narrative description of the content, features, and services that the new site will provide. For in-house projects the project sponsor usually supplies this statement of overall intent for the site. For projects offered to outside design firms the statement of work forms the core of the RFPs offered to potential contract bidders.

Business needs the site will support

This section answers the "why" of your project. It should be a short description of the sales, marketing, communications, or other business goals that will be accomplished by creating the new web site, along with a rationale and general metrics for determining the success and return on investment (ROI) for the proposed web site. Think of it as a written version of your "elevator speech" to senior managers who must approve the project: your most concise, to-the-point rendition of your top three reasons why the new or redesigned web site should exist. This section should end with a short strategic statement that places the site project within the context of the sponsoring organization's missions and existing web presence.

Success metrics

Most web site projects have measurable goals: to increase traffic, boost sales, improve client relations, reduce support emails, and so on. Many of these measures rely on preexisting data to enable before-and-after comparisons of

SATISFICING IN DESIGN

The economist Herbert Simon coined the term "to satifice" by combining "satisfy" and "suffice." Satisficing is consciously choosing not to find one perfect design solution and instead aiming at a balanced approach that roughly satisfies ("satisfices") all major design requirements. Complex or lengthy design iteration is expensive and necessarily involves the combinations of many unknown factors with no clear promise of a single optimum design solution. Although satisficing may sound like settling for mediocrity, satisfice strategies have produced some of the most successful designs of the past century.

The Douglas DC-3 was not the best competitor in any single performance class: all its competitors could best it in some category of speed, engine power, range, and carrying capacity. Yet the DC-3 was such a successful satisfice of all design factors that today, more than seventy-five years after it was designed, more than thirteen hundred DC-3 airframes are in daily use.

Don't allow contention over single points of your site design to paralyze the design process or to plunge your team into endless rounds of "Would it be better if . . . ?" *All* projects are in some measure satisfices, because there's no practical way to know if there is a single best solution to every problem for every user. *Don't let the perfect become the enemy of the very good.*

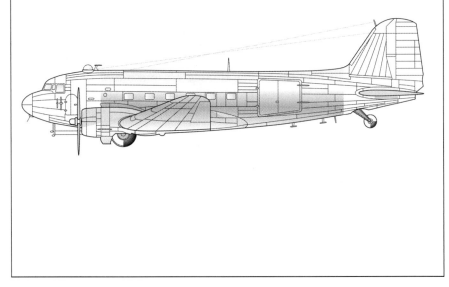

the site's success. Before you begin a site development project, determine how you will measure the impact of your efforts, and include details of success metrics in your project charter. It is important to establish success metrics before you begin because you may need to be proactive about collecting "before" data before launching the site.

Project scope and description

Here you detail the "what" of the proposed site. In as much detail as possible for each stage of the project, describe the web site to be created. Early in the planning process this statement will have to be general and should concentrate on the core "must-have" features, content, and purposes of the site. Avoid specifying the use of specific technologies (such as, "We're using Ajax for everything") that really should be determined after the web site team has made a thorough assessment. The project scope description should be a living document early in the planning stages of the project but should become a fixed specification *before hard budget numbers or schedule deadlines are assigned to the project.* Ironically, it is often useful (and sometimes easier) to make a careful statement of what your project *is not.* This form of "is/is not" scope statement is particularly useful where your new site may have aspects that are similar to existing organizational sites or where your project sponsors may not immediately grasp your intent in creating the web site.

Roles and responsibilities

Your charter should name the major sponsors, the project, design, technical, and editorial team members, and any other strategic stakeholders within the enterprise. There is no single correct way to structure a web site development effort, but everyone involved should be clear at the start about who is responsible for each aspect of the site development. This is an opportunity to make the point that the project requires an ongoing commitment, beyond the site launch. It is also another opportunity to clarify for sponsors and stakeholders that *they* have responsibilities and deadlines too, and that the team will be dependent on everyone's contributions. You should also outline a proposed project governance and approvals process, so everyone involved is clear about how each major project milestone will be communicated and formally approved by the sponsors or major stakeholders (fig. 1.11).

FIGURE 1.11
overleaf
A more detailed look at a typical web site development project. Note that although many people and disciplines may contribute to building a site, not everyone is busy at the same time. Project management is essential to bring the right resources to bear when they are needed.

	10	20	30	40

Goals, strategies, business case

Requirements

Budget, schedule, team logistics — Project kick-off   Budget, schedule

Content inventories — Catalog existing content resources

Content analysis and development — Create or obtain new text and graphic content

Editorial management for content — Set standards, review existing content   Assign new content, supervise creation

Content placement into site

Task analysis for interactivity — User interviews, focus groups, personas   Explore use cases

Site map, wireframes — Map and final wireframe

Interface, page graphic design — Interface design, accessibility

Engineering use cases — Why, how, where interactive elements will be used, explore use cases, accessibility

Programming and site engineering

Page engineering (XHTML, CSS) — Wireframes to templ

Page production, content assembly

QA testing of programming

QA review of links and functionality

Staging server; final server prep

Launch logistics

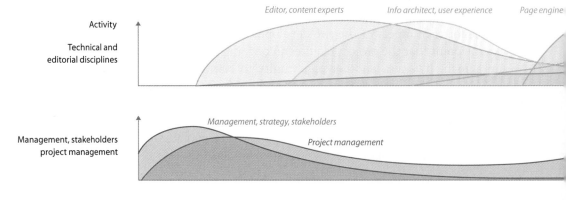

Activity

Technical and editorial disciplines

Editor, content experts   *Info architect, user experience*   *Page engine*

Management, stakeholders project management

Management, strategy, stakeholders

Project management

50	60	70	80	90	100%

Final reviews

Final reviews

Status reviews, adjustments, final planning

Final reviews

Review content in context, editorial quality control, search optimization

Final editorial reviews

Page build-out, text and graphics onto web pages, page linking, content accessibility

...age template graphics and visual design   Content graphics and design

Freeze new development and features well before QA testing phase

...ll code and core graphic identity

Page code validity, new XHTML, CSS, and JavaScript coding, web search

...e is built on a staging server, hidden from general Internet search

Site to delivery server for testing and launch

Final tests and launch

Graphic designer   *Engineering, programming*   *Editorial staff, page build-out*

Project budget

Your project budget should account for all of the expense categories outlined in *Site Definition and Planning,* above. Make your best calculations on your people, hardware, software, content, and technology development expenses, and then add a hefty contingency budget. Web projects always grow, often by as much as 10 percent or more, even in tightly managed projects. It happens to everyone, and *it will happen to you, too.* Plan for it rationally, or deal with the pain later.

Project risk assessment

Every good project plan should outline the risks of failure in major components of the project. Although your whole project is unlikely to melt down, take a hard look at the various make-or-break components of the plan and think about "Plan B" alternatives. For example, what happens if your content development and site design work out well, but your programmers don't meet expectations on interactive features? Will the site be viable? What happens to the project team if your designers and technologists do everything right but the client fails to produce the site content on time? What financial, schedule, quality-assurance, or other contingencies could be written into the contract and project charter to mitigate those risks?

Common risk points in web projects
- Schedule, budget, and scope of work: Let these drift and you're doomed.
- Quality assurance: QA becomes a problem when other schedules run long but the launch date doesn't change and QA testing is squeezed into the last few days before the site goes live.
- Content development: This is the most commonly underestimated factor in web publishing—ask any editor.
- Application development: Web projects rarely fail because an application does not function properly. Instead they fail because the intended audience hates to use it or doesn't find its features useful.

Security audits and managing security risk

Databases and applications that deal with e-commerce, or sensitive personal, financial, or health-related information should be scrupulously maintained and periodically audited for data security threats. Even a minor security leak or unchecked programming error could allow a hacker to access your database records, cause malicious damage, or take over your server to support email spamming or other illegal Internet schemes. The data security environment changes daily, and what was perfectly secure six months ago might be hopelessly vulnerable today if your servers, databases, and applications are not under active management and maintenance. Any web-based application or web database must operate with a plan for periodic security audits, as well as the normal timely application and web server patching and maintenance that you'd expect in any well-management data center or commercial web hosting service.

Ongoing technical support for hosting, databases, applications
Nontechnical managers are often unpleasantly surprised by the expenses of hosting and maintaining web sites that require substantial database or programming support. Although basic hosting of "static" web sites is an inexpensive commodity, web sites that depend on databases and the complex interactive features of web applications must usually be hosted on two or more tightly interrelated servers for security and technical reasons. The multiple servers must be maintained and updated, regularly backed up to prevent data loss, and housed in a secure networked data center environment for maximum reliability and "up time." Make sure that your technical team lead has accounted for these ongoing system maintenance costs as well as the initial development and start-up costs.

Editorial maintenance
Your brand-new web site starts aging the day you launch it into the world. If you don't maintain the site, technical changes, content changes, and the inevitable entropic "link rot" will degrade your site over time. Even a simple site with relatively stable content will deteriorate over time without basic maintenance, and business environment changes that affect your content will certainly happen. Plan for it, make sure you can clearly identify who is responsible for which content on the site, and make ongoing maintenance part of the original site planning.

GENERAL ADVICE ABOUT RUNNING WEB PROJECTS

Ready, fire, aim

The prospect of creating a new or revised web site is exciting, and many teams will find it irresistible to jump in and start "sketching" or prototyping site designs long before anyone on the team knows:

- What your goals and strategies are
- Who exactly you're designing the site for and what *those users* want
- What essential content structures, navigation, and interactive features are needed

Don't let the process get hijacked by eager beavers who "just want to make some pages." Decide the big strategic things first, and make pages only when you have all the important answers in place to guide the rest of the design process intelligently.

Stay away from visual design until everything else is planned

The fastest way to run a web project off the rails is to start your planning process by discussing the home page visuals or what the overall graphic design of the site should look like. Pour the foundation and build the walls before you let anyone fuss about the color of the drapes. The visual form of your site should flow from careful and informed decisions about site structure, navigation, content and interactivity requirements, and overall business goals. Detailed visual design should always come last in site planning: premature graphic design decisions will confound you at every turn.

Small is good

Often the easiest way to "manage" a site project is by adding content or features to avoid contention on the team, particularly if you look only at the initial programming or design costs. Large web sites are expensive to maintain, and it's easy to bite off more than you can chew. Every new page, link, or application feature requires a long-term maintenance commitment. Stay small if you can, and stay focused. A small, high-quality site is infinitely better than a giant contraption with old content and broken links. The Kiva site is a model of simple, straightforward design and functionality—staying small while accomplishing enormous good (fig. 1.12).

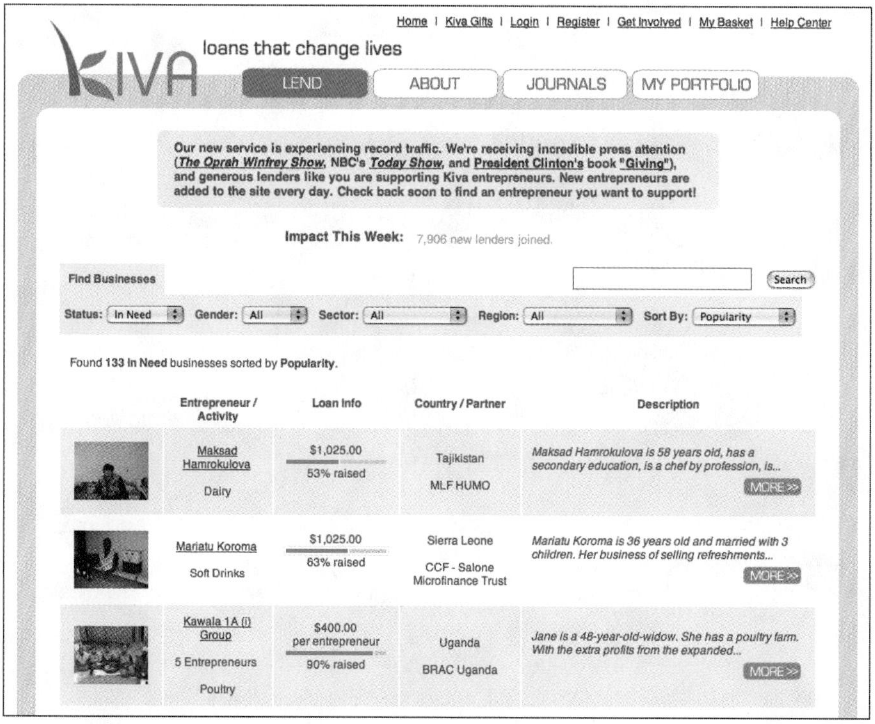

FIGURE 1.12
Elegant sites are never more complex than they need to be.

Plan the work, then work the plan

The oldest joke in project management is, "Good, fast, or cheap? Pick any two." If you are developing anything more than a small web site, make sure you have an experienced web project manager.

To err is human, to forgive—design.

—Andrew Dillon

Universal Usability

U sability is a measure of effectiveness. It describes how effective tools and information sources are in helping us accomplish tasks. The more usable the tool, the better we are able to achieve our goals. Many tools help us overcome physical limitations by making us stronger, faster, and more sharp-sighted. But tools can be frustrating or even disabling. When we encounter a tool that we cannot work with, either because it is poorly designed or because its design does not take into account our needs, we are limited in what we can accomplish.

In designing web sites our job is to reduce functional limitations through design. When we aim for *universal* usability, we improve the quality of life for more people more of the time. On the web, we can work toward universal usability by adopting a universal design approach to usability.

Here we cover the concepts, principles, and processes for universal usability. Specific techniques for universal usability are woven into context in the chapters that follow.

A BASIS FOR UNIVERSAL USABILITY
The concept of universal usability is informed by several initiatives, primarily accessibility, usability, and universal design.

ACCESSIBILITY
Since the World Wide Web Consortium established the Web Accessibility Initiative in 1999, the imperative of web accessibility has gained the attention of individuals, organizations, and governments worldwide. WAI promotes best practices and tools that make the web accessible to people with disabilities. They also safeguard universal web access by providing expert input for development initiatives to ensure that accessible designs can be accomplished using current and future web technologies.

Web accessibility is a critical element of universal usability. The guidelines produced by WAI and other accessibility initiatives provide us with

51

techniques and specifications for how to create universally usable designs. They ensure that designers have the tools and technologies needed to create designs that work in different contexts.

USABILITY AND USER-CENTERED DESIGN

Usability is both a qualitative measure of the experience of using a tool and a phenomenon that can be measured and quantified as a concrete means to judge a design's effectiveness. Quantitative usability metrics include how quickly we complete tasks and how many errors we make in the process. But usability can also be measured by qualitative measures, such as how much satisfaction we derive in using a tool. "Learnability" is another important measure: how quickly we learn to use a tool and how well we remember how to use it the next time. Usability has an impact not only on our effectiveness but also on more fundamental qualities, such as loyalty. The more usable the tool, the better we feel about using it and, in the case of web sites, the more likely it is that we will return to the site.

The most common method for achieving usability is user-centered design (UCD). UCD includes user-oriented methods such as task analysis, focus groups, and user testing to understand user needs and refine designs based on user feedback. UCD involves determining what functionality users want in a product and how they will use it. Through iterative cycles of design, testing, and refinement, UCD practitioners continuously check in to make sure they are on track—that users like and will be successful using the design.

Universal usability arises from user-centered design, but with a broad and inclusive view of the user. UCD is applied to the task of designing web sites that are easy to learn and use by a diversity of users, platforms, and usage contexts.

UNIVERSAL DESIGN

Universal design incorporates access requirements into a design, rather than providing alternate designs to meet specific needs, such as large print or Braille editions for vision-impaired readers. A common example of universal design in the built environment is ramped entryways, which can be used by everyone and eliminate the need for a separate, handicapped entrance. Universal design has many benefits. A single design that meets broad needs is often less costly than multiple designs. And designs that anticipate a diverse user population often have unanticipated benefits. For example, curb cuts in sidewalks are intended to help mobility- and vision-impaired users, but many others benefit, including people making deliveries, pushing a stroller, or riding a bike.

UNIVERSAL USABILITY GUIDELINES

Human-computer interaction (HCI) pioneer Ben Shneiderman defines universal usability as "having more than 90% of all households as successful users of information and communications services at least once a week." Note that Shneiderman is not calling for *any* use of technology but rather *successful* use. He goes on to explain that, to achieve universal usability, designers need to "support a wide range of technologies, to accommodate diverse users, and to help users bridge the gap between what they know and what they need to know."

It's important to think about universal usability as a goal and not an outcome. Clearly, no web site can accommodate every possible use context, any more than a potato peeler can be used successfully by every individual. The web provides an environment that is far more flexible than the built world, making the goal of universal access more feasible.

MOVING BEYOND THE "TYPICAL" USER

The first step toward the goal of universal usability is to discard the notion that we are designing for a "typical" user. Universal usability accounts for users of all ages, experience levels, and physical or sensory limitations. Users also vary widely in their technical circumstances: in screen size, network speed, browser versions, and specialized software such as screen readers for the visually impaired. Each of us inhabits multiple points on the spectrum, points that are constantly shifting as our needs and contexts change. For example, virtually all adults over fifty have some form of mild to moderate visual impairment. And within that context our needs change as we move from viewing web pages from the back of an auditorium to sitting in front of a large desktop display monitor to walking down the street peering at a small mobile display. A broad user definition that includes the full range of user needs and contexts is the first step in producing universally usable designs.

SUPPORTING ADAPTATION

Next we need a design approach that will accommodate the diversity of our user base, and here we turn to the principle of adaptation. On the web, uni-

UNIVERSAL DESIGN PRINCIPLES

Universal design is informed by a set of principles and guidelines developed by the Center for Universal Design at North Carolina State University's College of Design (www.design.ncsu.edu/cud/about_ud/udprinciples.htm). The following are the principles and guidelines that are most applicable to the web environment.

Principle One: Equitable Use "The design is useful and marketable to people with diverse abilities. Provide the same means of use for all users: identical whenever possible; equivalent when not." The virtual environment is far more flexible than the physical one. A single book cannot serve multiple readers because of the limitations of the printed page. An online book can be made larger, smaller, colored, copied, printed, read aloud. The flexibility of the web provides an excellent opportunity to design for "same means of use."

Flexibility and user control allow users to adapt designs to meet their needs and preferences

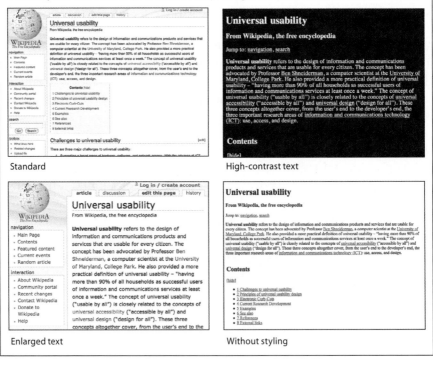

Standard

High-contrast text

Enlarged text

Without styling

Principle Two: Flexibility in Use   "The design accommodates a wide range of individual preferences and abilities. Provide choice in methods of use." The web is flexible by nature, and users have choice regarding platform, software, and settings. Users can choose to view web pages without images or in a variety of layouts and typefaces.

Principle Three: Simple and Intuitive Use   "Use of the design is easy to understand, regardless of the user's experience, knowledge, language skills, or current concentration level. Eliminate unnecessary complexity and arrange information consistent with its importance." Most web pages have low signal-to-noise ratios, with much of the page given over to organizational identity, advertising, and navigation. Simplicity and direct access to salient features and information is essential in an effective design strategy.

Principle Four: Perceptible Information   "The design communicates necessary information effectively to the user, regardless of ambient conditions or the user's sensory abilities. Use different modes (pictorial, verbal, tactile) for redundant presentation of essential information and provide compatibility with a variety of techniques or devices used by people with sensory limitations." Because text on web pages is machine-readable, it can be adapted to different contexts. For instance, text is accessible to people who can't see because software can read text aloud. Web technologies include provisions for supplying equivalent text for nontext items, such as alt-text for images, captions for spoken audio, and audio descriptions for video files.

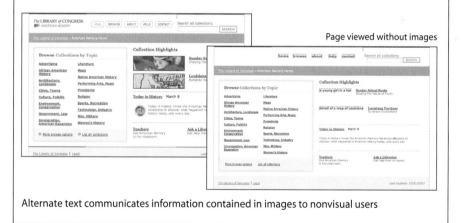

Page viewed without images

Alternate text communicates information contained in images to nonvisual users

versal usability is achieved through adaptive design, where documents transform to accommodate different user needs and contexts. Adaptive design is the means by which we support a wide range of technologies and diverse users. The following guidelines support adaptation.

Flexibility

Universal usability is difficult to achieve in a physical environment, where certain parameters are necessarily "locked in." It would be difficult to make a book, and a chair to read it in, that fit the needs and preferences of every reader. The digital environment is another story. Digital documents can adapt to different access devices and user needs based on the requirements of the context.

A web page contains text, with pointers to other types of documents, such as images and video. Software reads the page and acts on it by, for example, displaying the page visually in the browser. But because of the nature of the web, the same page can be accessed on a cell phone, using a screen reader, or printed on paper. The success of this adaptation depends on whether the page design supports flexibility. Pages designed exclusively for large displays will not display well on the small screens of cell phones (fig. 2.1).

The web environment is flexible, with source documents that adapt to different contexts. When considering universal usability, we need to anticipate diversity and build flexible pages that adapt gracefully to a wide variety of displays and user needs.

User control

In many design fields, designers make choices that give shape to a thing, and these choices, particularly in a fixed environment, are bound to exclude some users. No one text size will be readable by all readers, but the book designer must make a decision about what size to set text, and that decision is likely to produce text that is too small for some readers. In the web environment, users have control over their environment. Users can manipulate browser settings to display text at a size that they find comfortable for reading.

Flexibility paired with user control allows users to take control of their web experience and shape it into a form that works within their use context.

Keyboard functionality

Universal usability is not just about access to information. Another crucial component is interaction, in which users navigate and interact with links, forms, and other elements of the web interface. For universal usability, these actionable elements must be workable from the keyboard. Many users cannot use a mouse, and many devices do not support point-and-click interaction. For example, nonvisual users cannot see the screen, and many mobile devices only support keyboard navigation. Some users use software or other input devices that only work by activating keyboard commands. For these users, elements that can only be activated using a mouse are inaccessible.

Make actionable elements workable via the keyboard to ensure that the interactivity of the web is accessible to the broadest spectrum of users.

FIGURE 2.1
Page designs optimized for screen displays don't always fare well on mobile devices.

Text equivalents

Text is universally accessible. (Whether text is universally *comprehensible* is another discussion!) Unlike images and media, text is readable by software and can be rendered in different formats and acted upon by software. When information is presented in a format other than text, such as visually using images or video or audibly using spoken audio, the information is potentially lost on users who cannot see or hear. Web technology anticipates format-related access issues and supplies methods for providing equivalent text. With equivalent text, the information contained in the media is also available as text, such as a text transcript or captions along with spoken audio (fig. 2.2).

Text equivalents allow universal usability to exist in a media-rich environment by carrying information to users who cannot access information in a given format.

UNIVERSAL USABILITY IN THE DESIGN PROCESS

The World Wide Web is now more than eighteen years old—time enough for basic design conventions to have emerged. In designing web pages we often base initial designs on widely used page layout and navigation patterns, and use best practices such as consistency, modularity, and simplicity in creating our web interfaces. However, the best method for making design decisions is a combination of design best practices and familiar web layout conventions, developed in close consultation with users at each stage of the design process. Involving users in the development process helps us understand user requirements, which allows us to make informed design decisions and produce more effective designs.

Web technology collects metrics about users: what operating system and browser they use, their screen resolution, what page they visited just before their arrival at your site. And although it's certainly useful to know these attributes, they are not that helpful in defining the audience for your web site. Web metrics will not tell you precisely why users visit your site, what they hope to find from your site, or whether they are visually impaired in some way, expert or novice, young or old.

In the end, even with the best web analytics, many things about your audience's hopes, motivations, and expectations will remain a mystery if you rely solely on web metrics to understand your users.

In contrast, a *target* audience is a group of users that you have identified as critical to the success of your site. For instance, you may be designing for a certain age group, such as grade-school children, teens, or retirees. Or you may be designing for a specific technology, such as mobile devices. Bear in mind that your target audience may share common interests, but they are

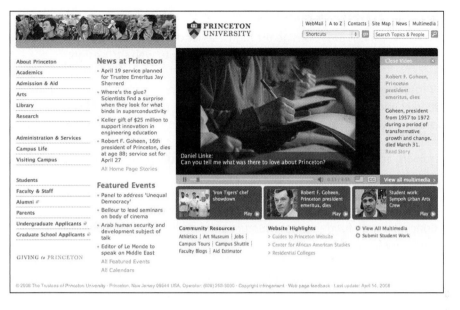

FIGURE 2.2
Equivalent text for
spoken audio in the
form of captions.

not likely to share access requirements. Some may be experts and others first-time users. Some may be have low or no vision, and others may have mobility or dexterity issues. The same person may access your site on a laptop, workstation, PDA (personal digital assistant), and cell phone. And although you may target a certain audience, others will come. For example, an investment service for retirees will also draw visits from investors, competitors, family members, and those lucky enough to enjoy an early retirement. It would be a mistake to design such a site to meet only the needs of older users.

And there is much at stake by excluding users. Even if your web logs show that only 2 percent of your users use a specific brand of browser, don't make the mistake of using technology that excludes those users. It's bad business to exclude anyone from access to your information and services, and there is no way to place a value on those users who you have excluded. Who knows? Your next major donor might be one of the 2 percent you turned away at the door!

THE DEVELOPMENT CYCLE

All development processes go through a series of stages that together form the classic "design cycle," here related particularly to web site design.

Requirements In larger projects the requirements phase may involve formal market and user research, web analytics research, focus groups of current or prospective users, and formal usability testing. In smaller projects the requirements phase often takes the form of team meetings with users, project stakeholders, and project sponsors to develop lists of functional requirements.

Design Design transforms lists of requirements into concrete form, first as rough layouts and page wireframes, navigation interfaces, and site diagrams. Concentrate on fundamental structure and function, and save detailed graphic design for later.

Development Development is the actual building of HTML pages and coding of any associated web applications. Even if you use an iterative design process (most web teams do), don't get too far into development until all major issues of design are settled.

Testing All site designs require both functional testing (link checks, browser compatibility issues, cross-platform issues) and editorial quality control. Too often web teams dominated by technologists short-change the editorial considerations, forgetting that content also requires an extensive quality-assurance process to produce a good product.

Classic design cycle

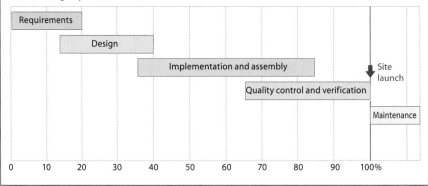

Linear or "waterfall" development Classic linear design projects march through each phase one at a time, completing each before moving on to the next. Linear development works best where tried and true methods exist and where the detailed specifications have been used successfully in the past. In less certain circumstances, linear development can seem brittle and plodding.

Iterative model of design Most projects deal with complex sets of unknowns by moving through a series of partial analyze-design or design-build stages, progressively building complexity and design consensus into the developing system, especially in the early planning and design phases of the cycle. The iteration model begins to break down when cycles of design-build-redesign continue too far into the development phase. These *development iterations* can result in production churning and much wasted time and effort.

A hybrid approach Good project management uses the strengths of both iterative and linear models, where many design iterations are encouraged early in the process but are strongly discouraged later in the development and testing phases, when efficient development effort and control of the overall project scope and schedule become paramount.

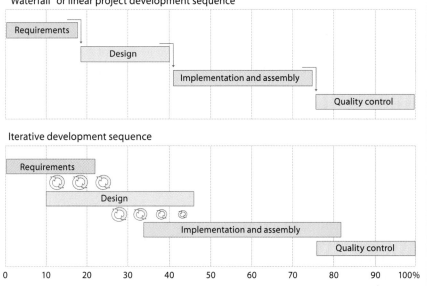

USER RESEARCH

The first step in any web site design process is to gather information about users—who they are, what their goals are—and identify their requirements for working with the site. The research phase is normally the most time-consuming phase of any design project, but that imbalance is due in large part to the fact that the design and evaluation phase moves more rapidly because of the time spent on research. With good user research, the decisions that drive the design are based on a solid understanding of users' goals and requirements and therefore are far more likely to hit the mark without many cycles of iteration.

Surveys

Several techniques exist for collecting feedback directly from users about their goals and behaviors. The information gathered from these collection techniques is subjective; it represents what users say they do, which is not necessarily the same as what they actually do and care about.

Surveys are helpful for collecting a large and broad range of responses about demographics and goals. Web site surveys typically ask initial questions to help define the user: age, gender, audience type (customer, potential customer, buyer, seller). Then there might be questions related to frequency of use: first-time visitor, sometimes visitor, frequent visitor. The meat of the survey is likely to be determining which elements of the site are most used, along with some assessment of the effectiveness and enjoyment derived from using them. This question might be represented as a list of site sections, each with a sliding scale measuring the success of use. Finally, an open-ended question inviting general feedback is always a good idea. Although the information is difficult to analyze, a simple read of the responses will yield common themes that may be useful for planning.

Interviews

In-person techniques open the door to more accurate and detailed information gathering because of the opportunity for interaction and exchange. In an interview, you inquire into user goals, interests, needs, and behaviors. One effective method for understanding user behaviors is to ask users to give a verbal walkthrough that describes their typical interaction and task flow when accomplishing a goal. For example, in designing a new dating web site, you might ask users from your target audience to describe their current process when interacting with a similar web site and how they make connections without the help of the web. The key is to get the user talking and keep him or her talking. Ask clarifying questions, pursue important details, and periodically sum up the important elements of the conversation. Don't be too quick to speak when the conversation lags; pause, and give the user the opportunity to continue the discussion thread. Also, don't be too rigid in sticking to the script; digressions may lead to valuable insights.

Focus groups

Focus groups have a very different dynamic. Whereas the interview is all about the individual, the focus group is about the collective—a group of users who share common concerns. Focus groups have a number of benefits, not the least of which is economy; it's an opportunity to hear many different perspectives at once. Also, the collaborative nature of focus groups helps people contribute insights that they may not have been aware of on their own. One user raises an issue that resonates with another, and the second user picks up the issue and takes it further, and the next, further.

Web analytics

With each page served, web servers collect basic information about the user and save the information in a server log file. Web analytics involves using the data in the server logs to study user behaviors. More advanced web analytics make use of additional tracking techniques that usually involve embedding something on the client—a "bug" on the page or a session cookie—that enables collection of additional information. With web analytics, it's possible to reconstruct elements of a web site session, such as:

- Where the user was before arriving at your site
- If the user used a search engine, which keywords were used
- The sequence of pages the user visited while on your site
- Attributes of the user's configuration, including browser, operating system, and screen dimensions and color settings
- Whether the user was a new or repeat visitor
- The last page in the session before the user left your site (fig 2.3)

FIGURE 2.3

Web analytics can help you analyze usage patterns in your site.

These and other site-specific metrics (the number of page requests helps determine which pages are most used; the number of distinct hosts helps determine how many site visitors there are) offer important insights into how users are working with your site, which is essential to any redesign process. Just bear in mind that, although web analytics appear to measure what is happening on your site, the reality is far more complicated. Many factors skew the data, such as browser caching, in which pages are stored locally on the client machine. When a user visits a cached page, that visit will not be logged in the server log file since the server was not asked for the page. Use web analytics, but don't treat them as the last word on user behaviors. Use them to complement the other user-centered techniques described in this chapter.

Field studies

Observing users in their natural setting yields valuable insights and objective information about user behaviors and the efficacy of designs. With observational methods, we move beyond self-reported goals and behaviors to observed goals and behaviors.

In a field study, you observe users working with a system, typically in their own context. For example, in designing a library catalog system, observing library patrons navigate the library is an excellent way to understand how they work with online catalog systems and how such systems help or hinder them in achieving their goals. Field studies are particularly helpful at the beginning of a project. For a redesign, observe users working with your current system to identify points of conflict between the design and user goals. For a new web site project, observe users working with a similar web site.

DESIGN AND EVALUATION

The next step in the design process is to apply what is learned in the research phase to creating designs that support the diversity of the target audience in accomplishing their goals. The design phase is an iterative one in which we conceptualize designs to create mockups, which we then evaluate and refine, often repeatedly, before arriving at a final design and finished web site.

Personas

Personas are fictional narratives describing particular representative users and serve as a stand-in for real users during the design process. Personas arise from the research phase and are informed by surveys, interviews, focus groups, and other research methods. Personas typically include a name, demographic information, level of expertise, and platform details such as connection speed, operating system, and browser software. Personas also include detailed information about user goals and motivations.

For universal usability, personas should push the boundaries of the fictional "average user" to include a range of use contexts and user motivations. Personas should represent the full range of age groups, computer expertise, and access technologies, including mobile devices, the wide but short screens of typical laptop computers, and screen reader software for nonvisual access (fig 2.4).

Goal analysis

Users of a system do so in response to specific goals they are trying to achieve. When we roll out of bed and into the shower in the morning, our goal is not turning on the water; our goal is to get clean and wake up. It's the tasks we

Emily Johnson
Veteran investor, novice web user

Age: 72
Residence: Cape Cod, Massachusetts
Internet experience: Novice
Primary uses: Banking, email
Favorite sites: Fidelity, AOL
Average time online: 3 hours/day

Quote
"I love the independence of the web,
but I wish it wasn't so hard."

Profile

Emily has been retired for eight years. She taught grade school in the Watertown school system for 40 years. She learned to budget her finances by raising a large family on a small, public school teacher's salary. When she retired, she sold her house of 43 years and moved to an inexpensive condo. With the income from her house sale, she began to explore investing. Initially she worked through an agent, but then she began managing her own investments through the web. Emily has had great success, more than doubling her initial investment over the course of ten years.

Emily is often frustrated when using web sites. She has an intuitive sense about investing and thoroughly understands the mechanics of the process. However, she sometimes makes mistakes when managing her accounts online. When she encounters difficulties, she blames her physical shortcomings—her arthritis, which makes it difficult to manipulate interface elements, and her failing vision, which makes it difficult to read.

undertake to accomplish this goal that involve water, faucets, and soap. In design, it's important to focus on goals rather than tasks in making design decisions. A focus on goals helps us think outside the box and create better designs. Instead of designing a shower from the perspective of the tasks it needs to support, we can focus on the goal of getting clean and waking up, which opens the door to new approaches.

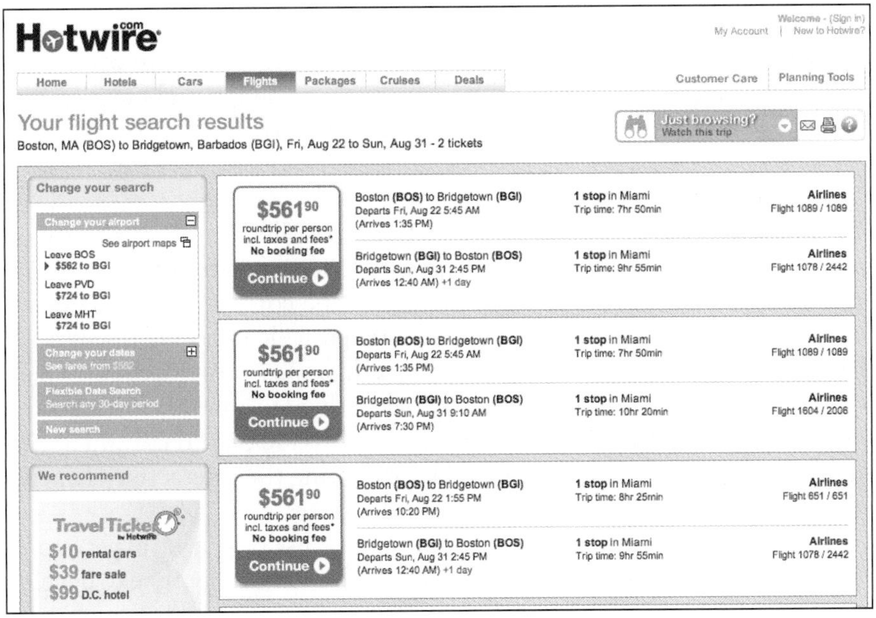

FIGURE 2.5
Complex data displays can easily overwhelm the reader. Keep the display focused on the information most important to the user's current task.

For example, let's say our goal when interacting with a travel web site is to get from Boston to Barbados without spending too much time or money. To accomplish our goal, our tasks are to compare flight schedules and prices. The designer who designs for our goal will understand that time spent in transit and cost are the primary factors and will design an interface that shows information in a way that permits easy comparisons. Other information related to the trip, such as meals served or type of aircraft, is secondary and available on request (fig. 2.5).

Goals come in many shapes and sizes and emerge from different perspectives. Users have both personal and practical goals: being more productive, having fun, saving time and money. Institutional goals also play a part: increase revenue, recruit more and better employees, offer more services. With any web site project, goals should be the driving factor behind design decisions and the compass to steer by throughout the design process.

Scenarios

Scenarios, or use cases, are brief narratives that tell the story of a particular user's path in accomplishing his or her goals. To construct a scenario, we use personas representing our users and walk them through the various tasks necessary with the web site in order to accomplish their goals. In composing a scenario, we can play out different approaches to design and functionality and in the process identify possible problems with each approach.

Prototypes and wireframes

Paper prototypes are an inexpensive method for collecting user feedback on an evolving design. A paper prototype typically illustrates the location of page elements, such as site navigation, search, and content, and includes the labeling that will be used for these elements (page elements are discussed in detail in the Wireframes section of chapter 3, *Information Architecture*). These low-resolution mockups can be used in user testing to determine whether the organization of the page and the navigation labels are easy to use and understand. They are obviously less helpful for exploring the interactive elements of the page. For that we need functional wireframes.

Functional wireframes use the same minimalist design of paper prototypes, but on a functional web site (fig. 2.6). They take more time to develop than paper prototypes but are well worth the effort, particularly for sites that are built on complex information architectures and for web applications that contain a high level of interaction. For a functional wireframe, several layers of the web site are established to model the site's architecture, navigation, and functionality. For interactive sites, such as web applications, the wireframe should include a basic user interface in order to play out and test the flow of the application with users.

User testing

User testing is a controlled and directed observation of user behaviors when working with a design. User testing is used throughout the design process to evaluate different design approaches by observing how well, or how poorly, they work in helping users accomplish tasks.

A typical user testing session has a tester and a participant who represents the target audience. The user is assigned a set of tasks intended to put specific elements of a design to the test and reveal any shortcomings of the approach. During the session, the user is asked to think aloud so that the tester can understand the rationale behind his or her choices. The session normally ends with an open-ended interview in which the user is given the opportunity

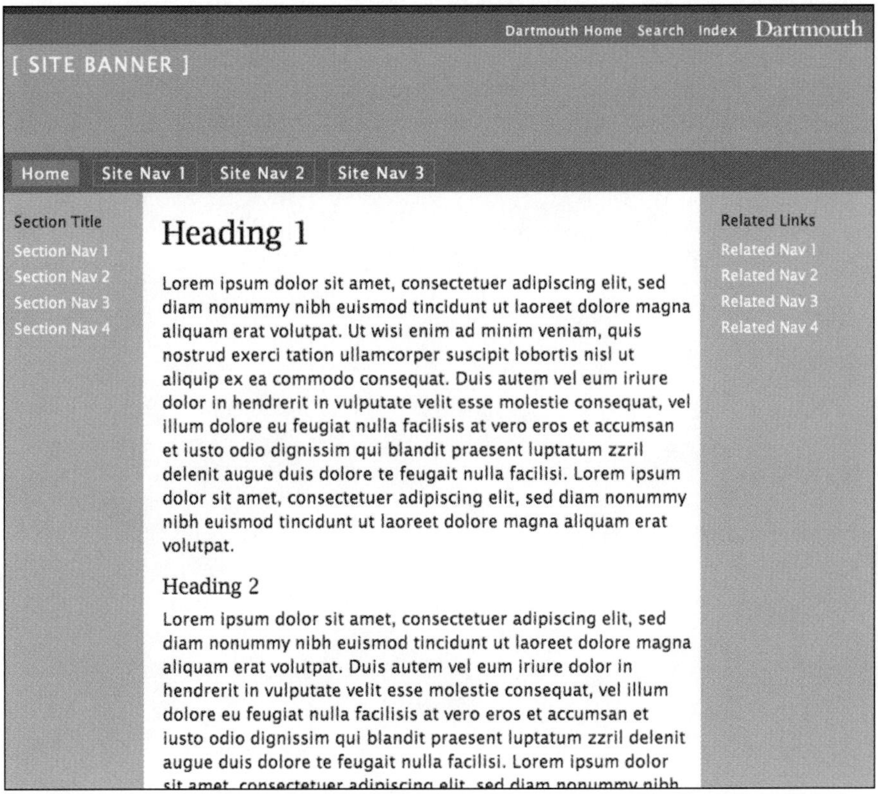

FIGURE 2.6
An example of a
basic template for
building functional
wireframes.

to discuss his or her experience with the system more broadly and provide insights and suggestions on how the system might be improved.

User testing is useful throughout the design process to help identify usability problems. The lessons learned from user testing can be used in refining the design and improving its universal usability.

Design informs even the simplest structure, whether of brick and steel or prose.

— E. B. White

CHAPTER 3

Information Architecture

I n the context of web site design, information architecture describes the overall conceptual models and general designs used to plan, structure, and assemble a site. Every web site has an information architecture, but information architecture techniques are particularly important to large, complex web sites, where the primary aims are to:

- Organize the site content into taxonomies and hierarchies of information;
- Communicate conceptual overviews and the overall site organization to the design team and clients;
- Research and design the core site navigation concepts;
- Set standards and specifications for the handling of HTML semantic markup, and the format and handling of text content; and
- Design and implement search optimization standards and strategies.

Information architecture encompasses a broad range of design and planning disciplines, and the boundaries among information architecture, technical design, user interface, and graphic design are necessarily blurred by the need for all of these communities of practice to cooperate to produce a cohesive, coherent, and consistent experience for the site user. Architecture is an appropriate metaphor for the assembling of complex multidimensional information spaces shared by many different users and readers, where the underlying structure of information must first be framed out before more specific disciplines such as interface and graphic design can operate effectively. The user interface and visual design of the site may be much more visible to the user initially, but if the underlying organization of the site and its content is poorly constructed, visual or interactive design will not fix the problems.

In large web projects the role of information architect will probably be filled by an individual with long experience in organizing and presenting information, particularly in the context of the web. However, in many projects the information architecture of the site will become a joint project among the design, editorial, and technical teams. Regardless of how the role is filled, the information architecture tasks form the crucial planning bridge between your general discussions of site goals and audiences and the specific design, user interface, and technical solutions you'll use in the finished site designs.

ORGANIZING YOUR INFORMATION

Our day-to-day professional and social lives rarely demand that we create detailed architectures of what we know and how those structures of information are linked. Yet without a solid and logical organizational foundation, your web site will not function well even if your basic content is accurate, attractive, and well written.

There are five basic steps in organizing your information:

1　Inventory your content: What do you have already? What do you need?
2　Establish a hierarchical outline of your content and create a controlled vocabulary so the major content, site structure, and navigation elements are always identified consistently;
3　Chunking: Divide your content into logical units with a consistent modular structure;
4　Draw diagrams that show the site structure and rough outlines of pages with a list of core navigation links; and
5　Analyze your system by testing the organization interactively with real users; revise as needed.

CONTENT INVENTORIES

A content inventory is a detailed listing of basic information about all the content that exists in a site to be redesigned or, in some cases, a site to be newly created from existing content resources. Although a content inventory is often tedious and time-consuming to create, it is an essential component of any rational scope planning for a web project. Content inventories are most useful in the initial project planning and information architecture phases, but a detailed content inventory will be useful throughout the project for both planning and build-out of the site. The work of moving through an existing site and recording information on each page is detailed, but it's also easy to divide up among team members who work through different subsections or directories of the site. The team members making the site inventory must both have access to the site pages in a web browser and be able to view the site file structure on the server to ensure that all sections of content are inventoried.

Web content inventories of existing sites commonly take the form of a spreadsheet file with multiple worksheets, containing long listings of every page in the site, along with such essential characteristics as the page title, URL, people responsible for the content, and so on. Each page typically gets a row on the spreadsheet, with columns listing such basic information as:

- Unique ID number for project purposes
- Page title
- Page template or type
- URL
- General type of content
- Person responsible for the content
- Keep/revise/discard decisions
- Create new content?
- Review status

Hierarchies and taxonomies

Hierarchical organization is a virtual necessity on the web. Most sites depend on hierarchies, moving from the broadest overview of the site (the home page), down through increasingly specific submenus and content pages. In information architecture you create categories for your information and rank the importance of each piece of information by how general or specific that piece is relative to the whole. General categories become high-ranking elements of the hierarchy of information; specific chunks of information are positioned lower in the hierarchy. Chunks of information are ranked in importance and organized by relevance to one of the major categories. Once you have determined a logical set of priorities and relations in your content outlines, you can build a hierarchy from the most important or general concepts down to the most specific or detailed topics.

Taxonomies and controlled vocabularies

Taxonomy is the science and practice of classification. In information architecture, a taxonomy is a hierarchical organization of content categories, using a specific, carefully designed set of descriptive terms. As any experienced editor or librarian can tell you, one of the biggest challenges of organizing large amounts of information is developing a system for always referring to the same things the same way: a controlled vocabulary, in library science parlance. One of the most important jobs of the information architect thus is producing a consistent set of names and terms to describe the chief site content categories, the key navigation site links, and major terms to describe the interactive features of the site. This controlled vocabulary becomes a foundational element of the content organization, the user interface, the standard navigation links seen on every page of the site, and the file and directory structure of the site itself.

Brainstorming

When designing a new web site or extensively overhauling an existing one, it can be useful to step back from the details of the content inventory and take a fresh look at both how your information is organized and the underlying paradigms that drive conversations about content and site organization.

Some common underlying paradigms for site organization are:

- Identity sites: Dominated by projected identity and marketing
- Navigation sites: Dominated by navigation and links
- Novelty sites: Dominated by news and "what's new"
- The org chart site: Designed around the organization of the enterprise
- Service sites: Organized around service, content, or products categories
- Flashy sites: Use interaction and visual flash to draw an audience
- Tool-oriented sites: Organized around the latest technology, such as XML, Ajax, or "Web 2.0"

Some paradigms or mindsets are clearly better than others: it's rarely wise to fall in love with a particular technology before you have a clear rationale for using it or for projecting your identity to the extent that you ignore the motivations and concerns of your potential readers and users. However, good sites are a balance of meeting your users' needs and delivering your message to the world. There is no formula for finding the right organizational paradigm, but in the early planning you should always examine your standing prejudices and explicitly justify them. Why is it a good idea to organize your navigation around your business units? How does that match your users' needs and concerns? Clumsy "org chart sites" are a standing joke among web

FIVE HAT RACKS: THEMES TO ORGANIZE INFORMATION

In *Information Anxiety* (1989), Richard Saul Wurman posits that there are five fundamental ways to organize information: the "five hat racks" on which you can hang information.

Category   Organization by the similarity of characteristics or relatedness of the items. This is a particularly useful approach when all the things being organized are of equal or unpredictable importance. Examples include topics of books in a bookstore or library and items in a department or grocery store.

Time   Organization by timeline or history, where elements are presented in a sequential step-by-step manner. This approach is commonly used in training. Other examples include television listings, a history of specific events, and measuring the response times of different systems.

Location   Organization by spatial or geographic location, most often used for orientation and direction. This most graphic of the categories obviously lends itself to maps but is also used extensively in training, repair, and user manual illustrations and other instances where information is tied to a place.

Alphabetic   Organization based on the initial letter of the names of items. Obvious examples are telephone and other name-oriented directories, dictionaries, and thesauri, where users know the word or name they are seeking. Alphabetic systems are simple to grasp and familiar in everyday life. This method of organization is less effective for short lists of unrelated things but is powerful for long lists.

Continuum   Organization by the quantity of a measured variable over a range, such as price, score, size, or weight. Continuum organization is most effective when organizing many things that are all measured or scored the same way. Examples include rankings and reviews of all kinds, such as the *U.S. News and World Report* ranking of colleges and universities, the best movies in a given year, darkest or lightest items, and other instances where a clear weight or value can be assigned to each item.

designers, but sometimes users really *do* want to know how you are organized and will find services and content more easily with navigation based on business units. If you see these underlying mindsets driving or distorting early site organization discussions, put them on the table for discussion and brainstorming. Everyone has paradigms: just be sure you've examined and chosen yours as the best solution for your site.

Card sorting and whiteboard sessions

Even if the major categories of your content organization are clear to the design team, it still may be hard to sort through where each piece of content belongs or what organization scheme will seem intuitive and predictable to your users.

Card sorting is a common technique for both creating and evaluating content organization and web site structures. In classic card-sorting techniques, index cards are labeled with the names of major and secondary content categories, and individual team members or potential site users are then asked to sort through the cards and organize them in a way that seems intuitive and logical. Users may also be asked to suggest new or better names for categories. The resulting content outline from each participant is recorded, usually in a spreadsheet, and all the individual content schemes are compared for commonalities and areas of major disagreement. The best card-sorting data comes from individual sessions with representative current or potential users of your site. If you have enough participants, combining the results of each card-sorting session produces a powerful "wisdom of crowds" aggregation of many individual judgments about what content organization makes sense.

For smaller or less formal site projects you can have group whiteboard sessions with techniques similar to card sorting. Participants are asked to sort through cards or sticky notes labeled with the names of major content elements, which are then posted on a whiteboard and sorted by the group until there is consensus about what overall organization makes the most sense. In most cases you'll achieve quick consensus on the major categories of content and navigation, and the whiteboard organization becomes a useful first look at the site org chart that can help the group resolve the more problematic questions of what content belongs in which category.

For successful content organization sessions, make sure that you:

- Name the major categories as clearly as possible, without duplications or redundancies in terminology
- Have a complete inventory of all your major categories and subcategories of content
- Prepare thorough instructions for individual card-sorting sessions
- Refrain from prompting or coaching individual participants
- Refrain from discouraging ideas, and allow free brainstorming
- Have plenty of supplies for new categories and improved terminology
- Bring a digital camera to record the proposed organizations and whiteboard layouts

Individual card-sorting and group whiteboard sessions are fast, inexpensive ways to create and evaluate your proposed site content organization. The techniques have been used for many years, and if you involve actual or potential users of your site, they offer "real world" validation of ideas from your sponsors, stakeholders, and team members.

CHUNKING INFORMATION

Most information on the World Wide Web is gathered in short reference documents that are intended to be read nonsequentially. This is particularly true of sites where the contents are mostly technical or administrative documents. Long before the web was invented, technical writers discovered that readers appreciate short chunks of information that can be located and scanned. This method of presenting information translates well to the web for several reasons:

- Few web users read long passages of text onscreen. Most users save long documents to disk or print them for more comfortable reading.
- Discrete chunks of information lend themselves to web links. The user of a web link usually expects to find a specific unit of relevant information, not a book's worth of general content.
- Chunking can help organize and present information in a modular layout that is consistent throughout the site. This allows users not only to apply past experience with a site to future searches and explorations but also to predict how an unfamiliar section of a web site will be organized.

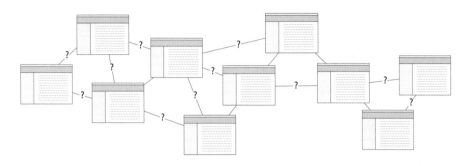

FIGURE 3.1
Don't make a
confusing web of
links. Designers
aren't the only ones
who make models
of sites. Users try
to imagine the site
structure as well,
and a successful
information
architecture will
help the user build a
firm and predictable
mental model of
your site.

- Concise chunks of information are better suited to the computer screen, which provides a limited view of long documents. Long web pages tend to disorient readers; they require users to scroll long distances and to remember what has scrolled off-screen.

The concept of a chunk of information must be flexible and consistent with common sense, logical organization, and convenience. Let the nature of the content suggest how it should be subdivided and organized. Although short web documents are usually preferable, it makes little sense to divide a long document arbitrarily, particularly if you want users to be able to print easily or save the document in one step.

SITE STRUCTURE

When confronted with a new and complex information system, users build mental models. They use these models to assess relations among topics and to guess where to find things they haven't seen before. The success of the organization of your web site will be determined largely by how well your site's information architecture matches your users' expectations. A logical, consistently named site organization allows users to make successful predictions about where to find things. Consistent methods of organizing and displaying information permit users to extend their knowledge from familiar pages to unfamiliar ones. If you mislead users with a structure that is neither logical nor predictable, or constantly uses different or ambiguous terms to describe site features, users will be frustrated by the difficulties of getting around and understanding what you have to offer. You don't want your user's mental model of your web site to look like figure 3.1.

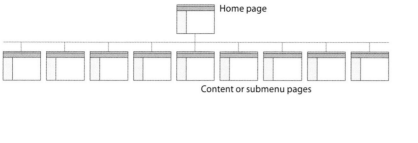

Home page

Content or submenu pages

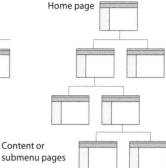

Home page

Content or submenu pages

THE BROWSE FUNCTIONALITY OF YOUR SITE

Once you have created your site in outline form, analyze its ability to support browsing by testing it interactively, both within the site development team and with small groups of real users. Efficient web site design is largely a matter of balancing the relation of major menu or home pages with individual content pages. The goal is to build a hierarchy of menus and content pages that feels natural to users and doesn't mislead them or interfere with their use of the site.

Web sites with too shallow an information hierarchy depend on massive menu pages that can degenerate into a confusing laundry list of unrelated information. Menu schemes can also be too deep, burying information beneath too many layers of menus. Having to navigate through layers of nested menus before reaching real content is frustrating (fig. 3.2).

If your web site is actively growing, the proper balance of menus and content pages is a moving target. Feedback from users (and analyzing your own use of the site) can help you decide if your menu scheme has outlived its usefulness or has weak areas. Complex document structures require deeper menu hierarchies, but users should never be forced into page after page of menus if direct access is possible. With a well-balanced, functional hierarchy you can offer users menus that provide quick access to information and reflect the organization of your site.

FIGURE 3.2
Examples of the "Goldilocks problem" in getting the site structure "just right." Too shallow a structure (left) forces menus to become too long. Too deep a structure (right) and users get frustrated as they dig down through many layers of menus.

SITE SEARCH AS NAVIGATION

If your site has more than a few dozen pages, your users will expect web search options to find content in the site. In a larger site, with maybe hundreds or thousands of pages of content, web search is the only efficient means to locate particular content pages or to find all pages that mention a keyword

FIGURE 3.3

The "long tail" of
web search. Large
sites are just too
large to depend
solely on browsing.
Heavily used pages
are likely to appear
on browsing menus
pages, but obscure
pages deep within
the site will only
be found and read
through web search
technologies.

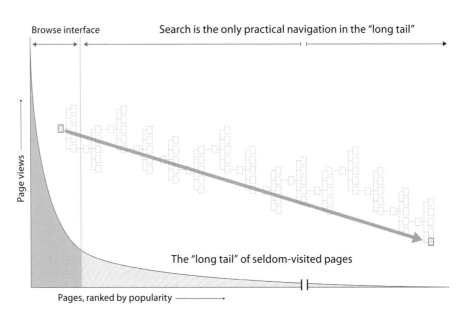

or search phrase. Browse interfaces composed of major site and content land-marks are essential in the initial phases of a user's visit to your site. However, once the user has decided that your site may offer what he or she is looking for, the user crosses a threshold of specificity that only a search engine can help with:

- No browse interface of links can assure the user that he or she has found all instances of a given keyword or search phrase.
- Search is the most efficient means to reach specific content, particularly if that content is not heavily visited by other users and is therefore unlikely to appear as a link in a major navigation page.

As with popular books at the library or the hit songs on iTunes, content usage on large web sites is a classic "long-tail" phenomenon: a few items get 80 percent of the attention, and the rest get dramatically less traffic. As the user's needs get more specific than a browser interface can handle, search engines are the means to find content out there in the long tail where it might otherwise remain undiscovered (fig. 3.3).

a. Straight linear sequence

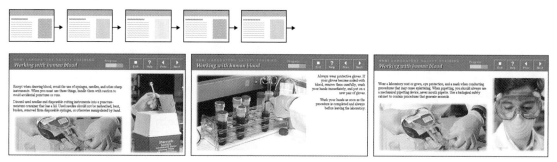

b. Linear sequences with supporting digressions

FIGURE 3.4

Some web sites, such as this training site, are meant to be read in a linear sequence (a). Programming logic can offer customized content for particular audiences and allow digressions from the main sequence of pages (b).

SITE STRUCTURAL THEMES

Web sites are built around basic structural themes that both form and reinforce a user's mental model of how you have organized your content. These fundamental architectures govern the navigational interface of the web site and mold the user's mental models of how the information is organized. Three essential structures can be used to build a web site: sequences, hierarchies, and webs.

Sequences

The simplest and most familiar way to organize information is to place it in a sequence. This is the structure of books, magazines, and all other print matter. Sequential ordering may be chronological, a logical series of topics progressing from the general to the specific, or alphabetical, as in indexes, encyclopedias, and glossaries. Straight sequences are the most appropriate organization for training or education sites, for example, in which the user is expected to progress through a fixed set of material and the only links are those that support the linear navigation path (fig 3.4a).

FIGURE 3.5

Hierarchies are simple and inevitable in web design. Most content works well in hierarchical structures, and users find them easy to understand.

a. Simple hub-and-spoke structure

b. More complex hierarchy

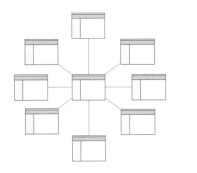
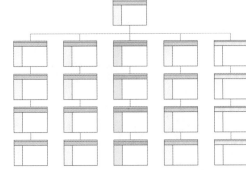

More complex web sites may still be organized as a logical sequence, but each page in the sequence may have links to one or more pages of digressions, parenthetical information, or information on other web sites (fig. 3.4b).

Hierarchies

Information hierarchies are the best way to organize most complex bodies of information. Because web sites are usually organized around a single home page, which then links to subtopic menu pages, hierarchical architectures are particularly suited to web site organization. Hierarchical diagrams are very familiar in corporate and institutional life, so most users find this structure easy to understand. A hierarchical organization also imposes a useful discipline on your own analytical approach to your content, because hierarchies are practical only with well-organized material.

The simplest form of hierarchical site structure is a star, or hub-and-spoke, set of pages arrayed off a central home page. The site is essentially a single-tier hierarchy. Navigation tends to be a simple list of subpages, plus a link for the home page (fig 3.5a).

Most web sites adopt some form of multitiered hierarchical or tree architecture. This arrangement of major categories and subcategories has a powerful advantage for complex site organization in that most people are familiar with hierarchical organizations, and can readily form mental models of the site structure (fig. 3.5b).

Note that although hierarchical sites organize their content and pages in a tree of site menus and submenus off the home page, this hierarchy of content subdivisions should not become a navigational straitjacket for the user

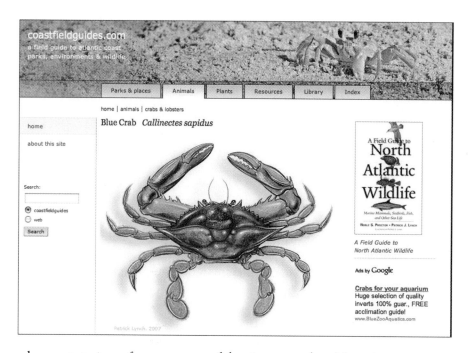

FIGURE 3.6
Local (left column)
and global (tabs)
navigation systems
provide a flexible and
easy to understand
navigation system.

who wants to jump from one area of the site to another. Most site navigation interfaces provide global navigation links that allow users to jump from one major site area to another without being forced to back up to a central home page or submenu. In figure 3.6, tabs in the header allow the user to move from one major content area to another, the left navigation menu provides local topic categories, and a search box allows the user to jump out of categorical navigation and find pages based on a web search engine.

Webs

Weblike organizational structures pose few restrictions on the pattern of information use. In this structure the goal is often to mimic associative thought and the free flow of ideas, allowing users to follow their interests in a unique, heuristic, idiosyncratic pattern. This organizational pattern develops with dense links both to information elsewhere in the site and to information at other sites. Although the goal of this organization is to exploit the web's power of linkage and association to the fullest, weblike structures can just as easily propagate confusion. Ironically, associative organizational schemes are often the most impractical structure for web sites because they are so hard for

FIGURE 3.7
A simple web of
associated pages.

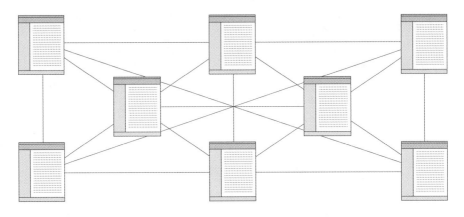

the user to understand and predict. Webs work best for small sites dominated by lists of links and for sites aimed at highly educated or experienced users looking for further education or enrichment and not for a basic understanding of a topic (fig. 3.7).

SUMMARY

Most complex web sites share aspects of all three types of information structures. Site hierarchy is created largely with standard navigational links within the site, but topical links embedded within the content create a weblike mesh of associative links that transcends the usual navigation and site structure. Except in sites that rigorously enforce a sequence of pages, users are likely to traverse your site in a free-form weblike manner, jumping across regions in the information architecture, just as they would skip through

FIGURE 3.8
We structure sites as
hierarchies, but users
seldom use them
that way. A clear
information structure
allows the user to
move freely and
confidently through
your site.

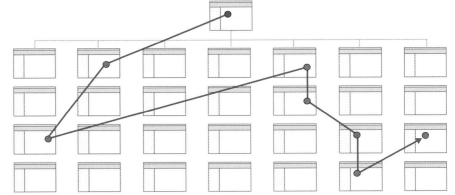

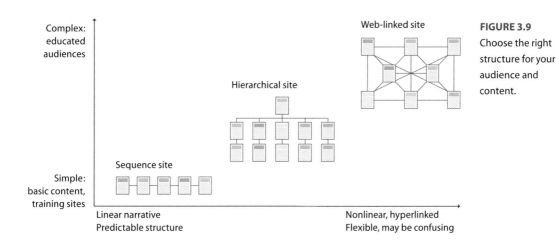

FIGURE 3.9
Choose the right
structure for your
audience and
content.

Complex: educated audiences

Simple: basic content, training sites

Web-linked site

Hierarchical site

Sequence site

Linear narrative
Predictable structure

Nonlinear, hyperlinked
Flexible, may be confusing

chapters in a reference book. Ironically, the clearer and more concrete your site organization is, the easier it is for users to jump freely from place to place without feeling lost (fig. 3.8).

The nonlinear usage patterns typical of web users do not absolve you of the need to organize your thinking and present it within a clear, consistent structure that complements your overall design goals. Figure 3.9 summarizes the three basic organization patterns against the linearity of the narrative and the complexity of the content.

PRESENTING INFORMATION ARCHITECTURE

Site planning with a team is often easier if you base your major structural planning and decisions on a shared master site diagram that all members of the group can work with. The site diagram should evolve as the plan evolves and act as the core planning document as changes are proposed and made in the diagram. Site diagrams are excellent for planning both the broad scope of the site and the details of where each piece of content, navigation, or interactive functionality will appear.

For major planning meetings consider printing at least one large diagram of the site organization, so that everyone can see the big picture as it develops from meeting to meeting. The site diagram should dominate the conference table, becoming a tactile, malleable representation of the plan. Everyone should be free to make notes and suggest improvements on the printed plan, and the revised diagram becomes the official result of the meeting.

FIGURE 3.10

Jesse James Garrett's
visual vocabulary for
site design diagrams
(www.jjg.net/ia/
visvocab).

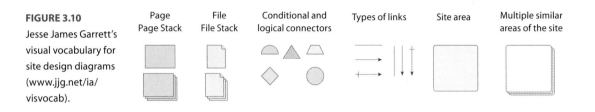

SITE DIAGRAMS

As your team works out the information architecture and major categories of content, site diagrams visualize the developing information hierarchy and help communicate the organizational concepts to the team and to stakeholders and project sponsors. This communications role is crucial throughout the project, as the site diagram evolves in iterations from a brainstorming and planning document into a blueprint for the actual site as it will be developed.

Site diagrams can range from simple hierarchical "org chart" diagrams to more complex and information-rich maps that show both the major divisions of the site as the user experiences them, but also act as an overview of the site directory and file structure. The well-known information architect Jesse James Garrett developed a widely used visual vocabulary for site diagrams that has become the de facto standard, and the symbols are broadly useful for portraying site structure and interactive relationships and user decision points (fig. 3.10).

Major elements of a mature site diagram include:

- Content structure and organization: major site content divisions and subdivisions
- Logical functional grouping or structural relationships
- The "click depth" of each level of the site: How many clicks are required to reach a given page?
- Page type or template (menu page, internal page, major section entry point, and so on)
- Site directory and file structure
- Dynamic data elements like databases, RSS, or applications
- Major navigation terms and controlled vocabularies
- Link relationships, internal and external to the site
- Levels of user access, log-ins required, or other restricted areas

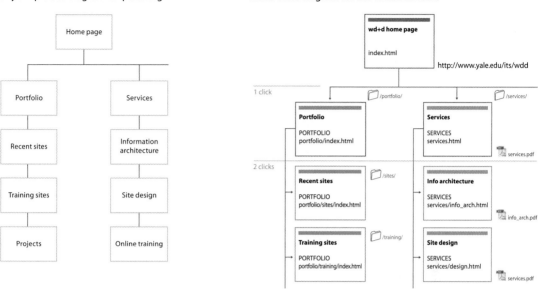

Early simple site diagram for planning

Mature site diagram for the technical team

Site diagrams start simply, and may evolve into two distinct variations: conceptual site diagrams that communicate at a general level the evolving site structure to clients and stakeholders, and more complex blueprint diagrams that are used by the technical, editorial, and graphic design teams as a guide to the structure of both the user interface and the directories and files.

Figure 3.11 depicts a simple site diagram for use in presentations and general overviews and the same site shown in greater detail for use by the site development team. These site diagrams can be developed with drawing software such as Adobe Illustrator but are usually developed with specialized diagrammatic software such as Microsoft Visio, ConceptDraw, or OmniGraffle.

FIGURE 3.11
Keep irrelevant technical details out of early planning diagrams. Diagrams gradually incorporate more details as the focus shifts from clients and content experts to the technical team who will build the site.

Site file and directory structures

Site diagrams are also useful when your project moves from planning to web page production. As the new site is built up in a directory on the web server, the site diagram is often the first place programmers look to gain an understanding of how the site files should be subdivided into directories (folders) on the server. The pattern of directories and subdirectories of the site files

FIGURE 3.12

Ideally the
information
architecture will be
consistently reflected
in the actual
organization of files
and directories in the
site structure.

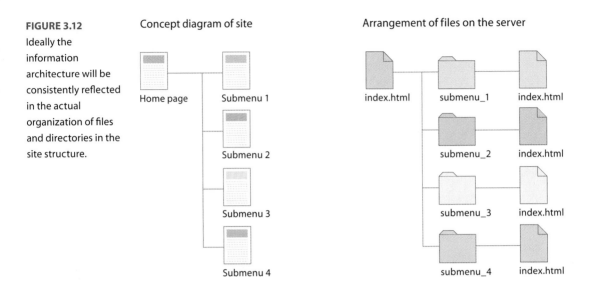

Concept diagram of site

Home page   Submenu 1

Submenu 2

Submenu 3

Submenu 4

Arrangement of files on the server

index.html   submenu_1   index.html

submenu_2   index.html

submenu_3   index.html

submenu_4   index.html

should mirror the major content divisions and structures as shown on the site diagram.

As the site directories and subdirectories are organized on the server, information on the exact names used for major directories and files should be added to the site diagram, so that everyone on the team has a ready current reference to the naming conventions and file locations in the site (fig. 3.12).

WIREFRAMES

The information architecture process is fundamentally one of avoiding the particular while insisting on the general. At various points in this conceptual phase, stakeholders, clients, and even members of your design team may find it irresistible to launch into specific proposals for the visual design of pages. In particular, concern about the possible look and feel of the home page is notorious for throwing planning processes off the rails and into detailed discussions of what colors, graphics, or general character the home page should have, long before anyone has given serious thought to the strategic goals, functions, and structure of the site. Wireframes force teams to stay focused on the information architecture and structural design without getting sidetracked by the distraction of the visual layer.

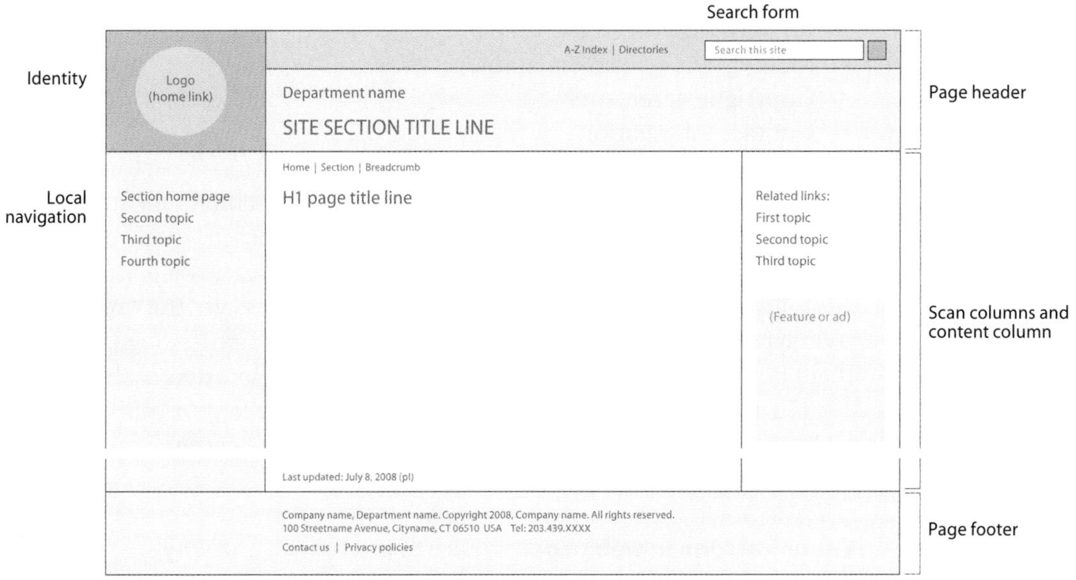

Search form

Identity

Logo
(home link)

A-Z Index | Directories   Search this site

Page header

Department name

SITE SECTION TITLE LINE

Local
navigation

Section home page
Second topic
Third topic
Fourth topic

Home | Section | Breadcrumb

H1 page title line

Related links:
First topic
Second topic
Third topic

Scan columns and
content column

(Feature or ad)

Last updated: July 8, 2008 (pl)

Company name, Department name. Copyright 2008, Company name. All rights reserved.
100 Streetname Avenue, Cityname, CT 06510 USA   Tel: 203.439.XXXX

Contact us | Privacy policies

Page footer

If site diagrams provide the global overview of the developing web site, then wireframes are the "rough map" that will eventually be used by graphic and interface designers to create preliminary and final page designs for the site. Wireframes are rough two-dimensional guides to where the major navigation and content elements of your site might appear on the page. They bring a consistent modular structure to the various page forms of your site and provide the fundamental layout and navigation structure for the finished templates to come (fig. 3.13).

Things that might appear as standard elements of a web page wireframe include:

- Organizational logo
- Site identity or titles
- Page title headlines
- Breadcrumb trail navigation
- Search form
- Links to a larger organization of which you are a part
- Global navigation links for the site
- Local content navigation

FIGURE 3.13
A typical page
wireframe diagram.

- Primary page content
- Mailing address and email information
- Copyright statements
- Contact information

To keep the discussion focused on information architecture and navigation, keep your wireframe diagrams simple and unadorned. Avoid distinctive typography, use a single generic font, and use gray tones if you must to distinguish functional areas, but avoid color or pictures. Usually the only graphic that appears in a mature wireframe will be the organization logo, but even there it may be better simply to indicate the general location of the logo.

The page wireframe will acquire more complexity as your thinking about global and local navigation matures and you are more certain about the nature and organization of the primary site content.

Canonical form in web pages: Where to put things, and why

What governs how people scan pages of information, print or screen? According to classical art composition theory the corners and middle of a plane attract early attention from viewers. In a related compositional practice, the "rule of thirds" places centers of interest within a grid that divides both dimensions in thirds. These compositional rules are purely pictorial, however, and are probably most useful for displays or home pages composed almost entirely of graphics or photography. Most page composition is dominated by text, and there our reading habits are the primary forces that shape the way we scan pages. In Western languages we read from top to bottom, scanning left to right down the page in a "Gutenberg z" pattern. This preference for attention flow down the page—and a reluctance to reverse the downward scanning—is called "reading gravity" and explains why it is rarely a good idea to place the primary headline anywhere except the top of a page. Readers who are scanning your work are unlikely to back up the page to "start again." Search engines also have a well-known bias toward items near the top of a page (fig. 3.14).

Eye-tracking studies by the Poynter Institute of readers looking at web pages have shown that readers start their scanning with many fixations in the upper left of the page. Their gaze then follows a Gutenberg z pattern down the page, and only later do typical readers lightly scan the right area of the page (fig. 3.15a). Eye-tracking studies by Jakob Nielsen show that web

Middle and corners

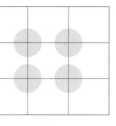
Rule of thirds

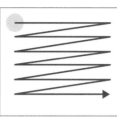
Gutenberg Z

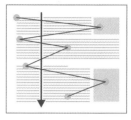
Reading gravity

pages dominated by text information are scanned in an "F" pattern of intense eye fixations across the top header area, and down the left edge of the text (fig. 3.15b).

When readers scan web pages they are clearly using a combination of classic Gutenberg z page scanning, combined with what they have learned from the emerging standards and practices of web designers. As the web nears its twentieth anniversary some clear trends have emerged that will eventually form the basis for "best practice" recommendations in web page composition. Human interface researchers have done studies on where users expect to find standard web page components and have found clear sets of expectations about where some items are located on web pages (fig. 3.16).

FIGURE 3.14
Classic rules of composition and our reading habits combine to govern how we approach information displays.

a. Poynter eye-tracking study

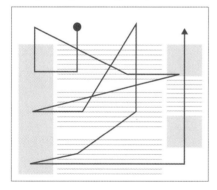

b. "F" pattern and the "golden triangle"

FIGURE 3.15
Eye-tracking studies show that our page-scanning patterns are dominated by top-left scanning for the most important words and links on a page.

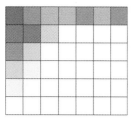
Home link

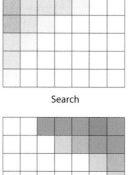
Search

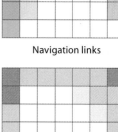
Banner ads

Navigation links

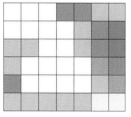
External links

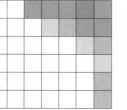
Shopping cart

Help link

About us

FIGURE 3.16
Users have developed clear expectations about where common content and interface elements are likely to appear. Violate these expectations at your peril.

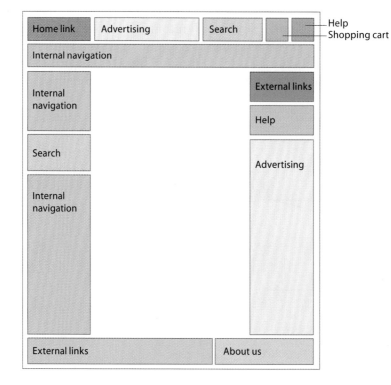

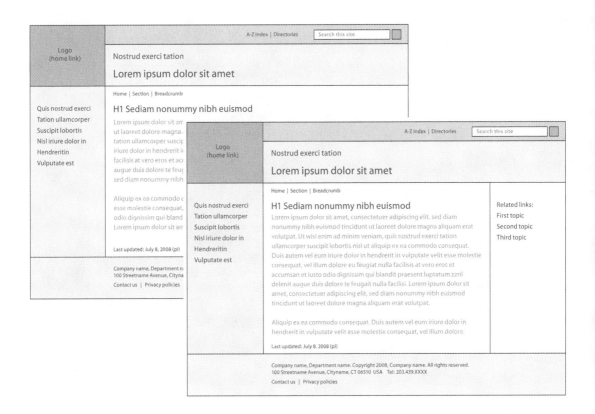

The web is still a young medium with no standards organizations to canonize existing typical page layout practices. Until we have a *Chicago Manual of Style* for the web, we can at least combine current mainstream web design practice, user interface research, and classic page composition to form recommendations for the location of identity, content, navigation, and other standard elements of pages in text-dominant, information-oriented web sites (fig. 3.17).

FIGURE 3.17
Always consider web conventions and user expectations as you develop the basic structure of page designs.

Navigation isn't just a *feature* of a web site, it *is* the web site, in the same way that the building, the shelves, and the cash registers *are* Sears. Without it, there's no *there* there.

—Steve Krug

CHAPTER 4

Interface Design

U sers of web documents don't just look at information, they interact with it in novel ways that have no precedents in paper document design; therefore, web designers must be versed in the art and science of interface design. The graphic user interface (GUI) of a computer system comprises the interaction metaphors, images, and concepts used to convey function and meaning on the computer screen. It also includes the detailed visual characteristics of every component of the graphic interface and the functional sequence of interactions over time that produce the characteristic look and feel of web pages. Graphic design and visual "signature" graphics are not used simply to enliven web pages—graphics are integral to the user's experience with your site. In interactive documents, graphic design cannot be separated from issues of interface design.

NAVIGATION AND WAYFINDING

In his book *The Image of the City* (1960), Kevin Lynch coined the term "wayfinding" to describe his concept of environmental legibility—that is, the elements of the built environment that allow us to navigate success-fully through complex spaces like cities and towns. The most fundamental underlying metaphor of the World Wide Web is navigation through a space populated by places we call web "sites," and thus the wayfinding metaphor is perfect for thinking about web navigation (fig. 4.1).

Wayfinding has four core components:

1 Orientation: Where am I am right now?
2 Route decisions: Can I find the way to where I want to go?
3 Mental mapping: Are my experiences consistent and understandable enough to know where I've been and to predict where I should go next?
4 Closure: Can I recognize that I have arrived in the right place?

FIGURE 4.1

Venice is beautiful, but without the churches and campaniles that tower over the city and provide landmarks for navigation through the neighborhoods, the streets and canals would be a confusing warren of twists and turns to the visitor.

In interviews conducted in various cities, Lynch had local residents draw maps of their cities from memory. The mental maps that residents create are crucial to wayfinding in their environment. An individual's map of the local environment is unique, but Lynch found that most people's maps were populated by five types of elements:

1 Paths: Familiar streets, walkways, subway routes, bus lines
2 Edges: The physical barriers of walls, fences, rivers, or shorelines
3 Districts: Places with a distinct identity, such as, in New York, Chinatown, Wall Street, and Greenwich Village
4 Nodes: Major intersection or meeting places, such as the clock in New York's Grand Central Terminal
5 Landmarks: Tall, visible structures that allow you to orient over long distances

Although you can readily see the parallels with navigation on the web, the web is a special kind of space that often doesn't provide the concrete spatial and navigational clues we take for granted in the real world of walking through a town. Web *navigation* has many similarities to physical movement, but actual *travel* on the web is magical: you just appear at the next point in your journey from page to page, and there is no experience of the landscape unfolding before you as a series of landmarks.

There's no sense of scale or movement in space
We don't pass familiar landmarks unless we're deliberately browsing through a site hierarchy. Most of the time we just suddenly appear in a new place, and the "journey" itself provides no information on our new location.

There's no compass
There are no directions and often no clear sense of heading a particular direction. This lack of abstract direction is what makes links to home pages so crucial in web navigation: your orientation to home and whether you are heading away from the home page or toward the home page is about all the sense of "direction" there is in many sites.

You are here
All of this argues for concrete, visible, easy-to-understand navigational cues on web pages. Print designers and editors often chafe at the heavy interface framing of web pages—do we really need such a burden of headers and footers and buttons and links? Well, yes, we do. Without that navigation interface, and all the "you are here" markers it provides, we'd all be back to that lost-in-space feeling that was so common in the early days of the web.

PATHS: LEADING THE WAY
In web sites paths are the consistent, predictable navigational links that appear the same way throughout the web site. Paths can be purely in the user's mind, as in your habitual navigation through a favorite newspaper site. Paths can also be explicit site navigation elements such as breadcrumb trails that show you where you are in relation to the overall site (fig. 4.2).

FIGURE 4.2
Two examples of breadcrumb trails in site headers.

FIGURE 4.3
In large sites users
should be able to
readily see when
they have passed
important regional
boundaries. If all the
pages look identical,
it's harder to tell
where you are within
a large site.

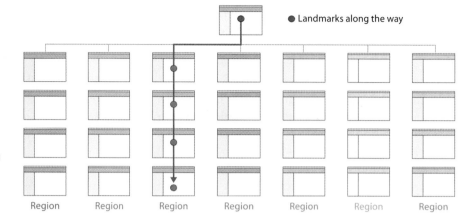

DISTRICTS AND EDGES: THE PARADOX OF CONSISTENCY

Consistency is the golden rule of interface design and wayfinding, but there is a paradox at the heart of consistency: if everything looks the same, *there are no edges.* How can you tell where you are or when you have moved from one space to another? A well-designed site navigation system is built on a consistent page grid, terminology, and navigation links, but it also incorporates the visual flexibility to create identifiable regions and edges within the larger space. In a corporate site, if you move from one region to another—say, from marketing to human resources—you ought to notice that you just passed an important regional boundary (fig. 4.3).

NODES: THE LOCAL COFFEE SHOP OR TIMES SQUARE?

Coffee used to be easy: it was regular or black. Now with six kinds of mocha skim lattes on offer, coffee has become yet another potential point of stress in your day. In Western societies we equate freedom with a range of choices, but as psychologist Barry Schwartz points out in his book *The Paradox of Choice,* an overwhelming range of choices causes stress, slows our decision-making, makes us generally less satisfied (did I make the *right* choice from my eighty-nine options?), and makes us more likely to walk away from making any choice at all. "Give the user choices" is a constant mantra in user interface design, but too many choices delivered simultaneously leave most users overwhelmed and likely to abandon the problem altogether (fig. 4.4).

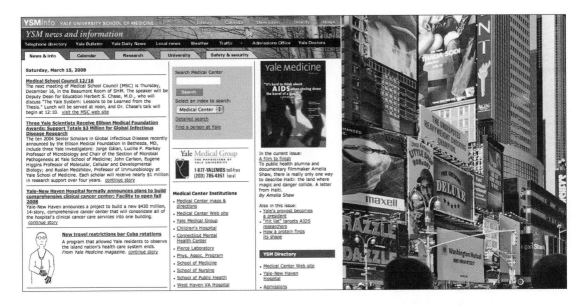

LANDMARKS: "YOU ARE HERE"

Orientation cues are particularly important in the web interface, since users often arrive at a page without having followed a deliberate and repeatable path. For example, one point of web wayfinding that is quite unlike navigation in physical space is search, which cuts across all the normal wayfinding boundaries to provide a view of every occurrence of a keyword or phrase across the web site. Search is more than an automated directory function; search can deliver you directly from one point in a site to another, and that direct connection makes the user all the more dependent on "you are here" cues from the user interface of the site.

FIGURE 4.4

As pages get more complex, you risk overwhelming the user with the "Times Square effect" of too many competing visual stimuli.

SUMMARY: PRINCIPLES FOR WAYFINDING IN WEB SITES

- Paths: Create consistent, well-marked navigation paths
- Regions: Create a unique but related identity for each site region
- Nodes: Don't confuse the user with too many choices on home and major menu pages
- Landmarks: Use consistent landmarks in site navigation and graphics to keep the user oriented

FIGURE 4.5
Multiple and
complementary "you
are here" markers
help users stay
oriented in complex
sites.

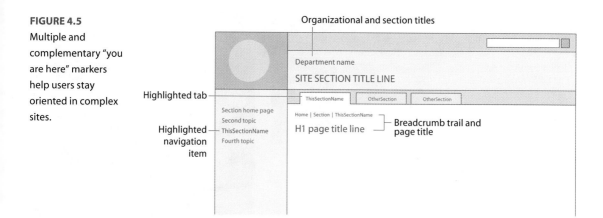

Organizational and section titles

Highlighted tab

Highlighted navigation item

BROWSE VERSUS SEARCH

User interface research shows that about half of web users prefer to browse through menu lists of links to find information, and the other half will go straight to the search box to enter keywords for search. All readers will use both the browse and search features of a site at some point, so supporting both navigation paradigms is important to user interface design. As the web has become larger and more complex, the dependence on search technology has become greater, both for users seeking information and for web publishers hoping users will find their content.

ORIENTATION

Both the browse and search aspects of navigation must support the user's sense of location and orientation to the major landmarks of a site. Core page components and interface elements (see *Interface Design*, below) are relevant to both browsing and searching; they establish and maintain a broad sense of a web site as a navigable space and provide a "you are here" sense of local placement within the larger dimension of the site. Breadcrumb trails, tabs or links that change color to indicate the current location, and section titles all contribute to a firm sense of place within a site (fig. 4.5).

These landmark and wayfinding elements are especially important to users who navigate by searching. The browse interface allows users to move gradually through a site, seeing various landmarks as they pass through the site hierarchy (fig. 4.6). Web search allows a user to cut directly into a site

User's path from the home page

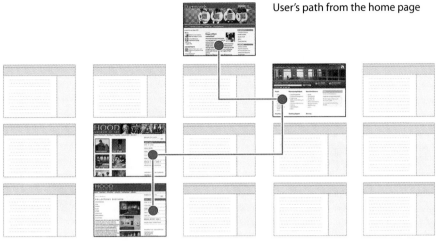

FIGURE 4.6
Interface consistency
is essential in
institutional
web design, but
distinctive graphic
variations in
regions of a site can
form wayfinding
"landmarks" that
readers pass by as
they browse through
the site, much as
distinctive real-world
buildings, streets,
and signs help
travelers navigate
through towns.

hierarchy with no preamble. Users who come to your site from a general Internet search engine like Yahoo! or Google may arrive directly at a page deep within the organization of your site. As web search becomes the way most of your audience reaches your site, the percentage of users who see your home page is decreasing all the time (fig. 4.7).

Direct link to a deep page within
the site, bypassing most potential
navigation landmarks

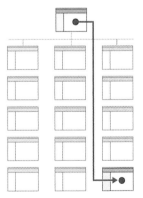

Search links directly to deep
page, bypassing most potential
navigation landmarks

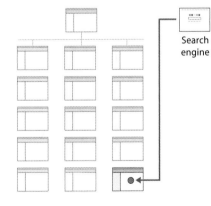

Search
engine

FIGURE 4.7
Your home page
is not the only
gateway to your site.
Search engine users
increasingly arrive
at a site on internal
content pages, not
the home page.

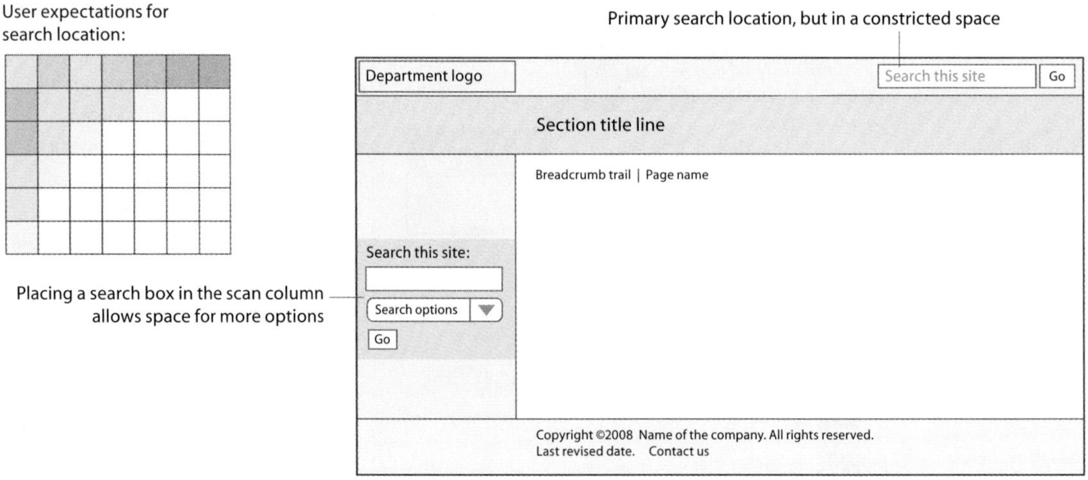

User expectations for
search location:

Primary search location, but in a constricted space

| Department logo | | Search this site | Go |

Section title line

Breadcrumb trail | Page name

Search this site:

Search options ▼

Go

Placing a search box in the scan column
allows space for more options

Copyright ©2008 Name of the company. All rights reserved.
Last revised date.   Contact us

FIGURE 4.8

Conventions are
your friends. Always
put the search box
where users expect
to find it.

SUPPORTING WEB SEARCH USERS

The most fundamental support for users who prefer to search is to make
search easily available from every page of your site. Users expect that any
site of more than a few pages will have a search feature. Research shows that
there are specific areas of the page where users expect to see a search box
(fig. 4.8).

Always be sure you let users know the scope of what they are searching.
It's confusing when users enter a keyword thinking that they are searching
only the current web site but then get search results from the whole company
or the whole Internet ("Results 1–100 of about 5,100,000,000 for 'help'").
In simple search forms you can make the scope of the search clear in the field
label. Where there is more room on the page the search form can offer more
options to control the scope of the search (fig. 4.9).

To preserve the user's sense of place within your site, the results of a user's
search query should appear on a page that looks like the rest of the web site.
For large institutions, as long as the larger institutional site is well organized
and graphically consistent, every small subsite does not need to have a custom search page.

Search is powerful, but web search is no substitute for a coherent site architecture, carefully expressed in your page design and navigation. Ironically,
search navigation is heavily dependent on those interface elements and page

Input field text informs user of scope of search

Calendar | A-Z Index | Search ITS sites | Go | Y

Select menu allows user to control scope of search

computing | Medical_Center [↕] (Search) Advanced Search / Search Tips

Yale_University
Yale_Libraries
✓ Medical_Center
Medical_Library
Yale_College
Yale_News_Releases
ITS

design features that we think of as part of the standard browsing interface. By cutting out the intermediate steps in browsing through an information hierarchy, search can deliver the user to pages deep inside a web site, where only the "browsing" interface of site graphics, page titles, breadcrumb trails, and navigation links can supply the cues that allow users to establish their "you are here" location within the site.

INTERFACE DESIGN

Readers need a sense of context of their place within an organization of information. In paper documents this sense of where you are is a mixture of graphic and editorial organizational cues supplied by the graphic design of the book, the organization of the text, and the physical sensation of the book as an object. Electronic documents provide none of the physical cues we take for granted in assessing information. When we see a web hypertext link on a page we have few clues to where we will be led, how much information is at the other end of the link, and exactly how the linked information relates to the current page. Even the view of individual web pages is restricted for many users. Most web pages don't fit completely on a standard office display monitor; there is usually a lower part of the page that the user cannot see. Users of small-screen mobile devices have an even more limited view-port, and a big-picture view of a web page is impossible for screen reader users, who access pages an element at a time. Web pages need to give the user explicit cues to the context and organization of the site because only a small segment of any site is available at one time (fig. 4.10).

FIGURE 4.10
No matter how big
your site is, users
only see one page at
a time.

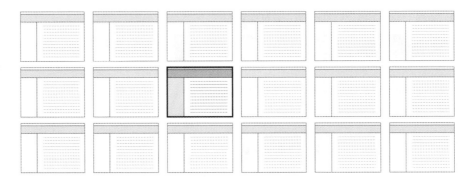

CLEAR NAVIGATION AIDS

Most user interactions with web pages involve navigating hypertext links between documents. The main interface problem in web sites is the lack of any sense of where you are within the local organization of information. Clear, consistent icons, graphic identity schemes, page titles and headings, and graphic- or text-based overview and summary screens can give users confidence that they can find what they are seeking without wasting time.

Users should always be able to return easily to your home page and to other major navigation points in the site. These basic links should be present and in consistent locations on every page. Headers provide basic navigation links and create an identity that tells users they are within the site domain.

In the Digital Web Magazine site, for example, the header appears on every page (fig. 4.11). The header is efficient (offering multiple choices in a small space) and predictable (it is always there, at the top of every page), and it provides a consistent identity throughout the site.

FIGURE 4.11
Headers are essential
for both site identity
and consistent
navigation.

NO DEAD-END PAGES

Web pages often appear with no preamble: users can make or follow links directly to subsection pages buried deep in the hierarchy of web sites. They may never see your home page or other introductory site information. If your

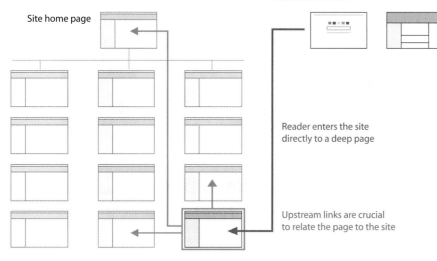

Site home page

Link originates from a search engine
or another web site

FIGURE 4.12
Users can enter a site
anywhere and need
instant cues to site
identity and "you are
here" markers.

Reader enters the site
directly to a deep page

Upstream links are crucial
to relate the page to the site

subsection pages do not contain links to the home page or to local menu pages, the user will be locked out from the rest of the web site (fig. 4.12).

Make sure all pages in your site have *at minimum* a link back to the home page or, better yet, a home page link along with links to other main sections of the site. In addition to user interface considerations, these links are crucial for search engine visibility.

DIRECT ACCESS

Users want to get information in the fewest possible steps. This means that you must design an efficient hierarchy of information to minimize steps through menu pages. Studies have shown that users prefer menus that present at least five to seven links and that they prefer a few pages of carefully organized choices over many layers of oversimplified menu pages. Design your site hierarchy so that real content is just a click or two away from the main menu pages of your site.

SIMPLICITY AND CONSISTENCY

Users are not impressed with complexity that seems gratuitous, especially those users who may be depending on the site for timely and accurate information. Your interface metaphors should be simple, familiar, and logical—if

FIGURE 4.13
The Opera site is
a masterpiece of
balancing high
functionality with
low-key interface
elements.

you need a metaphor for collections of information, choose a familiar genre, such as file folders. Unusual or peculiar "creative" navigation and home page metaphors always fail because they impose an unfamiliar, unpredictable interface burden on the user. Baffle users with a weird home page, and they will quickly hit the "back" button and move on to the next item on the Google results page, and you'll have lost a potential reader or customer. Let your content shine, and let the interface recede. Opera is a master of balancing bold content with a minimal but highly usable interface (fig. 4.13).

The best information designs are never noticed. Once you know where the standard links are on the page header graphics, the interface becomes almost invisible. Navigation is easy and never competes with content for your attention (fig. 4.14).

For maximum functionality and legibility, your page and site design should be built on a consistent pattern of modular units that all share the same basic layout grids, graphic themes, editorial conventions, and organi-

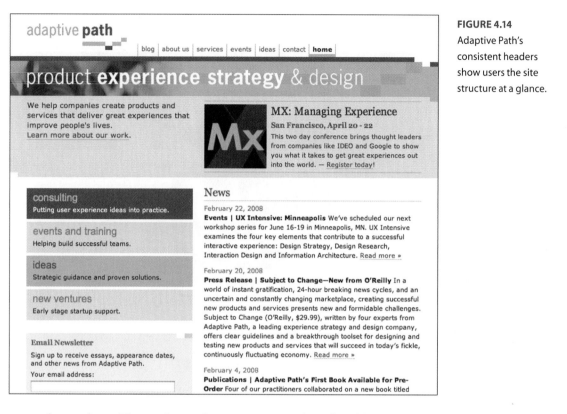

FIGURE 4.14
Adaptive Path's consistent headers show users the site structure at a glance.

zation hierarchies. The goal is to be consistent and predictable; your users should feel comfortable exploring your site and confident that they can find what they need. The graphic identity of a series of pages in a web site provides visual cues to the continuity of information. The header menu present on every page of the Capgemini site creates a consistent user interface and corporate identity (fig. 4.15).

Even if your site design does not employ navigation graphics, a consistent approach to the layout of titles, subtitles, page footers, and navigation links to your home page or related pages will reinforce the user's sense of context within the site. To preserve the effect of a "seamless" system of pages you may wish to bring important information into your site and adapt it to your page layout scheme rather than using links to send the reader away from your site (but be sure there are no copyright restrictions on copying the information into your site).

FIGURE 4.15
Capgemini offers
strong site identity
and navigation that
never competes with
page content for the
reader's attention.

DESIGN INTEGRITY AND STABILITY

To convince your users that what you have to offer is accurate and reliable, you will need to design your web site as carefully as you would any other type of corporate communication, using the same high editorial and design standards. A site that looks sloppily built, with poor visual design and low editorial standards, will not inspire confidence.

Functional stability in any web design means keeping the interactive elements of the site working reliably. Functional stability has two components: getting things right the first time as you design the site, and then keeping things functioning smoothly over time. Good web sites are inherently interactive, with lots of links to local pages within the site as well as links to other sites on the web. As you create your design you will need to check frequently that all of your links work properly. Information changes quickly on the web, both in your site and in everyone else's. After the site is established you will need to check that your links are still working properly and that the content they supply remains relevant.

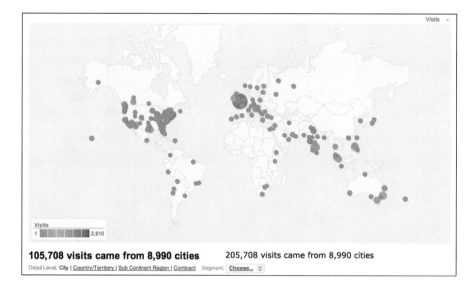

105,708 visits came from 8,990 cities   205,708 visits came from 8,990 cities

FIGURE 4.16
Web traffic analysis programs like Google Analytics are a goldmine of information on who is using your site and what their technical capabilities are.

FEEDBACK AND DIALOG

Your web design should offer constant visual and functional confirmation of the user's whereabouts and options, via graphic design, navigation links, and uniformly placed hypertext links. Feedback also means being prepared to respond to your users' inquiries and comments. Well-designed web sites provide direct links to the web site editor or webmaster responsible for running the site. Planning for this ongoing relationship with users of your site is vital to the long-term success of the enterprise.

BANDWIDTH AND INTERACTION

Users will not tolerate long delays. Research has shown that for most computing tasks the threshold of frustration is about ten seconds. Web page designs that are not well "tuned" to the network access speed of typical users will only frustrate them. Check your web site logs to be sure that you understand your typical user's location and network connections. If you have many international users, for example, you may want to be more conservative about large graphics on your pages (fig. 4.16).

Also beware of potentially slow dynamic content components in your site, such as RSS feeds, text from content management systems, or other data sources that can slow the loading of web pages.

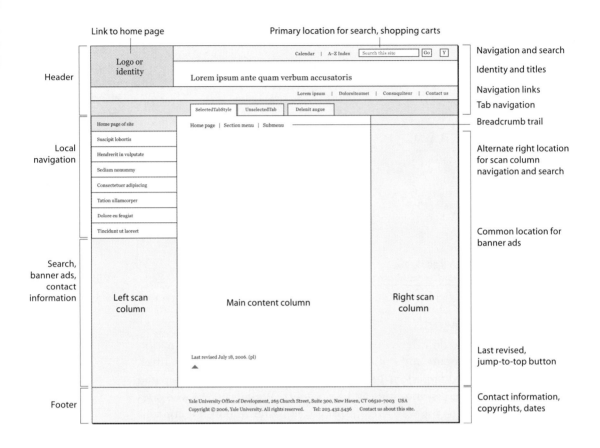

Link to home page — Primary location for search, shopping carts

Header

Logo or identity

Lorem ipsum ante quam verbum accusatoris

Calendar | A–Z Index | Search this site | Go | Y

Lorem ipsum | Dolorsiteamet | Consuquiteur | Contact us

SelectedTabStyle | UnselectedTab | Delenit augue

Home page of site
Suscipit lobortis
Hendrerit in vulputate
Sediam nonummy
Consectetuer adipiscing
Tation ullamcorper
Dolore eu feugiat
Tincidunt ut laoreet

Local navigation

Home page | Section menu | Submenu

Search, banner ads, contact information

Left scan column

Main content column

Right scan column

Last revised July 18, 2006. (pl)
▲

Footer

Yale University Office of Development, 265 Church Street, Suite 300, New Haven, CT 06510-7003 USA
Copyright © 2006, Yale University. All rights reserved.   Tel: 203-432.5436   Contact us about this site.

Navigation and search
Identity and titles
Navigation links
Tab navigation
Breadcrumb trail

Alternate right location for scan column navigation and search

Common location for banner ads

Last revised, jump-to-top button

Contact information, copyrights, dates

FIGURE 4.17

A canonical page layout. Not every page includes every element shown here.

Ideally your company webmaster should be able to supply reports and data on your typical users and their equipment. If you don't have easy access to this information from your organization's web server logs, you may be able to use a free service like Google Analytics to better understand your users.

INTERFACE DESIGN CONVENTIONS

Most text-oriented informational web sites are converging on a relatively consistent layout of header, footer, local navigation, and content elements that together make a useful, familiar starting point for web interface designs. In general, people find the familiar easier to use and remember, and if your site follows these familiar patterns, users will quickly adapt and begin to focus on your unique content, features, or products (fig. 4.17).

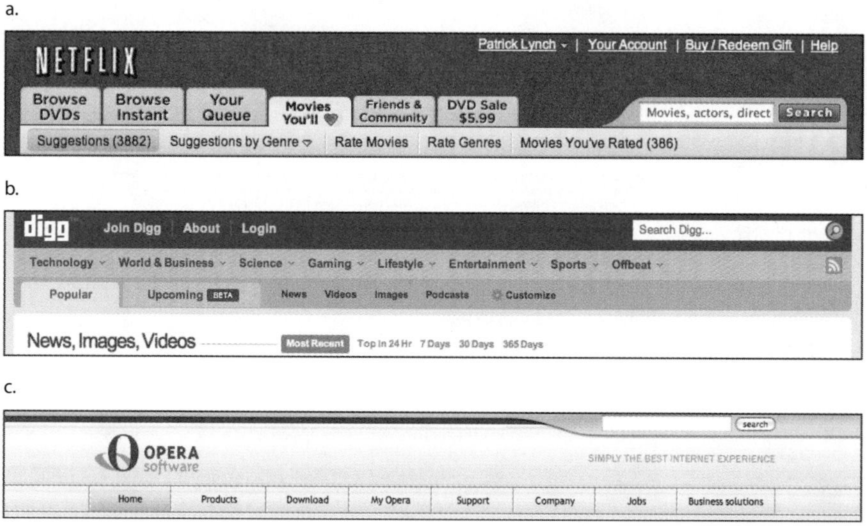

a.

b.

c.

FIGURE 4.18

Various header
navigation designs
and "you are here"
markers.

As you design the interface for your site, remember that the ideal web interface should never compete with the page content for the user's attention. The interface is the frame, not the painting.

What goes in the header area?

Web page headers convey the site identity, provide major navigation links, and often offer a search box. The header is where people expect to see a consistent statement of your organizational identity, and the header graphics and text are probably the most important elements in making a collection of web pages feel like an identifiable "site" rather than a random assemblage of files.

User research shows overwhelmingly that users expect that the top left area of your page header will contain both a visual indication of who you are, plus a link back to your site's home page. Users also expect that the header may play an important role in global navigation within your site. Important navigation links are often arrayed horizontally within the page header.

"Folder tabs" are ideal when your site has relatively few (five to seven) major navigation categories. If you have more than seven major categories, consider dropping the tab metaphor in favor of a well-organized set of plain text links (fig. 4.18a). When carefully designed, header tabs can also handle complex navigation (fig. 4.18b).

FIGURE 4.19
Classic left local
navigation, with
hierarchical lists.

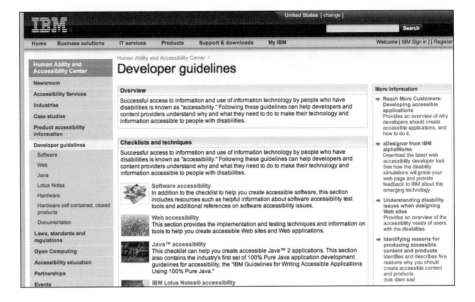

Semantically, header navigation lists should always be marked up as HTML lists, even if what appears on the page looks more like a collection of folder tab graphics. This semantic handling of header lists has powerful advantages for universal accessibility and helps clarify your site organization for search engines. Designers can use Cascading Style Sheets to style lists of navigation links to look like tabs. Opera's page headers are minimalist tabs but convey every essential page header function in a compact design (fig. 4.18c).

Right or left columns for navigation links?

According to most user interface and eye-tracking studies, users quickly adapt to content navigation within either the left column or far-right column of web pages—just be consistent in how you lay out your navigation on all pages. Left navigation columns are much more common and therefore have an edge in usability because all web users are familiar with them (fig. 4.19).

Right navigation columns are more often dominated by external or more parenthetic "related links" or by advertising. The dominant user expectation that right columns contain advertising suggests that any right-column navigation links you use should look very different from advertising, or your navigation may be ignored by many users.

FIGURE 4.20
Two examples of breadcrumb trails within or just under the page header.

Breadcrumb trails for navigation

Over the past decade breadcrumb trails have emerged as a powerful yet easy-to-understand navigation device of web pages. The name is derived from the metaphor of leaving breadcrumbs along your path to find your way back where you came from. In practice a breadcrumb trail is a simple hierarchical list of web links showing the structure of a site, usually starting with the home page and ending with the major navigation page closest to your current location within the site (fig. 4.20).

Each step in the breadcrumb trail is a clickable web link, so users have both a visual indication of their current location within the site and a clickable menu of major navigation sections for the site. In addition to its user interface advantages, the breadcrumb trail plays a potentially powerful role in adding major linked keywords to each web page, increasing the search visibility and keyword relevance of a page.

INFORMATION DESIGN

Concepts about structuring information today stem largely from the organization of printed books and periodicals and the library indexing and catalog systems that developed around printed information. The interface standards of books in the English-speaking world are well established and widely agreed-upon, and detailed instructions for creating books may be found in such publications standards manuals as *The Chicago Manual of Style*. Every feature of the printed book, from the contents page to the index, has evolved over centuries, and readers of early books faced some of the same organizational problems that users of hypermedia documents confront today. Johannes Gutenberg's Bible of 1456 is often cited as the first mass-produced book, yet even after the explosive growth of publishing that followed Gutenberg's invention of printing with movable type, more than a century passed before page numbering, indexes, tables of contents, and even title pages became expected and necessary features of books. Web documents are undergoing a similar—albeit faster—evolution and standardization.

Although networked interactive hypermedia documents pose novel challenges to information designers, most of the guidance needed to design, create, assemble, edit, and organize multiple forms of media does not differ radically from current practice in print media. Most web documents can be designed to conform to *The Chicago Manual of Style* conventions for editorial style and text organization. Much of what an organization needs to know about creating clear, comprehensive, and consistent internal publishing standards is already available in such general publishing style guides as the *Franklin Covey Style Guide for Business and Technical Communication* and *The Gregg Reference Manual*. Don't get so lost in the novelty of web pages that basic standards of editorial consistency, business communications, and graphic design are tossed aside.

FREESTANDING PAGES

Web pages differ from books and other documents in one crucial respect: hypertext links allow users to experience a single web page separate from its context. For this reason web pages need to be more independent than pages in a book. For example, the headers and footers of web pages should be more informative and elaborate than those on printed pages. It would be absurd to repeat the copyright information, author, and date of a book at the bottom of every printed page, but individual web pages often need to provide such information because a single web page may be the only part of a site that some users will see. This problem of making documents freestanding is not unique to web pages. Journals, magazines, and most newspapers repeat the date, volume number, and issue number at the top or bottom of each printed page because they know that readers often rip out articles or photocopy pages and will need that information to be able to trace the source of the material.

Given the difficulties inherent in creating web sites that are both easy to use and full of complex content, the best design strategy is to apply a few fundamental document design principles consistently in every web page you create. The basic elements of a document aren't complicated and have almost nothing to do with Internet technology. It's like a high school journalism class: who, what, when, and where.

Who

Who is speaking? This question is so basic, and the information is so often taken for granted, that authors frequently overlook the most fundamental piece of information a reader needs to assess the provenance of a web document. Whether the page originates from an individual author or an institution, always tell the reader who created it and what institution you are associated with. The flood of web sites that propagated incorrect or intentionally misleading material in the 2004 American presidential election offers a vivid example of how "information" of no known origin and of dubious authenticity can quickly cloud legitimate inquiry and discussion.

What

All documents need clear titles to capture the user's attention, but for several reasons peculiar to the web, this basic editorial element is especially crucial. The page title and major headings are also crucial for search engine visibility. The page title element is the most important determinant of keyword relevance for search engines, so craft your titles carefully if you want users to find your content.

When

Timeliness is an important element in evaluating the worth of a document. We take information about the age of most paper documents for granted: newspapers, magazines, and virtually all office correspondence are dated. Date every web page, and change the date whenever the document is updated. This is especially important in long or complex online documents that are updated regularly but may not look different enough to signal a change in content to occasional readers. Corporate information, personnel manuals, product information, and other technical documents delivered as web pages should always carry version numbers or revision dates. Remember that many readers prefer to print long documents from the web. If you don't include revision dates, your audience may not be able to tell whether the version they have in hand is current.

Where

The web is an odd "place" that has huge informational dimensions but few explicit cues to the place of origin of a document. Click on a web link, and you could be connected to a web server in Sydney, Chicago, or Rome—anywhere, in fact, with an Internet connection. Unless you are well versed in parsing URLs, it can be hard to tell where a page originates. This is the World Wide Web, after all, and the question of where a document comes from is sometimes inseparable from whom the document comes from. Always tell the user where you are from, with (if relevant) your corporate or institutional affiliations.

Incorporating the "home" URL within the page footer is an easy way to maintain the connection to where a page originated. Once the user has saved the page as a text file or printed the page onto paper, this connection may be lost. Although newer versions of the most common web browsers allow users to include the URL automatically in anything they print, many people never take advantage of this optional feature. Too many of us have stacks of printed web pages with no easy way of locating the web sites where they originated.

SUMMARY: INFORMATION DESIGN GUIDELINES

Every web page needs:

- An informative title (which also becomes the text of any bookmark to the page)
- The creator's identity (author or institution)
- A creation or revision date
- A copyright statement, Creative Commons statement, or other statement of ownership to protect your intellectual property rights
- At least one link to a local home page or menu page, in a consistent location on all pages
- The home page URL

Most web pages should also incorporate these additional elements:

- An organization logo or name near the upper left corner, with a link back to your home page
- Navigation links to other major sections of your site
- At least one heading to identify and clarify the page content
- Mailing address and contact information or a link to this information
- Alternate ("alt") text identifying any graphics on the page

Include these basic information elements and you will have traveled 90 percent of the way toward providing your users with an understandable web user interface.

THE ENTERPRISE INTERFACE

The web can provide a powerful framework for promoting group cohesion and identification with the large missions and goals of an enterprise, but only if the user interface, information architecture, and graphic design of the enterprise's web sites consistently promote a common purpose and shared identity across all the major elements of the public-facing web sites and the organization's internal sites and intranet. Most large corporations have well-established corporate identity programs that now include comprehensive web design and interface standards.

THE ORGANIZATIONAL CONTEXT OF INTERFACES

Many smaller companies, federal, state, and local government sites, college and university sites, and nonprofit institutions produce chaotic, poorly organized web sites because the institutions lack consistent, widely implemented web publishing standards. Nobody sets out to produce a chaotic enterprise web presence, but an insistence on trying to optimize each little site within the larger organization is a guarantee of disorder and confusion for users. You can't optimize a library by writing a great book, and no single web site—no matter how well designed—will ever improve an enterprise's overall web presence.

The only long-term approach to improving an organization's web presence is a consistent approach to web interface design, one that explicitly recognizes the larger context of the enterprise and the web in general. Ideally this set of consistent standards becomes the "enterprise interface" across all forms of web information publishing and web-based access to applications. In today's large organizations web content can flow from dozens of major information sources. A consistent, comprehensive approach to the enterprise interface is the best way to maximize the return for the enormous investments that companies make in web publishing and web applications.

A chaotic web presence sends one consistent message about an organization: contempt for the user. Users spend 99.99 percent of their time on web sites other than yours, and potential readers could care less that you want to look unique. If your organization has web standards, always incorporate them into your site design and user interface. If you don't have standards, lead an effort to create them. Research on the most effective corporate intranets and portals shows that users are most productive, efficient, and overwhelmingly more satisfied with sites that employ a consistent, comprehensive interface and design standard throughout the organization's web presence.

Enterprise interface programs have three primary aims: coherence, symbolism, and positioning.

Coherence

A coherent interface presents the enterprise clearly and comprehensively, conveying an understandable picture of the organization's structure and functioning, products and services to clients, internal communications and management policy, and overall mission and goals. Building a legible, easily navigable corporate web structure is more than just a graphic user interface issue. A well-structured site rich with useful content directly represents the depth and breadth of an enterprise more comprehensively than any previous medium.

IBM's overall web presence is a masterpiece of comprehensive visual and interface design across a massive organizational web presence (fig. 4.21).

Symbolism

As networked work environments become the norm and various forms of telecommuting and remote access become routine, web-based work environments will become the dominant force in creating and maintaining the corporate ethos, attitudes, and values. For most employees the organizational web presence has become the most visible and functional evidence of social cohesion and common purpose across the enterprise.

Positioning

A clear and recognizable identity program helps distinguish an enterprise from peers and competitors. This is especially critical on the Internet, where everyone has a web site and all web sites appear in the same limited venue (a browser window on the user's screen). A user may visit a dozen organizational sites in a browsing session and be exposed to many graphic themes. Web users' expectations of the Internet as a communications medium are determined mainly by what they have seen in other sites, and what they've seen is mostly like confetti: weightless, colorful, and chaotic. Will users remember your pages if your site looks like nothing else they've seen in your larger enterprise?

Cohesive, comprehensive design transcends immediate commercial objectives. Enterprises need to differentiate themselves not only in the products and services they offer but also as social entities. In too many corporate, university, and government sites, the lack of a comprehensive group identity and shared sense of mission are made painfully obvious by the chaotic condition of their web sites. An effective web presence can be a powerful tool for enhancing the status and competitive positioning of an enterprise, but only if the web site effectively projects a feeling of trust in the knowledge and competence of the organization that produced it.

FIGURE 4.21

A comprehensive design system across the massive IBM web presence.

Design is not just what it looks like and feels like.
Design is how it works.

—Steve Jobs

CHAPTER 5

Site Structure

Much as foundational concrete and piles define the stability and longevity of buildings, so the structural underpinnings of web sites affect their success in ways that, though not visible on the surface, are ultimately far more important than color and typography. Site structure determines how well sites work in the broader context of the web. The methods you use to mark up pages determine whether they can be read well by software and indexed well by search engines. The logic and stability of the underlying files and directories that your web site rests on affect its functionality, as well as its potential for growth and expansion. Attention to these behind-the-scenes structural components from the start produces a web site that will hold up over time, work effectively within the larger web environment, and adapt and grow as needed.

SEMANTIC CONTENT MARKUP

Proper use of HTML is the key to getting maximum flexibility and return on your investment in web content. From its earliest origins, HTML was designed to distinguish clearly between a document's hierarchical outline structure (Headline 1, Headline 2, paragraph, list, and so on) and the visual presentation of the document (boldface, italics, font, type size, color, and so on). HTML markup is considered semantic when standard HTML tags are used to convey *meaning and content structure*, not simply to make text look a certain way in a browser.

This semantic approach to web markup is a central concept underlying efficient web coding, information architecture, universal usability, search engine visibility, and maximum display flexibility. Web content is accessed using web browsers, mobile computing devices of all kinds, and screen readers. Web content is also read by search engines and other computing systems that extract meaning and context from how the content is marked up in HTML.

```
<h1>This is the most important headline</h1>
<p>This is ordinary paragraph text within the body of
   the document, where certain words and phrases may be
   <em>emphasized</em> to mark them as <strong>particularly
   important</strong>.</p>
<h2>This is a headline of secondary importance to the headline
   above</h2>
<p>Any time you list related things, the items should be marked
   up in the form of a list:</p>
<ul>
   <li>A list signals that a group of items are conceptually
      related to each other</li>
   <li>Lists may be ordered (numbered or alphabetic) or unordered
      (bulleted items)</li>
   <li>Lists may also be menus or lists of links for navigation
      </li>
   <li>Cascading Style Sheets can make lists look many different
      ways</li>
</ul>
```

Even in the simple example above, a search engine would be able to distinguish the importance and priority of the headlines, discover which keywords were important, and identify conceptually related items in list form. A Cascading Style Sheet designed particularly for mobile phones could display the headlines and text in fonts appropriate for small screens, and a screen reader would know where and how to pause or change voice tone to convey the content structure to a blind reader.

HTML DOCUMENT STRUCTURE

Properly structured HTML (or XHTML) documents may contain the following elements:

- HTML document structure (`<head>`, `<body>`, `<div>`, `<span>`)
- Text content
- Semantic markup to convey meaning and content structure (headlines, paragraph text, lists, quotations)
- Visual presentation (CSS) to make content look a certain way

- Links to audiovisual content (GIF, JPEG, or PNG graphics, QuickTime or other media files)
- Interactive behavior (JavaScript, Ajax elements, or other programming techniques)

Document structure

In properly formed HTML, all web page code is contained within two basic elements:

- Head (`<head>`...`</head>`)
- Body (`<body>`...`</body>`)

In the past these basic divisions in the structure of page code were there primarily for good form: strictly correct but functionally optional and invisible to the user. In today's much more complex and ambitious World Wide Web, in which intricate page code, many different display possibilities, elaborate style sheets, and interactive scripting are now the norm, it is crucial to structure the divisional elements properly.

The `<head>` area is where your web page declares its code standards and document type to the display device (web browser, mobile phone, iPod Touch) and where the all-important page title resides. The page head area also can contain links to external style sheets and JavaScript code that may be shared by many pages in your site.

The `<body>` area encompasses all page content and is important for CSS control of visual styles, programming, and semantic content markup. Areas within the body of the page are usually functionally divided with division (`<div>`) or span (`<span>`) tags. For example, most web pages have header, footer, content, and navigation areas, all designated with named `<div>` tags that can be addressed and visually styled with CSS.

The HTML document type declares which version and standards the HTML document conforms to and is crucial in evaluating the quality and technical validity of the HTML markup and CSS. Your web development technical team should be able to tell you which version of HTML will be used for page coding (for example, HTML4 or XHTML1) and which document type declaration will be used in your web site. HTML is the current basic standard for web page markup. XHTML is very similar to HTML, but XHTML is a subset of XML and has more exacting markup requirements. Although HTML is the most broadly used web markup standard, there are powerful advantages in using XHTML as your standard for page markup, including:

- Compatibility with XML techniques, XML content, and hybrid JavaScript/XML techniques such as Ajax
- Compatibility with non-HTML web markup standards such as MathML for scientific documents, SMIL (Synchronized Multimedia Integration Language) for interactive audiovisual content, and Scalable Vector Graphics (SVG)
- Future compatibility with newer XML content techniques, content management systems, and other evolving web technologies that will benefit from the greater consistency and structure of XHTML markup standards

Content markup

Semantic markup is a fancy term for common-sense HTML usage: if you write a headline, mark it with a heading tag (`<h1>`, `<h2>`). If you write basic paragraph text, place the text between paragraph tags (`<p>`...`</p>`). If you wish to emphasize an important phrase, mark it with strong emphasis (`<strong>`... `</strong>`). If you quote another writer, use the `<blockquote>` tag to signal that the text is a quotation. *Never choose an HTML tag based on how it looks in a web browser.* You can adjust the visual presentation of your content later with CSS to get the look you want for headlines, quotations, emphasized text, and other typography.

A few exclusively visual HTML tags such as `<b>` (boldface) and `<i>` (italics) persist in HTML because these visual styles are sometimes needed for other reasons, such as to italicize a scientific name (for example, *Homo sapiens*). If you use semantically meaningless tags like `<b>` or `<i>`, ask yourself whether a properly styled emphasis (`<em>`) or strong emphasis (`<strong>`) tag would convey more meaning.

HTML also contains semantic elements that are not visible to the reader but can be enormously useful behind the scenes with a team of site developers. Elements such as classes, IDs, divisions, spans, and meta tags can make it easier for team members to understand, use, visually style, and programmatically control page elements. Many style sheet and programming techniques require careful semantic naming of page elements that will make your content more universally accessible and flexible.

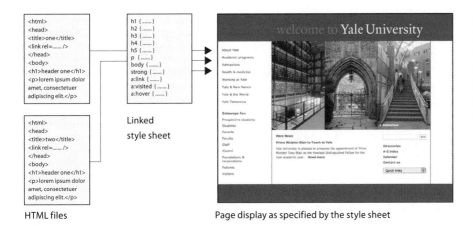

HTML files Linked style sheet Page display as specified by the style sheet

FIGURE 5.1
Style sheets translate HTML code into a particular layout for viewing, in this case for a full-sized computer screen.

Cascading Style Sheets

Cascading Style Sheets allow web publishers to retain the enormous benefits of using semantic HTML to convey logical document structure and meaning while giving graphic designers complete control over the visual display details of each HTML element. CSS works just like the style sheets in a word-processing program such as Microsoft Word. In Word, you can structure your document with ranked headlines and other styles and then globally change each one just by changing its style. CSS works the same way, particularly if you use linked external style sheets that every page in your web site shares. For example, if all of your pages link to the same master CSS file, you could change the font, size, and color of every <h1> heading in your site just by changing the <h1> style in your master style sheet (fig. 5.1).

Audiovisual content

Web page files don't contain graphics or audiovisual material directly but use image or other pointer links to incorporate graphics and media into the final assembly of the web page in the browser. These links, and the alternate text ("alt" text) or long description ("longdesc") links they contain, are critical for universal usability and search engine visibility. Web users don't just search for text. Search engines use the alternate text descriptions to label images with keywords, and visually impaired users depend on alternate text to describe the content of images. Proper semantic markup will ensure that your audiovisual media are maximally available to everyone in your audience and to search engines.

Interactive scripting

JavaScript is a language commonly used to create interactive behaviors. JavaScript is also a key technology in web page content delivery strategies such as Ajax. All JavaScript code belongs in the "head" area of your web page, but if your code is complex and lengthy, your "real" page content will be pushed dozens of lines down below the code and may not be found by search engines. If you use page-level JavaScript scripting (also called client-side scripting), you should place all but the shortest bits of code in a linked file. This way you can use lengthy, complex JavaScript without losing search page ranking.

Other document formats

The web supports document formats other than HTML. PDF (Portable Document Format), Flash, and Shockwave are formats commonly used to provide functionality that is not available using basic HTML. PDF files are favored for documents that originated in word-processing and page layout programs and retain the appearance of the original document. Flash and Shockwave provide interactivity beyond what is available using standard HTML. In general, the best approach is to offer documents as plain HTML because the markup offers greater flexibility and is designed to enable universal usability. At times, however, the additional features and functionality offered by these other formats is essential; in this case, be sure to use the software's accessibility features. Adobe in particular has made efforts to incorporate accessibility features into its web formats by supporting semantic markup, text equivalents, and keyboard accessibility.

WATCH FOR BROWSER VARIATIONS

HTML and CSS for tables, forms, positioning, and alignment sometimes work slightly differently in each brand or operating system version of web browser. These subtleties normally pass unnoticed, but in very precise or complex web page layouts they can lead to nasty surprises. Never trust the implementation of HTML, CSS, JavaScript, Java, or any plug-in architecture until you have seen your web pages displayed and working reliably with each major web browser and across operating platforms.

Check your web logs or use a service such as Google Analytics to be sure that you understand what browser brands, browser versions, and operating systems (Mac, Windows, mobile) are most common in your readership. If you encounter a discrepancy in how your pages render in different browsers, check that you are using valid HTML and CSS code (see chapter 1, *HTML and CSS code validation*). Not every browser supports every feature of CSS, particularly if that feature is seldom used or has recently been added to the official standards for CSS code. For example, although drop-shadowed text is a valid CSS option, not all browsers support it.

SUMMARY ON SEMANTIC MARKUP

Set careful markup and editorial standards based on semantic markup techniques and standard HTML document types, and adhere to those standards throughout the development process. Today's web environment is a lot more than just Internet Explorer or Firefox on a desktop computer—hundreds of mobile computing devices are now in use, and new ways of viewing and using web content are being invented every day. Ultimately, following semantic web markup practices and using carefully validated page code and style sheets is your best strategy for ensuring that your web content will be broadly useful and visible into the future.

SITE FILE STRUCTURE

Like the inner workings of a fine watch, the internal details of your site are craftwork that only other technologists will see, but your users will benefit from careful planning and thought. Discussions about site and page structure usually center around the most visible aspects of navigation, user interface, and content organization, but attention to the file and directory structure and how you name things within your site can produce big payoffs in:

- Understanding: Your current team, future site maintainers, and most site users will benefit from careful, consistent, plain-language site nomenclature
- Flexibility: If every object in your site has a name, everything can be found, styled, and programmatically manipulated much more easily
- Accessibility: Named objects are more accessible to programmatic and style sheet control across all media types and give you flexibility in implementing universal accessibility features in your site
- Search optimization: Careful site nomenclature makes it much easier to optimize a site for search engine visibility

- Future growth and change: you can't scale up or automate changes in a randomly named, haphazardly constructed collection of files and directories; a nonsystem can't be systematically managed or structurally expanded

THE HIDDEN SEMANTICS OF SITES

The goal of semantic organization of your site is to produce a consistent, logical system of classifications for HTML and other files, directories, CSS components, and the various logical and visible divisions within your page templates. A consistent, modular approach to site construction can be scaled from small sites containing a dozen pages all the way up to content-managed sites consisting of tens of thousands of pages. Although we can present general principles for site structure here, the technical environment and functional demands of many sites may require particular forms of file naming. The fundamental point is that, whatever your site environment, you should develop systematic rules for naming every component of your site, make sure that everyone in the team understands and follows those rules, and use plain language wherever possible.

NAMING CONVENTIONS

Never use technical or numeric gibberish to name a component when a plain-language name will do. In the early days of personal computing, clumsy systems like MS-DOS and Windows 3.x imposed an "eight-dot-three" file name convention that forced users to make up cryptic codes for file and directory names (for example, "WHTEVR34.HTM"). No word spaces and few non-alphanumeric characters were allowed in file names, so technologists often used characters like the underscore to add legibility (for example, "CATS_003.HTM"). Habits developed over decades can be hard to break, and looking into the file structure of another team's site can sometimes feel like cracking the German Enigma codes of World War II. Current file name conventions in Windows, Macintosh, and Linux systems are much more flexible, and there's no reason to impose cryptic names on your team members, site users, and colleagues who may one day have to figure out how you constructed your site. There's an old saying in programming that when you add explanatory comments to your code, the person you are mostly likely doing a favor for is *yourself*, three years from now. Three years from now, will *you* know what's in a directory called "x83_0001"?

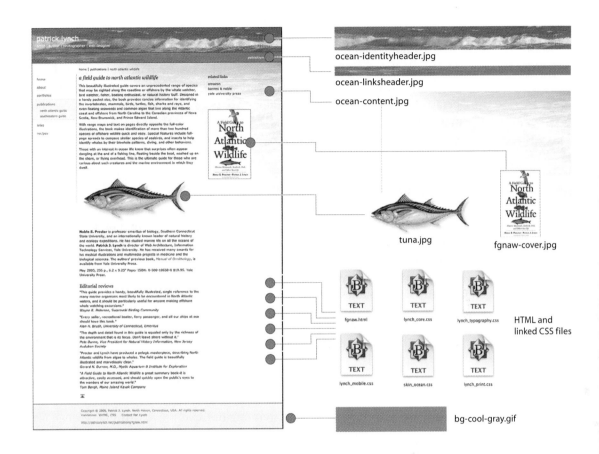

ocean-identityheader.jpg

ocean-linksheader.jpg

ocean-content.jpg

tuna.jpg

fgnaw-cover.jpg

fgnaw.html

lynch_core.css

lynch_typography.css

HTML and
linked CSS files

lynch_mobile.css

skin_ocean.css

lynch_print.css

bg-cool-gray.gif

Naming pages, directories, and supporting files

Although we think of web pages and their graphics as a unit, web page files do not contain graphics but consist instead of embedded links to separate graphics files. These embedded image links (`<img src="graphic.jpg" alt="example">`) are used by the web server to deliver a package consisting of an HTML file, plus all associated graphics, CSS or JavaScript files, and other media files. Most web "pages" are actually a constellation of files delivered to and assembled by the browser into the coherent page we see on our screens. Attention to file and directory names is essential to keeping track of the myriad pages and supporting files that make up a web site (fig. 5.2).

FIGURE 5.2
The constellation of twelve component files that form this web page.

Use language that anyone can understand

Use plain-language names for all of your files and directories, separating the words with "breaking" hyphen characters. This system is easy to read and understand, and since conventional word spaces are not allowed, the hyphens "break" the file name into individual words or number strings that can be analyzed by search engines and will contribute to the search rankings and content relevance of your pages. We recommend this convention for directory names, too.

Mirror your visible site structure wherever possible

Directory and file naming conventions that directly mirror the visible organization of your site are infinitely easier for your team and users to understand and will contribute to search engine rankings and relevance, because the whole URL becomes a useful semantic guide to your content structure. Each component of your page URL can contribute to search page ranking, but only if the names make sense in the context of your page content and relate to key words or phrases on the page.

This poorly named URL contributes nothing to search engine relevance or site structure legibility:

www.whatever.edu/depts1/progs2/org004/bio_424.HTML

In contrast, anyone (and any search engine) can parse this plain-language content arrangement at a glance:

www.whatever.edu/departments/biology/ornithology/
field-ornithology-bio-224.HTML

Always try to mirror the visible structure of your site's content organization in the directory and file structure you set up on the web server (fig. 5.3).

STRUCTURE FOR EFFICIENCY AND MAINTAINABILITY

Well-designed sites contain modular elements that are used repeatedly across many dozens or hundreds of pages. These elements may include the global navigation header links and graphics for the page header or the contact information and mailing address of your enterprise. It makes no sense to include the text and HTML code that make up standard page components in

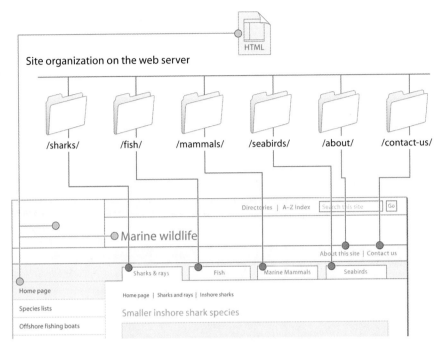

FIGURE 5.3
Try to mirror the
major interface and
content divisions
when you structure
the HTML and
directories of your
web site.

Site organization on the web server

/sharks/   /fish/   /mammals/   /seabirds/   /about/   /contact-us/

Directories | A–Z Index   Search this site   Go

Marine wildlife

About this site | Contact us

Sharks & rays   Fish   Marine Mammals   Seabirds

Home page   Home page | Sharks and rays | Inshore sharks

Species lists   Smaller inshore shark species

Offshore fishing boats

Page navigation wireframe

each file. Instead, use a single file containing the standardized element that repeats across hundreds of pages: when you change that one file, every page in your site containing that component automatically updates. HTML, CSS, and current web servers offer the power and flexibility of reusable modular components, and most large, sophisticated sites are built using dozens of reusable components.

Include files

Web servers allow site authors to create standardized pieces of HTML code, called "include files," that can be used across all pages in a web site. An include file is just a text file containing ordinary HTML page code. When a user requests a page, the web server combines the main page with whatever include files are specified in the main page file, and the assembled HTML page is then sent to the user's browser (fig. 5.4).

FIGURE 5.4
Include files are a
powerful way to
reuse standard
components across
many pages instead
of repeating the
HTML code over and
over again on each
page.

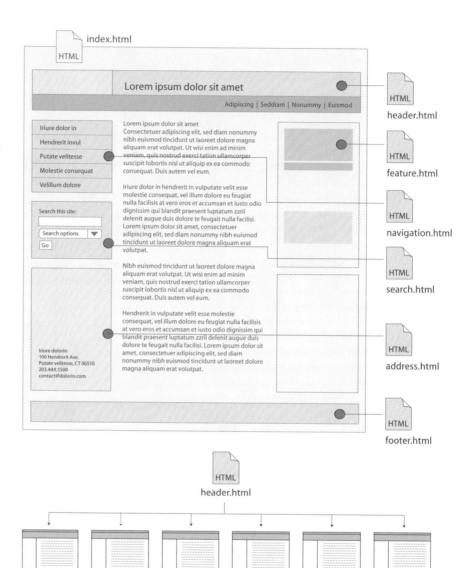

Many pages may share a single include file

Include files can also be handy for repeating standardized content such as payment policies, privacy policies, or other "boilerplate" business or legal language that is repeated in identical form in many places throughout a large site. Always look for opportunities to pull repeating content out of the page files and into an include file. If you ever have to change the boilerplate language, you'll be glad you have to change just one file to update every occurrence of the text throughout the site.

Using the cascade in CSS

Many users of Cascading Style Sheets know how to change the look of standard HTML components but don't pay much attention to the powerful cascade features of CSS. CSS is an extendable system, in which a related set of CSS instructions spread across multiple CSS files can cascade from very general style and layout instructions shared by all of your pages to extremely specific styles that only a handful of pages in your site may share. The CSS cascade has two major elements:

1. CSS cascade hierarchy

CSS has multiple hierarchical levels that cascade in importance and priority, from general CSS code shared by all pages, to code that is contained in a particular page file, to code that is embedded in specific HTML tags. General page code overrides shared site code, and CSS code embedded in HTML tags overrides general page code. This hierarchical cascade of CSS priorities allows you to set very general styles for your whole site while also permitting you to override the styles where needed with specific section or page styles (fig. 5.5).

2. Shared CSS across many pages

Multiple CSS files can work together across a site. This concept of multiple CSS files working together in a modular way is the heart of the cascade system of pages that all share code via links to master CSS files that control styles throughout the site. This system has obvious advantages: if all your pages share the same master CSS file, you can change the style of any component in the master CSS file, and every page of your site will show the new style. For example, if you tweak the typographic style of your <h1> headings in the master file, every <h1> heading throughout the site will change to reflect the new look.

FIGURE 5.5
Each level of the
style sheet "cascade"
overrides the one
below. Thus you can
use very general
styles but also add
code to customize
individual elements
where necessary.

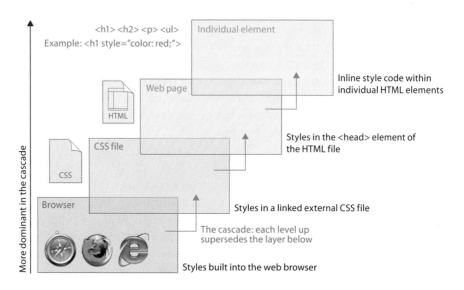

In a complex site, page designers often link groups of CSS files to style a site. Packaging multiple CSS files can have many practical advantages. In a complex site CSS code can run to hundreds of lines, and it's often more practical to subdivide such elements as the basic page layout CSS from the master site typography styles. It's easy to link to CSS files and let the master CSS layout and typography styles control all the pages in your site.

CSS "skin" files for specific graphic treatments

You may not want every page or section of your site to look the same. If so, you can add a third "skin" CSS file that provides specific graphics, colors, and header treatments for all pages in a site section that share the same visual design. Each CSS file in the multifile cascade adds information, moving from sitewide general layout and typographic styles to visual styles that may be specific to a few pages (fig. 5.6).

Media style sheets

Another advantage of CSS is the ability to provide context-appropriate designs using media style sheets. Support for media style sheets is not all that it could be, but there is sufficient support for screen, print, and, to a lesser degree, handheld devices. With media style sheets, it's possible to adapt a

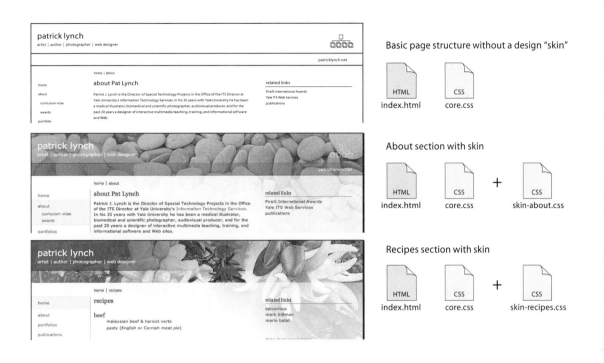

layout, for example, to hide navigation elements when printed or to minimize menu options when viewed on the small screen of a cell phone.

SEMANTIC STRUCTURE FOR HTML CONTENT CONTAINERS

As you plan the page wireframe templates for your site, consider the advantages of careful semantic HTML and CSS within the individual HTML files. Well-designed, standards-based web pages consist of many subdivisions that not only lay out functional regions of the page (header, footer, scan column, navigation, search box) but also provide unique name "IDs" for all standard page template elements. The content portions of web pages are subdivided by divisions (`<div>...</div>`) and spans (`<span>...</span>`) that label functional areas of the page, providing a "wrapper" around specific page elements or types of content. Divisions and spans should always be named carefully, and major repeating page elements should each have a unique ID.

FIGURE 5.6

A barebones page layout (top) and two different "skins" that use CSS to add customized graphics.

These named divisions and spans are crucial for three reasons:

1   Uniquely named page elements give you complete programmatic and style sheet control. You can't address a page element with css or JavaScript unless it has a name.
2   Uniquely named page divisions allow you to apply css visual styles more easily and powerfully to particular page areas or blocks of content.
3   Uniquely named page areas will give you many more options in the future, as new web content display devices and types of style sheets are developed. Someday you may want to convert your site to a new content management system. If all your pages and content are contained in consistent, systematically named page divisions, transforming your site will be much easier.

As you develop page wireframes and basic navigation, build in the power and convenience of careful semantic naming of your page regions and major page elements. It's easy to do in the beginning of a project and very hard or impossible to do later (fig. 5.7).

SEARCH ENGINE OPTIMIZATION

When the web first rose to popularity in the 1990s, people spoke of browsing or surfing the web, and users located interesting sites primary by finding and clicking on links listed on major web directory sites like Yahoo! and Netscape. As the size of the web has exploded over the past decade (Google now indexes well over twenty billion web pages), browsing through sites by following web links has become an increasingly inefficient means to initiate a search for new or very specific information. You may still browse the home page of the *New York Times* or a personal portal page like iGoogle or MyYahoo!, but if you need anything more specific, you will probably go straight to a search engine such as Google.

The way your pages appear to the automated "spider" software that search engines use to "crawl" links between web pages and create search indexes has become the most important factor in whether users will find the information you publish on the web. Search engine optimization isn't difficult and will make your site better structured and more accessible. If your site uses proper HTML structural markup, you've already done 80–90 percent of the work to make your site as visible as possible to search engines.

```
<body class="column3">
```

| Yale University | div id="yaleHeader" | | Directories | Yale Home | Search ITS sites | Go | Y |

div id="identityHeader"

ITS Media Services

INFORMATION TECHNOLOGY SERVICES

div id="itsLinksHeader"

div id="scanColumn"

div id="breadCrumb"

div id="navigationShow"
INCLUDE
(Navigation menu items)

div id="content"

div id="mainColumn"

div id="sideBar"

Search optimization techniques are not the magic sauce that will automatically bring your site to the top of Google's page rankings, however. SEO isn't a cure-all for an ineffective site—it can increase the traffic volume to your site and make things easier to find, but it can't improve the quality of your site content. SEO techniques ensure that your site is well formed and lessen the possibility that you have inadvertently hidden important information while constructing your site. Over the long run, though, only good content and many reference links from other highly ranked web sites will get you to the first page of Google search results and keep you there.

FIGURE 5.7
The top section of a detailed page wireframe diagram for the site technical team that shows all the various page divisions (divs).

THE LONG TAIL OF WEB SEARCH

Most patterns of web site use follow what is widely known as long-tailed distribution. That is, a few items are overwhelmingly popular, and everything else gets relatively little attention. If you ranked the popularity of every web page in your site, you will typically see a long-tailed curve, in which the home page and a few other pages get lots of views and most others get much less traffic. This long-tailed distribution pattern in popularity is true for products in stores, books for sale at Amazon, songs to download on iTunes, or DVDs for sale at Wal-Mart.

Although *Wired* magazine's Chris Anderson popularized the concept of the long tail on the Internet, interface expert Jakob Nielsen first used Zipf curves (the formal mathematical term for long-tailed phenomena) to describe the distribution patterns seen in web site usage. Long-tailed usage patterns are fundamental to explaining why web search has become the most popular tool for finding information on the web, whether you are making a general Internet search or merely searching your company's internal web site. Once users get past the home page and major subdivisions of a large site, they are unlikely to browse their way through all the links that may be required to find a specific page, even if every link is well organized, intuitively labeled, and working properly (fig. 5.8).

BASIC SEARCH ENGINE CONCEPTS
Links and individual web pages are the primary elements of web search. Search engines find web pages by following web links from one page to another. Search engine companies use an automated process to find and follow web links and to analyze and index web page content for topical relevance. These automated search programs are collectively called web spiders or web crawlers. This emphasis on links and pages is crucial to understanding how web search works: crawlers can find your pages only *if they have links to follow* to find them, and search engines do not rank web sites—they rank the popularity and content relevance *of individual web pages*. Each page of your site needs to be optimized for search and well linked to other pages, because from a search engine's point of view, each page stands alone.

So, what exactly are the rules?
We can't tell you, and the search engine companies won't give you the formulas either. If search engines like Google and Yahoo! told everyone how they rank pages and how they detect and ban search-scamming techniques, unscrupulous web publishers would instantly start to game the system, and soon we'd all be back to the pre-Google 1990s, when general web search had become almost useless. What we can say is what the search engines themselves gladly tell web content developers: create compelling page content with proper structural markup and good linkages to other pages and sites. Don't hide your content with poor page development techniques, and your pages will rank well in any search engine.

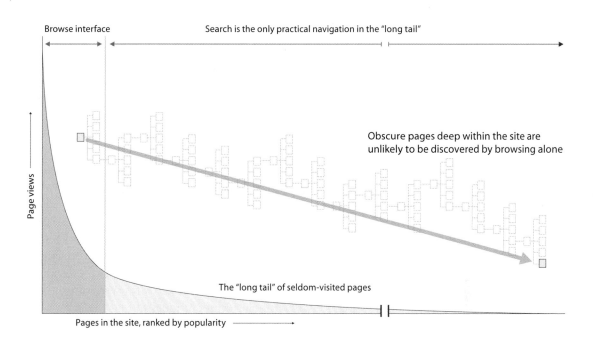

Browse interface

Search is the only practical navigation in the "long tail"

Page views

Obscure pages deep within the site are
unlikely to be discovered by browsing alone

The "long tail" of seldom-visited pages

Pages in the site, ranked by popularity

Internal versus external search factors

Current search engines use a combination of two information sources to rank the relevance of a web page to any given search term:

1   Internal factors: characteristics of the text and links within the page—the page title, content headings, the body text, the alternate text in image HTML tags, web links both internal to the site and external to other sites, and the frequency and distribution of topical keywords. Organized meta-information such as keyword and description HTML meta tags also factor in page ranking, although not as heavily as page titles, headings, and words within the page content. Even your domain name and the names of files and directories within the URL of your web page may count toward relevancy rankings.

2   External factors: the degree to which your page is linked with existing highly ranked pages on the same topic, how often people who get your page in their search results click on the link to your page, and other statistical factors that the search engines glean from their own data on the

FIGURE 5.8
Search is essential
to finding content in
large sites.

searches users perform and the link choices they make for a given topic or keyword. Links from popular pages that link to your page are essentially votes that your page is relevant to the search topic. Links from high-ranking pages are the most important factor in determining rank, but overall volume counts, too: the more links your page has from other pages and the more search users who click on your page link in search engine results, the higher your overall page ranking.

When web search services became popular in the 1990s, early search engines used internal content factors almost exclusively to rate the relevance and ranking of web pages. Rankings were thus childishly easy to manipulate. By inserting dozens of hidden keywords on a page, for example, an aggressive web page author could make a page seem richer in popular topic relevance than other web pages ("sex, sex, sex, sex"). By the late 1990s even the largest search engines were considered marginally useful in locating the best sources of information on a given topic, and the top-ranked sites were often those that used the most effective manipulation techniques to bias the search engines. The innovation that transformed web search in the late 1990s was Google's heavy use of external page factors to weigh pages' relevance and usefulness. Google's algorithms balance external ranking factors with statistical analysis of the page text to determine relevance and search ranking. Google's fundamental idea is similar to peer citations in academic publications. Every year thousands of science papers are published: How can you tell which articles are the best? You look for those that are most frequently cited ("linked") by other published papers. Important science papers get cited a lot. Useful web sites get linked a lot.

What search engines crawlers can and cannot "see" on your web pages
Search engine crawlers can only analyze the text, the web links, and some of the HTML markup code of your web page and then make inferences about the nature, quality, and topical relevance of your pages based on statistical analysis of the words on each page.

The following are not visible to a search engine:

- Display text within graphics, headers, banners, and company logos
- Flash animations, videos, and audio content
- Pages with little text content and lots of unlabeled graphics

- Site navigation that uses "rollover" or other graphic links or imagemaps
- Navigation links that depend on JavaScript or other dynamic code (crawlers do not execute JavaScript code)
- Content features such as RSS feeds and other text that depend on JavaScript to appear on the page
- Microsoft Office documents and Acrobat PDF files are read by some, *but not all,* web crawlers, and it is not always clear how these non-HTML content formats affect rankings

The following may cause search crawlers to bypass a web page:

- Pages with very complex structure: deeply nested tables, many frames, or unusually complex HTML
- Lengthy JavaScript or CSS code at the top of the page HTML code listing: crawlers give up on a page that seems to contain no content
- Pages with many broken links: crawlers abandon pages with many broken links, and they can't follow the broken links to find new pages
- Content with keyword spamming (repeating keywords many times in hidden text, alternate image text, or meta tags): search engines now ignore these primitive relevance-biasing schemes, and your page may even be banned from the search index if you use these techniques
- Server-side or meta-refresh redirects that are used to move a user from an old URL to a new one: many crawlers don't follow the redirect link to the new page
- Long, complex URLs with special characters (&, ?, %, $) that are often generated by dynamic programming or databases
- Slow-loading pages with inefficient dynamic links to content management systems or databases: if the page doesn't load in a few seconds, many crawlers give up and move on
- Pages that use frames or iframes: crawlers often ignore pages with complex frame schemes because they can't make sense of the individual HTML files that make up each framed "page" (avoid frames where possible, and never use frames for navigation purposes)
- Some dynamic pages that are assembled on request by a web application and database; be sure your developers know how you want to handle the search visibility of your content before they choose a development technology or content management tool for dynamic web sites

In addition to making your pages less searchable, these poor practices make your site less accessible, particularly to people who use screen reader software to access web content. SEO, structural markup of content, and universal usability are a wonderful confluence of worthy objectives: by using the best web practices for content markup and organizing your content and links with care, your site will be both more visible to search and more accessible to all users.

OPTIMIZING YOUR PAGES FOR SEARCH

Write for readers, not for search engines. The most popular sites for a given topic got that way by providing a rich mix of useful, interesting information for readers. Think about the keywords and phrases you would use to find your own web pages, and make a list of those words and phrases. Then go through each major page of your site and look at the page titles, content headers, and page text to see if your title and headers accurately reflect the content and major themes of each page. Put yourself in the user's place: How would a user find this page in your site? What keywords would they use to look for this content? Remember, search engines have no sense of context and no idea what other related content lies on other pages on your site. *To a search engine crawler, every page stands alone.* Every page of your site must explain itself fully with accurate titles, headers, keywords, informative linked text, and navigation links to other pages in your site.

Focus on your titles and keywords

The ideal optimized web page has a clear editorial content focus, with the key words or phrases present in these elements of the page, in order of importance:

- Page titles: titles are the most important element in page topic relevance; they also have another important role in the web interface—the page title becomes the text of bookmarks users make for your page
- Major headings at the top of the page (`<h1>`, `<h2>`, and so on)
- The first several content paragraphs of the page
- The text of links to other pages: link text tells a search engine that the linked words are important; "Click here" gives no information about the destination content, is a poor practice for markup and universal usability, and contributes nothing to the topical information of the page

- The alternate text for any relevant images on the page: accurate, carefully crafted alternate text for images is essential to universal usability and is also important if you want your images to appear in image search results such as Google Images and Yahoo! Images; the alternate text of the image link is the primary way search engines judge the topical relevance of an image
- The HTML file name and the names of directories in your site: for example, the ideal name for a page on Bengal tigers is "bengal-tigers.html"

Note that the singular and plural forms of words are different keywords, and adjust your keyword strategy accordingly. Thus "tiger" and "tigers" are different keywords. Search engines are not sensitive to letter case, so "Tiger" and "tiger" are exactly equivalent. Also think about context when you work out your content keywords. Search engines are the dumbest readers on the web: they don't know anything about anything, and they bring no context or knowledge of the world to the task of determining relevance. A search crawler doesn't know that Bengal tigers are carnivores, that they are large cats of the genus *Panthera,* or that they are also called Royal Bengal Tigers. Your optimized page on Bengal tigers might use all the following keywords and phrases, because a user could search with any of these terms:

- Tiger
- Tigers
- "Bengal Tiger"
- "Royal Bengal Tiger"
- "Panthera tigris tigris"
- "Panthera tigris bengalensis"

If your site has been on the web long enough to get indexed by Google or Yahoo!, use your chosen keywords to do searches in the major search engines and see how your site ranks in the search results for each phrase. You can also use the web itself to find data on the keywords and phrases that readers are currently using to find your site. Both Google and Yahoo! offer many tools and information sources to webmasters who want more data on how their site is searched, what keywords readers use to find their site, and how their site ranks for a given keyword or phrase:

- Google Webmaster Tools: www.google.com/webmasters/tools
- Goggle Analytics: www.google.com/analytics
- Google Adwords: Keyword Tool: adwords.google.com/select/KeywordToolExternal
- Yahoo! Site Explorer: siteexplorer.search.yahoo.com

Keyword frequency

Even in well-written content with a tight topical focus, the primary topical keywords are normally a small percentage of the words on the page, typically 5 to 8 percent. Because of the widespread practice of "keyword spamming" (adding hidden or gratuitous repetitions of keywords on a page to make the content seem more relevant), search engines are wary of pages where particular keywords appear with frequencies of over 10 percent of the word count. It is important to make sure your keywords appear in titles and major headings, but don't load in meaningless repetitions of your keywords: you'll degrade the quality of your pages and could lose search ranking because of the suspiciously high occurrence of your keywords.

Keyword placement on the page

There is some evidence that placing your keywords near the top and left edges of the page will (slightly) benefit your overall ranking, because, on average, those areas of pages are the most likely to contain important content keywords. The top and left edges also fall within the heaviest reader scanning zones as measured by eye-tracking research, so there are human interface advantages to getting your keywords into this page zone, too. For optimal headings, try to use your keywords early in the heading language. Search crawlers may not always scan the full text of very long web pages, so if you have important content near the bottom of long pages, consider creating a page content menu near the top of the page. This will help readers of long pages and will give you an opportunity to use keywords near the page top that might otherwise be buried at the bottom (fig. 5.9).

Use plain language and keywords in file and directory names

Use your major topical keywords in your file and site directory names. This helps a bit with search optimization, and it makes the organization of your site much more understandable to both your users and your partners on the web site development team. Always use hyphens in web file names, since

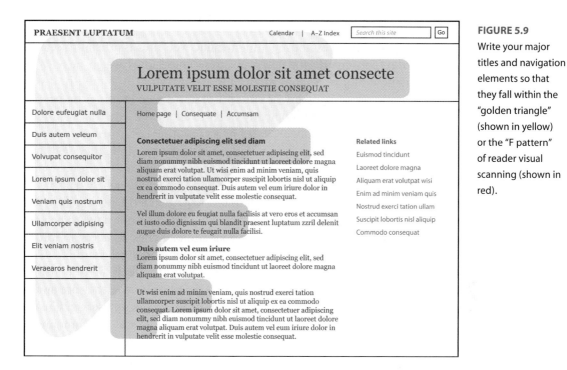

FIGURE 5.9
Write your major
titles and navigation
elements so that
they fall within the
"golden triangle"
(shown in yellow)
or the "F pattern"
of reader visual
scanning (shown in
red).

hyphens are "breaking" characters that divide words from each other. For example, in the file name "bengal-tiger-habitat.html" a search engine will see the words "Bengal," "tiger," and "habitat" because the words are separated by hyphens. If you use "nonbreaking" underscore characters as dividers or run the words together, the file name is seen as one long nonsense word that won't contribute to page ranking. The file names "bengal_tiger_habitat. html" or "bengaltigerhabitat.html" are equivalent, and neither is ideal for most search engines.

Both your readers and search crawlers can easily make sense of plain-language directory and file names in your URLs:

something.edu/cats/tigers/bengal-tiger-habitat.html

Requesting links from other web sites

Requesting links from established, high-traffic web sites is crucial to search optimization, particularly for new web sites. These links weigh heavily in search engine rankings, so they are well worth the effort to establish. If you work within a larger company or enterprise, start by contacting the people responsible for your primary company web site and make sure that your new site is linked from any site maps, index pages, or other enterprise-wide directory of major pages. Although it may not always be possible, the ideal link would be from your company's home page to your new site. Smart company web managers often reserve a spot on the home page for such "what's new" link requests because they know how to leverage their existing search traffic on the home page to promote a new site. The link does not have to be permanent: a few weeks of visibility after your site launches and gets an initial pass from the major search crawlers will be enough to get you started.

Your company's central web organization will also likely be responsible for any local web search capabilities, and you want to be sure they are aware of your new web site, particularly if it is housed on a new web server. Create a standard press release or email announcement, and send the announcement to colleagues, professional associations, partner companies, and the local press, requesting that related sites link to your site. The more links your site gets from established, high-traffic sites that already rank well in Google or Yahoo!, the faster your site will climb the search results rankings.

Submitting your new site to the major search engines

By far the best way to get your site listed in the major search engines is to request links from other existing sites that point to your new site. The two largest search engines offer pages that allow you to submit the URL for a new web site, but there is no guarantee that the search crawlers will find your site immediately. It could take several weeks or more for them to visit your new site and index it for the first time.

Site submissions pages:

- Google: www.google.com/addurl
- Yahoo!: search.yahoo.com/info/submit.html

HTML meta tags

Meta tags are a great intellectual notion that has largely fallen victim to human nature. The basic idea is excellent: use a special HTML header designation called a "meta" tag to hold organized bits of meta-information (that is, information about information) to describe your page and site, who authored the page, and what the major content keywords are for your page. The information is there to describe the page to search engines but is not visible to the user unless he or she uses the browser "View Source" option to check the HTML code. Unfortunately, in the 1990s, search scammers began to use meta tags as a means to load in dozens or even hundreds of hidden keywords on a page, often in many repetitions, to bias the results of web searches. Because of these fraudulent practices, recent generations of search engine software either ignore meta tags or give them little weight in overall search rankings. Current search crawlers will also down-rank or ban pages that abuse meta tags, so the practice of abusing meta tags has become pointless.

Should you use meta tags on your pages? We think they are still a useful structured means to provide organized information about your site. And although search engines may not give heavy ranking weight to meta tag information, most search engines will grab the first dozen or so words of a "description" meta tag as the descriptive text that accompanies your page title in the search results listing.

The basic forms of meta tags are useful, straightforward to fill out, and cover all the basic information you might want to describe your page to a search engine:

```
<meta name="author" content="Patrick J. Lynch" />
<meta name="description" content="Personal web site of artist,
    author, designer and photographer Patrick J. Lynch." />
<meta name="keywords" content="web design, web style guide, yale
    university, patrick j. lynch" />
```

The bottom line on meta tags: they never hurt, they might help a little, and they are a simple way to supply structured meta-information about your page content.

Make your site easy to navigate

Basic navigation links are an important part of search optimization, because only through links can search crawlers find your individual pages. In designing your basic page layout and navigation, be sure you have incorporated links to your home page, to other major subdivisions of your site, and to the larger organization or company you work in. Remember, each link you create not only gives a navigation path to users and search engine crawlers but associates your local site with larger company or other general Internet sites that have much higher user traffic than your site. The more you use links to knit your site into your local enterprise site and related external sites, the better off you'll be for search visibility.

Two kinds of site maps

In the context of search optimization, the term "site map" has several meanings, depending on its context:

- Site map pages: most web site maps are ordinary web pages with lists of links to the major elements of your web site (fig. 5.10). These master lists of the major pages in your site are an excellent resource for search engine crawlers, and site map pages are a great way to ensure that every important page of your site is linked in a way that search crawlers and users can easily find. Site map or "index" pages are a common element of web sites, and users who prefer to browse through lists of links know to look for site map or index pages in a well-organized site. In the earlier days of the web you'd see site maps that were laid out as diagrammatic charts or visual maps of the site, but the highly visual site map metaphors have largely faded in favor of the much more efficient link lists.
- XML site maps for search engines: the second common meaning for "site map" refers to a text file in XML format that sits at the level of your home page and informs web search crawlers about the major pages in your web site, how to find the pages, and how often the pages are likely to be updated (daily, weekly, monthly).

You should use both kinds of site maps to ensure maximum visibility of your site content.

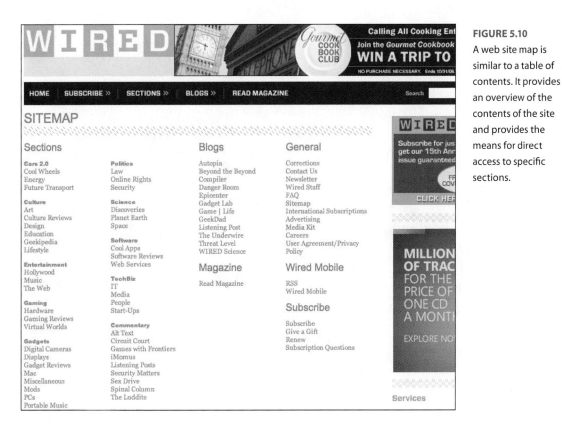

The experienced web designer, like the talented newspaper art director, accepts that many projects she works on will have headers and columns and footers. Her job is not to whine about emerging commonalities but to use them to create pages that are distinctive, natural, brand-appropriate, subtly memorable, and quietly but unmistakably engaging.

—Jeffrey Zeldman

CHAPTER 6

Page Structure

Book design and print typography are ancient and well-respected design disciplines. Both have a long tradition of creativity within the tight boundaries of our expectations for the form of books, page layout, letterform design, typography, and the harmonious confluence of visual design and content that characterizes the best print design. These deeply creative and intellectually demanding crafts are not hobbled by the 950 pages of rules and conventions in *The Chicago Manual of Style*. Book design, typography, and the larger world of print publishing are *enabled* by established conventions and standards for print publication. With "web standards" methods for building sites, with carefully validated and universally accessible XHTML and CSS, we now have excellent technical standards. Unfortunately we're still in an awkward, adolescent stage for web publishing, editorial, and design standards, but clear patterns and user expectations are emerging from the chaos.

It may seem odd to start a chapter on "design" with a plea for standards, rules, and conventions, but often site projects founder in the design stage because the larger norms of traditional publishing, editorial standards, and institutional practices are ignored in the pursuit of graphic, technical, or interactive eccentricities. "Prefer the standard to the offbeat." Take this timeless advice from William Strunk and E. B. White, and save your creative chops for the *real* work of developing interesting content.

SITE DESIGN IN CONTEXT

Web sites are composed of a hierarchy of elements that work together as a whole to shape user expectations. Site design is the point at which you assemble your planning work on information architecture, navigation elements, and user interface wireframes and begin to structure an actual site in HTML and CSS. But before you begin this process, situate your site appropriately within the context of the web and your organization.

THE WORLD WIDE WEB

The larger web environment shapes the expectations that users and readers bring to any site. As interface expert Jakob Nielsen points out, your readers spend the overwhelming majority of their time on sites other than yours. Any site design should consider the larger design norms and user expectations of the web and avoid self-indulgent exercises in interface or design novelty. Your site will succeed and draw visitors and customers if you provide great content and services. No site succeeds because it has a cool home page. Your site could easily fail if you ignore user expectations and create a peculiar, unusable framework for your content.

ENTERPRISE WEB IDENTITY

If you work within a larger organization, always make your relationship to the larger enterprise a clear and meaningful part of your site design. If your institution has an identity program or a web template system, use it. Adopting the design standards of the larger enterprise can save you a lot of time and money. Institutions notorious for poor governance—universities, government agencies, large nonprofit agencies—also often have chaotic web sites. Large companies sometimes have the same problems, but the standards and norms of corporate identity programs are well established in the business world, and most corporate sites start with the expectation that everyone will share a common look and feel and user interface and that each discrete corporate site will project a clear relationship to the parent enterprise.

PAGE STRUCTURE AND SITE DESIGN

Web "sites" are complete abstractions—they don't exist, except in our heads. When we identify a site as such, what we're really describing is a collection of *individual* linked pages that share a common graphic and navigational look and feel. What creates the illusion of continuity across a cohesive "site" is the design features that pages share. Individual HTML pages and how they are designed and linked are the atomic unit of web sites, and everything that characterizes site structure must appear in the page templates.

As the web has matured over the past decade, the structure of web pages in text-driven information sites has become more uniform and predictable. Although not all web pages share the exact layout and features described here, most web pages incorporate some or all of these basic components, in page locations that have become familiar to web users (fig. 6.1).

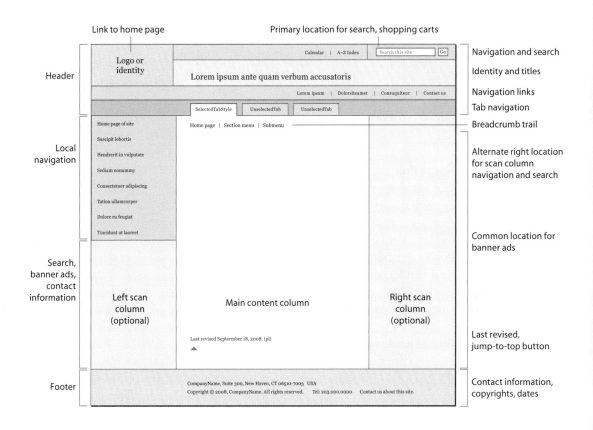

Link to home page   Primary location for search, shopping carts

Header	Logo or identity
	Lorem ipsum ante quam verbum accusatoris
	Calendar | A–Z Index Search this site Go

Navigation and search

Identity and titles

Navigation links

Tab navigation

Breadcrumb trail

Alternate right location for scan column navigation and search

Common location for banner ads

Last revised, jump-to-top button

Contact information, copyrights, dates

Local navigation

Home page of site
Suscipit lobortis
Hendrerit in vulputate
Sediam nonummy
Consectetuer adipiscing
Tation ullamcorper
Dolore eu feugiat
Tincidunt ut laoreet

Lorem ipsum \| Dolorsiteamet \| Consuquiteur \| Contact us

SelectedTabStyle   UnselectedTab   UnselectedTab

Home page \| Section menu \| Submenu

Search, banner ads, contact information

Left scan column (optional)

Main content column

Right scan column (optional)

Last revised Septermber 18, 2008. (pl)

Footer

CompanyName, Suite 300, New Haven, CT 06510-7003 USA
Copyright © 2008, CompanyName. All rights reserved.   Tel: 203.000.0000   Contact us about this site.

PAGE HEADERS

Page headers are like miniature versions of the home page that sit atop each page and do many of the things that home pages do, but in a limited space. Headers provide site identity and global navigation, with search and perhaps other tools. The exact location and arrangement of the components vary from site to site, but the overall design pattern has become fairly consistent.

Headers are the most visible component of site identity. What seems real is real: a collection of pages that share headers will be perceived as a "site" even if the pages originate from very different technical sources (php/Perl, jsp, .net, blog software, portal systems, SharePoint, web applications, content management systems, and so on).

FIGURE 6.1

A canonical page design and major page elements.

Possible header components (individual designs rarely use them all)   Variations on the basic header themes

Advertising		Search this site [Go]	Cart
Identity	Lorem Ipsum | Dolorsiteamet | Consuiquiteur | Eamet Dolorsit | Ipsum delit | Lorem Ipsum Dolor		
	Site titles, section identity, or advertising		
	SelectedTabStyle | UnselectedTab | UnselectedTab | UnselectedTab | UnselectedTab		

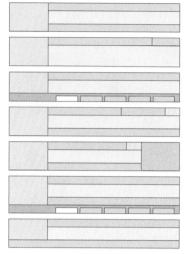

FIGURE 6.2

The canonical form of page headers is dominated by horizontal bands of links and tools, one or several identity graphics, and, in many sites, advertising. The cast of characters is fairly consistent, but the exact form of headers can vary quite a bit.

Home link

Placing your organization or site logo in the upper left corner of the page—and linking that logo to the home page—is a widely used convention and one you should adopt. If you are not using a logo or graphic in your header, at least put a "home" link near the upper left corner of the page, where 99 percent of users will expect to find it.

Global navigation

Headers are the most frequent location for global navigation links that span the site. The ideal arrangement is to use an HTML list of links, styled with CSS to spread horizontally across a section of the header. This gives you:

- Usability: global links where users most expect to see them
- Semantic logic: the collection of global links should be marked up as a list, because, well, it *is* a list
- Accessibility: the list format of links appears early in the code listing, where it should be
- Search visibility: a collection of your major navigation keywords, linked and at the top of the code listing, is ideal for search engine optimization

Tabs are another widely used, easily understood convention for global navigation. The best way to implement tabs is to style an ordinary HTML list with a more elaborate CSS treatment to form the "tab" graphic around each link. Be sure you get the graphic details right: the selected tab should be graphically unambiguous, and the remaining tabs should clearly be behind the selected tab. This type of "you are here" marker is essential in orienting

Google Webmaster Help Center   Change Language: English

Documentation   My site and Google   Search Help Center
Webmaster Guidelines
Getting started with   My site's ranking in Google search results   Search
Webmaster Tools

useit.com → Alertbox → Jan. 2008 Usability ROI   Search

Jakob Nielsen's Alertbox, January 22, 2008:

FIGURE 6.3
Locations for
breadcrumb trails.

users within the site. Tabs can also be used to implement a two-tiered navigation scheme, in which a secondary horizontal list of links appears under the selected tab, again as a simple HTML list with CSS styling, to keep things semantic, accessible, and search visible (fig. 6.2).

Breadcrumb navigation

Breadcrumb navigation is a widely used, easily understood navigation device that is particularly useful in large sites with deep levels of content organization (see chapter 4, *Interface Design Conventions*). Breadcrumbs integrated into the header are best at the top of the header, as in the Google and useit. com sites (fig. 6.3). Another popular location for breadcrumb navigation is just above the main page content.

Search

All sites with more than few dozen pages should offer local site search. The upper right area of the header is a popular location for search boxes, but a header search box must necessarily be simple to fit in this relatively small area (fig. 6.4). If you need more screen area to offer more controls and choices to the search user, consider locating your site search in the left or right scan columns of the page (see *Scan columns*, below).

Yale University   Calendar | A-Z Index   Search ITS sites   Go   Y

ITS INFORMATION TECHNOLOGY SERVICES

Find it   About ITS   Policies   Feedback   Search ITS   ITS A-Z Index   System Status

FIGURE 6.4
A header-based
search box.

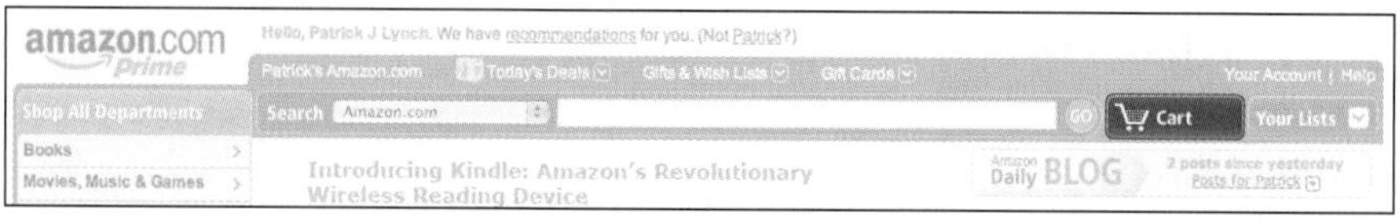

FIGURE 6.5

Put the shopping
cart where Amazon
puts it, because that's
where most people
will look for it.

"Checkout baskets," online shopping "carts"

Long ago, Amazon put its "cart" link in the upper right of the header, and that's where virtually all other shopping sites put it now, too. Don't buck the trend; it's one of the most firmly rooted interface conventions on the web (fig. 6.5).

Advertising

Ad-supported sites often reserve a large area above other header components for banner advertising, and research shows that users commonly expect to see banner ads in this area of the page. This layout convention has important implications, even if your site does not use banner ads, because of the widely observed phenomenon of "banner blindness." Readers commonly ignore areas of the screen that usually contain advertising, especially if the graphic content looks like a banner ad. Be sure your headers and other page graphics don't use the heavily boxed and graphically loud visual vocabulary of most banner ads, or your readers may ignore important elements of your user interface.

SCAN COLUMNS

Subdividing the page field into functional regions is a fundamental characteristic of modern graphic design. Early in the web's history, designers began using narrow "scan" columns at the edge of the page to organize navigation links and other peripheral page elements, much as scan columns have been used in print publications for a century or more. Research on web user expectations now supports the common practice of locating navigational links—particularly section navigation—in the left column.

Scan columns are also useful as locations for web search boxes, mailing address and contact information, and other more minor but necessary page elements. Research shows that the left scan column under the local navigation links is the second place most users will look for search features, after they look in the right header area (fig. 6.6).

FIGURE 6.6
Beyond the superficial visual style variations, scan column designs have become remarkably consistent in major content and sales web sites.

Left or right scan columns for navigation?

Extensive eye-tracking and user research says that it doesn't really matter whether you use left or right navigation columns. Users seem to do just fine either way, as long as you are consistent about where you put things. We favor the left column for navigation simply because that is the most common practice.

Mailing address and contact information

Basic "real world" information about who the company responsible for the site is, *where* the company is, and how to contact the company is often hard to find on otherwise well-designed sites. If you sell a product or service, don't hide from your customers. Display your contact information in a prominent location, such as the scan column, on every page.

Advertising and the scan columns

Our advice about ads in the scan column is the same as with header ads (above): beware! Users often ignore content that looks like advertising when they see it in a scan column. Use formats that don't scream "ADVERTISING!" Never make your scan column content or navigation look anything like a typical banner ad, or users may never notice it.

THE CONTENT AREA

Web content is so multifaceted that few general rules apply, but the following common practices make content areas easier to use:

- Page titles. Don't bury the lead. Every page needs a visible name near the top. For all kinds of logical, editorial, accessibility, search visibility, and *common-sense* reasons, use an <h1> heading at the top of the page to let users know what the page is about.
- Breadcrumb navigation. The top of the content area is the most common location for breadcrumb navigation.
- Jump-to-top links. Jump links are a nice refinement for long pages. These links don't need to be elaborate—just a top of page link will do, but a small up-arrow icon offers good reinforcement.
- Rules. These elements can easily be overused and lead to a cluttered design. Use css to keep page rules as unobtrusive as possible. When in doubt, skip rules and use a little white space to create visual content groupings or separations.
- Paging navigation. In multipage sequences it is convenient to have simple text links at the top and bottom of the page to move the reader to the previous or next pages in the sequence. In longer sequences it is helpful to provide information describing where they are in the series.
- Dates. Publication and update dates are useful for assessing the currency and relevance of content. In news and magazine sites the publication date should appear at the top of the page. Other sites should display a last-updated date at the bottom of the content area (fig. 6.7).

Page footers

Page footers are mostly about housekeeping and legal matters. These elements need to be on the page, but place them somewhere out of the way:

- Page author or, in large enterprise sites, responsible party
- Copyright statement
- Contact details, especially email
- Links to related sites or to the larger enterprise
- Redundant navigation links, for long pages

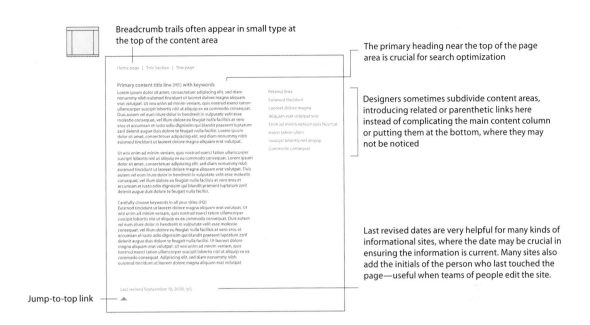

Breadcrumb trails often appear in small type at the top of the content area

The primary heading near the top of the page area is crucial for search optimization

Designers sometimes subdivide content areas, introducing related or parenthetic links here instead of complicating the main content column or putting them at the bottom, where they may not be noticed

Last revised dates are very helpful for many kinds of informational sites, where the date may be crucial in ensuring the information is current. Many sites also add the initials of the person who last touched the page—useful when teams of people edit the site.

Jump-to-top link

FIGURE 6.7
Typical content-area components.

PAGE TEMPLATES

Always start your template work with an internal page, because the internal page template will dominate the site. The home page is important, but the home page is inherently singular and has a unique role to play. Your internal page template will be used hundreds or thousands of times across larger sites, and the navigation, user interface, and graphic design of the internal pages will dominate the user's experience of your site. Get your internal page design and navigation right, and then derive your home and secondary page designs from the internal page template (fig. 6.8).

INTERNAL PAGE TEMPLATES

Internal page templates must accomplish these important functions:

- Global and local site navigation: make them logically consistent with the information architecture and structural organization of your site
- Design framework: organize content consistently throughout the site
- Graphic tone: establish the look and feel of the site, ideally with a system dominated by consistent visual elements, but with enough flexibility to create distinct regions within a large site

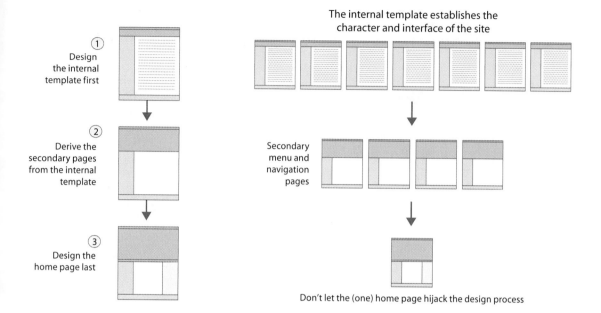

The internal template establishes the character and interface of the site

① Design the internal template first

② Derive the secondary pages from the internal template

③ Design the home page last

Secondary menu and navigation pages

Don't let the (one) home page hijack the design process

FIGURE 6.8

A logical ordering for internal, menu, and home page designs.

Types of internal pages

In larger sites containing a variety of content, your internal page template may be a set of templates that vary in details, such as the number of columns, to accommodate the range of content and user interface needs (fig. 6.9).

Sites that incorporate web applications, blog or wiki formats, or complex forms may need a simplified template variation that strips away some of the usual site navigation elements. Applications, complex forms, large data tables, and many kinds of highly graphic content (artwork, engineering drawings, repair manual graphics, and so on) usually require as much screen space as possible (fig. 6.10).

SECONDARY PAGE TEMPLATES

Most sites are organized in a multitiered hierarchy, with vertical dimensions (home, secondary pages, internal pages) and a horizontal spread of distinct content regions that graphically and organizationally help the reader navigate. Secondary page templates should be closely related to the internal page template but must accommodate these additional functions:

One column   Two columns 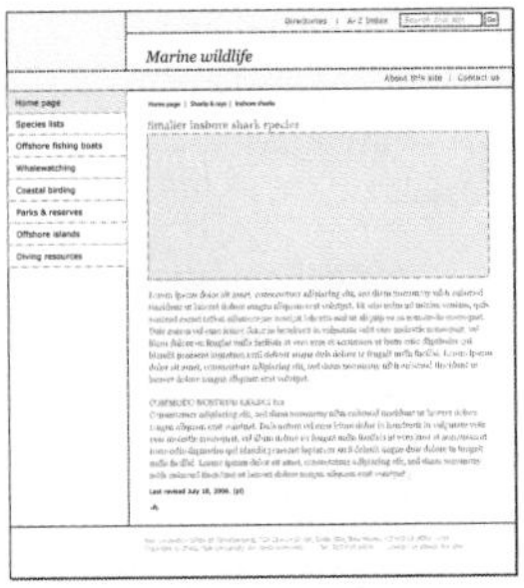   Three columns 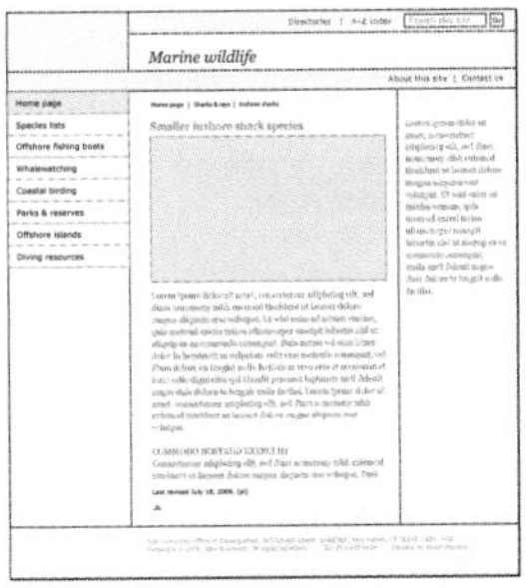   Menus plus tabs

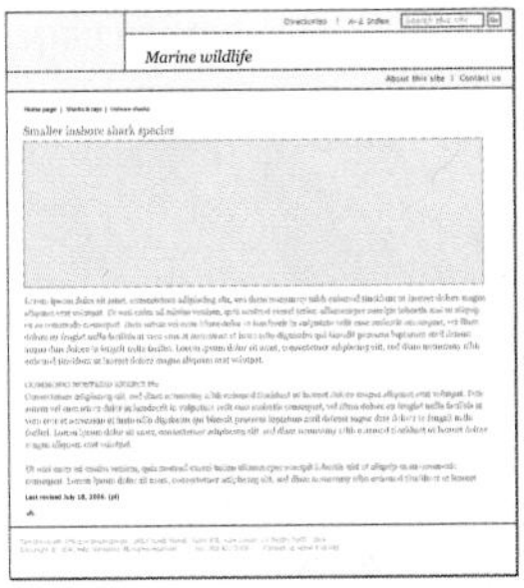

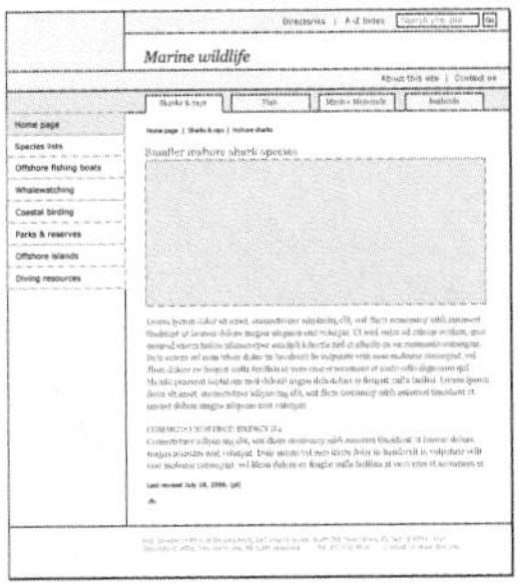

- Establish a tiered hierarchy of header labels that sets the relationship of the secondary page to the home page and larger enterprise site, as well as to the internal pages
- Provide a distinct look that identifies the secondary page as a special "sub-home page" and establishes a clear content theme

Secondary page templates help create a concrete sense of the vertical dimension of sites and may perform varied functions in the tiers between the home page and the internal content pages.

FIGURE 6.9

In larger sites the "template" is rarely a single layout and usually incorporates multiple variations to accommodate the full range of content and applications required.

Stripped-down interface for complex or specialized web content and applications

All the interface bells and whistles for maximum navigation flexibility

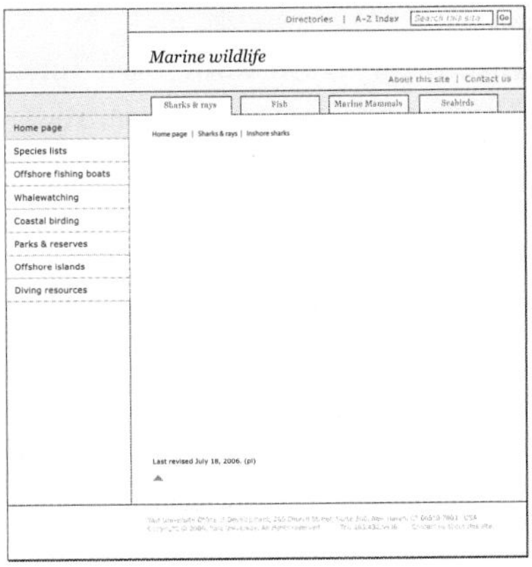

FIGURE 6.10

Always include a stripped-down version of the template (left) for large graphics, large data tables, or complex web applications.

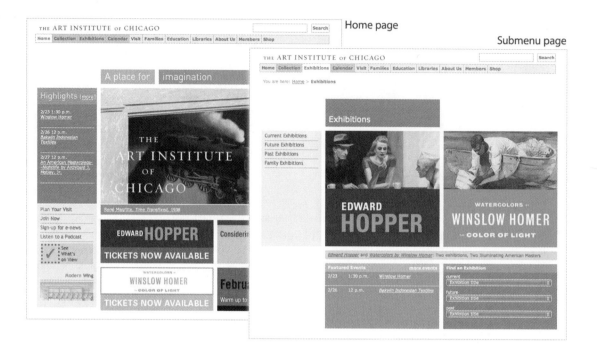

Home page

Submenu page

FIGURE 6.11

If you are featuring "Exhibitions" in your advertising, send visitors to a special submenu page that matches your ad campaign.

Navigation and submenu pages

Complex, multitiered sites usually need submenu pages to provide an organizing and navigational focal point for major subsections or regions of the site. These submenu pages are effectively the home page for that block of content.

Alternate "front doors" or "landing pages"

Many marketing or communications campaigns that point to web sites require a focused, immediately recognizable page to bring in visitors. These alternate entry points must bear a clear graphic and topical relation to the marketing graphics, featured product, or communications theme, but because they also function as alternate home pages, they should orient visitors to the larger site navigation as well (fig. 6.11).

Department or program home pages

Large corporate or enterprise sites require secondary or even tertiary levels of pages that act as home pages for the local department or program. In a multi-

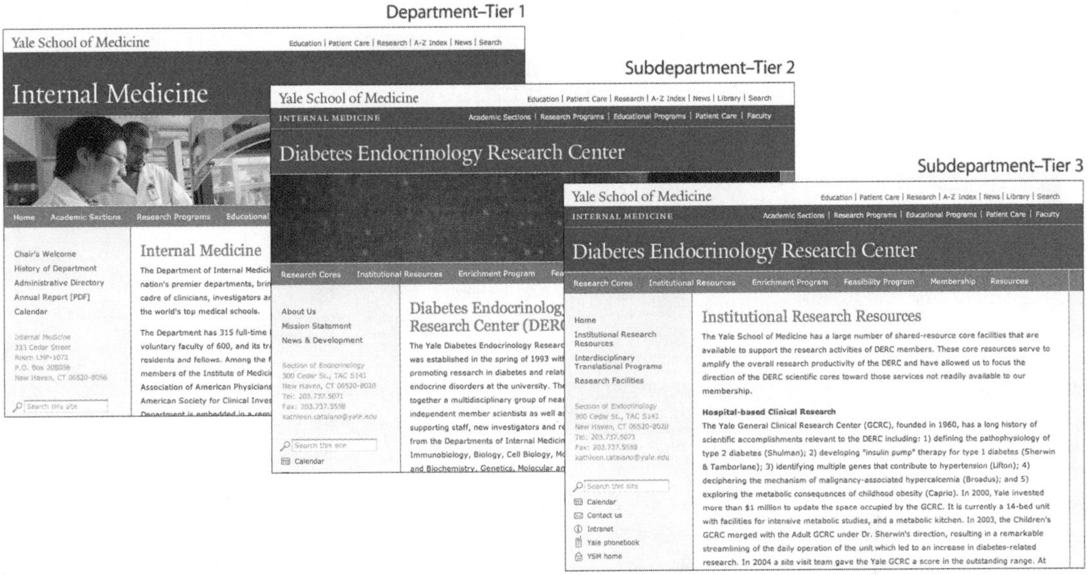

Department–Tier 1

Subdepartment–Tier 2

Subdepartment–Tier 3

tiered site your template system should establish a clear hierarchy of page header labeling and titles so that readers can see the relation of a department page to the larger enterprise (fig. 6.12).

THE HOME PAGE

Designing an effective home page can seem daunting, but if you've already thought through the fundamentals of your site navigation and have done the hard work of creating internal and secondary page templates, you have a great head start. Designing the home page layout *last* allows you to acknowledge the unique introductory role of the home page but places the design firmly within the larger navigational interface and graphic context of the site.

Home pages have four primary elements:

- Identity
- Navigation
- Timeliness, or content focus
- Tools (search, directories)

FIGURE 6.12

Department site templates should mirror the hierarchical structure of the departments in a carefully planned series of interrelated templates.

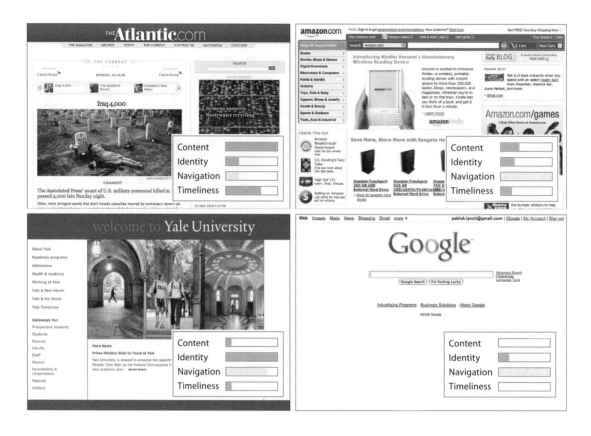

FIGURE 6.13

Four home page variations for very different institutions and purposes. Home page designs should always reflect a particular design strategy, depending on the nature and business intent of the web site.

Good home page designs always blend these four factors. *How* you blend them depends on the overall goals of your site, but most good home pages do not balance all four elements equally. Home pages often have a distinctive theme in which one factor dominates. Amazon's home page is all about navigation to products. Yale University's home page projects identity. The *Atlantic* is dominated by timeliness and content. Google's famously lean home page is all about tools. An effective home page can't be all things to all people. Decide what your priorities are, and build a home page that gives the user a clear sense of theme and priority (fig. 6.13).

Not all effective home pages have such singular emphasis. For example, Dartmouth College's home page strongly projects both identity and a lively sense of campus life. Navigation and tools aren't neglected, but they play a secondary role in the overall page impact (fig. 6.14).

FIGURE 6.14
Dartmouth's home design offers a good balance of identity, timeliness, navigation, and institutional identity.

Taglines

Too many sites project a strong brand image with logos and bold graphic design and then utterly fail to explain themselves to the new user. Unless you own one of the world's top one hundred brands, always put a brief explanatory comment, or tagline, prominently on the home page, so users understand instantly what you do and what you have to offer them. Taglines should be concise ("You'll find it at Alibris!"), but don't use a vague company motto. "We bring good things to life" is admirable but doesn't explain a thing about what General Electric can do for you. Users looking for content, services, or merchandise couldn't care less about your department's mission statement, so put that on your "about us" page, *not* on the home page.

Kiva's succinct service statement at the top of its home page is essential for a lesser-known brand and a novel service (fig. 6.15).

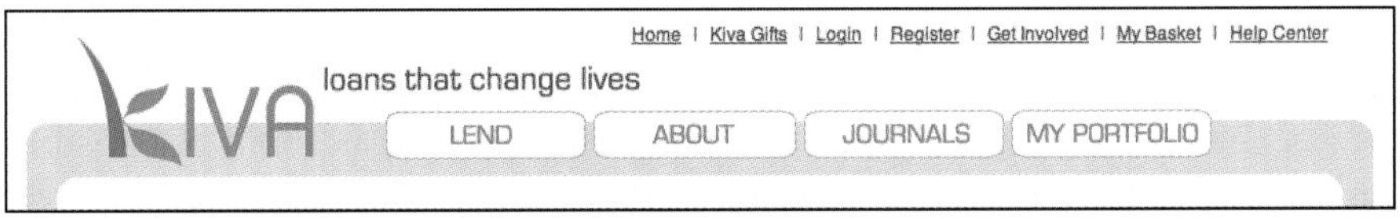

FIGURE 6.15
The purpose of the Kiva site is not self-evident to new users, and the header tag line ("loans that change lives") becomes a crucial explanation.

FIGURE 6.16
Page designs from
two complex, high-
traffic news sites.

Home page content and "the fold"

The roughly 65–75 square inches at the top of a home page comprise the
most visible area of the web site. Most users will be looking at your site on
19–22-inch monitors or laptop screens, and the top 6 or 7 vertical inches
are all that is sure to be visible on average screens, particularly on the short,
wide screens of most laptops. The "above the fold" metaphor refers to the
middle fold in classic broadsheet newspapers like the *New York Times* or *Wall
Street Journal*. Front-page stories above the fold are the most important and
visible.

In sites designed for efficient navigation the density of links at the top of
the home page should be maximal within the limits of legibility. Judging by
rwo of the top sites on the web, that maximum density is about one visible
link per square inch of screen space, or about seventy-five links in approximately seventy-five square inches (fig. 6.16).

FIGURE 6.17
The Denver Zoo
home page design
offers a full range of
options on the first
screen.

Of course, it's not likely that the average site needs anywhere near this much density of information. Some sites, such as the Denver Zoo, are designed to fit on the screen, with little or no need to scroll (fig. 6.17).

Dropdown menus

When there is a lot of content or merchandise categories to fit on the home page, there is the temptation to use dropdown menus to cram many choices into a small screen area. The space savings, though great, come at a cost to visibility and usability, because most choices are hidden until the user activates the menu. Careful navigation design can yield an effective hybrid strategy, in which you don't rely on dropdown menus but rather provide them as enhanced functionality for users who choose to explore them (fig. 6.18).

FIGURE 6.18

Opera uses classic
header-based global
navigation, coupled
with menus that
drop down as you
roll over each header
category.

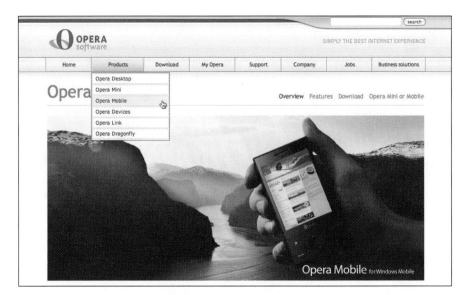

Dropdown menus are difficult to implement well using HTML and CSS. Although a standards-based HTML/CSS dropdown menu will be somewhat accessible and visible to search engines, the standard menu functionality that users expect from their Mac and Windows interfaces is not possible to reproduce using web tools alone. Web dropdowns tend to be slower and less forgiving of errors in mouse positioning than menus on Mac or Windows operating systems. Older users and users with less hand-eye coordination usually *hate* web dropdown menus, especially because they are often implemented with small font sizes and small cursor target areas.

Avoid dropdown menus that depend exclusively on JavaScript because they may not be accessible to keyboard users. Remember, too, that search engine spiders do not execute JavaScript code on the pages they scan, which is a huge disadvantage because navigation menu items make ideal keywords and linked keywords count heavily in search engine ranking. When using JavaScript to provide enhanced menu functionality, make sure the menus are workable from the keyboard and with JavaScript disabled.

Topical navigation versus path-splitting

Users usually arrive at a home page with specific topical or product interests or functional goals in mind. Most home pages thus feature prominent

FIGURE 6.19
Hiram College's header tabs "split paths," offering each major reader group (students, faculty, visitors) a special section tuned to its unique needs.

navigation lists or visual menus of topics, products, and services. Sometimes, however, users identify their interests by their identity or role. For example, it's common for university sites to "split paths" on the home page into prospective students, current students, parents, faculty, and other groups and then present various submenu pages oriented to the interests and needs of each group (fig. 6.19).

Web splash pages or "splash screens"

The two most useless words on the web are "Skip intro." For the vast majority of users, graphic or animated splash screens are an annoying extra mouse click on the way to real content. Splash pages are not accessible in any meaningful way, and if they depend on JavaScript, ActionScript, or other scripting to move the user to the real home page, *most web search engine spiders will never get past your splash page*, effectively preventing your highest-traffic page from contributing to your search rankings. Don't ever use an indulgent, functionally useless splash page as "eye candy" at the entrance to your site. Ever.

Simplicity is not the goal. It is the by-product of a good idea and modest expectations.

— Paul Rand

CHAPTER 7

Page Design

W e seek clarity, order, and trustworthiness in information sources, whether traditional paper documents or web pages. Effective page design can provide this confidence. The spatial organization of graphics and text on the web page can engage users with graphic impact, direct their attention, prioritize the information they see, and make their interactions with your web site more enjoyable and efficient.

Design creates visual logic and seeks an optimal balance between visual sensation and graphic information. Without the visual impact of shape, color, and contrast, pages are graphically uninteresting and will not motivate the viewer. Dense text documents without contrast and visual relief are also hard to read, particularly on low-resolution screens. But without the depth and complexity of text, highly graphic pages risk disappointing the user by offering a poor balance of visual sensation, text information, and interaction. In seeking the ideal balance, the primary constraints for page design are the limitations of the web medium, the diversity of individuals and technologies accessing web pages, and access speeds ranging from slow modems to high-speed wired and wireless connections.

Visual and functional continuity in your web site organization, graphic design, and typography are essential to convince your audience that your web site offers them timely, accurate, and useful information. A careful, systematic approach to page design can simplify navigation, reduce user errors, and make it easier for users to take advantage of the information and features of the site. But given the wide and diverse range of contexts that make up the experience of the web, the starting point for web page design begins under the surface of the page, with the structure of the underlying code.

DOCUMENT DESIGN

The documents that we produce for the web have a more complex purpose and functionality than those we create for a single medium, such as print. What works well in one context may be unusable in another. For instance,

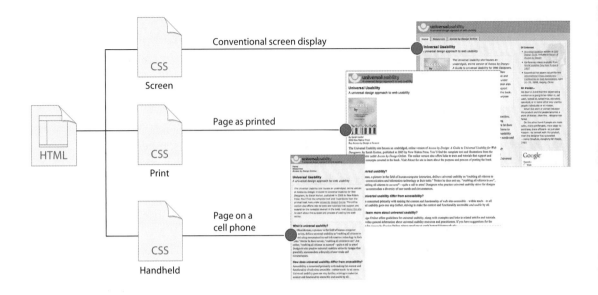

Conventional screen display

Page as printed

Page on a cell phone

CSS — Screen

CSS — Print

CSS — Handheld

HTML

FIGURE 7.1
Adapting the same HTML page for different display media, using CSS.

pages designed for viewing on a large display screen may not work well when printed on paper or viewed on a small cell phone display. When considering page design, look beyond the typical display screen and anticipate designs for other contexts, including print and mobile.

ADAPTIVE DESIGN

Done right, web pages can adapt to different contexts without requiring multiple versions of a document. A web document that employs adaptive design can be used successfully on a cinema or cell phone display, a television or a projection screen, printed in ink or Braille, read by a person or a software application. From the designer's perspective, there are two components to address to make this multipurpose system function effectively: the source document and media style sheets. With adaptive design, the source document contains all necessary information and functionality, and media style sheets adapt the source document for use in different contexts.

Defining styles

Styles can be defined in many ways: using the style attribute within element tags, in the head element of the page, or in an external style sheet. Generally speaking, external style sheets are the most effective; it's easy to modify, for example, the body background color for an entire site when the body background color property is defined in one location. With adaptive design, we create a different external style sheet for each context and then reference the style sheet using the "media" attribute of the `<link>` tag. Although there are many media attributes in the HTML specification, we focus here on the most widely used and supported media types: screen, print, and handheld (fig. 7.1).

```
<link rel="stylesheet" type="text/css" href="screen.css"
    media="screen" />
<link rel="stylesheet" type="text/css" href="print.css"
    media="print" />
<link rel="stylesheet" type="text/css" href="handheld.css"
    media="handheld" />
```

In practice, most consideration of media style sheets is after the fact. We often design first for conventional computer screens and then modify the design for print and handheld. This approach yields designs that are less than ideal, because we often don't address the requirements of the other media and viewing devices. To exploit the web environment fully, we need take a more holistic view from the start and create source documents that play well in multiple contexts.

DOCUMENT ORDER

Document order is the sequence in which elements, such as site identity, navigation, primary content, related content, and provenance information, appear in the document source code. Though not evident in the visual context, document order has a significant effect on the machine-readability of web pages. Many search engines give greater weight to content that appears at the top of a document. Screen readers begin reading web pages at the beginning of the page and read through the content in sequence. Many web browsers on small-screen devices collapse multicolumn layouts into one column for easier viewing. Print styling often makes use of a single-column layout to accommodate the aspect ratio of the page. The effectiveness of these contexts is largely dependent on document order.

Sequence is an important aspect of document order. Information is garbled when content elements do not follow a logical sequence—for example,

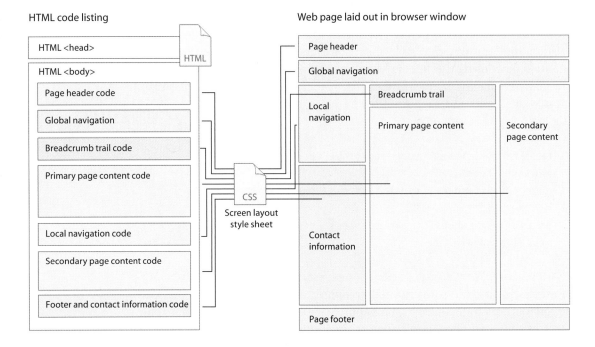

HTML code listing

Web page laid out in browser window

HTML <head>

HTML

HTML <body>

Page header code

Global navigation

Breadcrumb trail code

Primary page content code

CSS

Screen layout
style sheet

Local navigation code

Secondary page content code

Footer and contact information code

Page header

Global navigation

Breadcrumb trail

Local
navigation

Primary page content

Secondary
page content

Contact
information

Page footer

FIGURE 7.2

Code ordering within
the HTML code (left)
and how each code
block is arranged by
the style sheet.

when related links and advertising are jumbled in with the main content of
the page. Elements must follow a logical sequence in the document source
code, and each element must be fully articulated, without interruption by
other elements (fig. 7.2).

It's also necessary to consider the relative importance of elements and
to put the most important information at the beginning of the page. This
approach, called "front-loading," has many benefits. Nonvisual and small-
screen users have more direct access to main content when it appears early
in the source code, and keyboard users have more direct access to the functional elements of the page. And search engines do a better job of indexing
pages when the relevant content is at the top of the document (fig. 7.3).

SELECTIVE DISPLAY

Another aspect of document design is including elements that are relevant
to different contexts and coding the document to allow elements to display
or not, as appropriate. For example, although they are fundamental to any
screen design, navigation links are not helpful when printed on paper. With

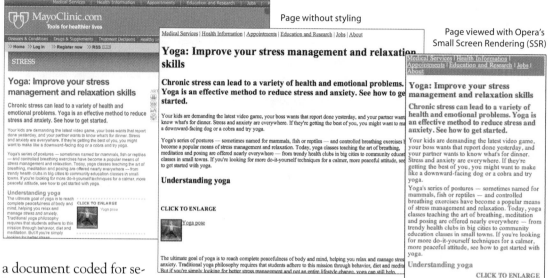

Page with the "screen" style sheet

Page without styling

Page viewed with Opera's Small Screen Rendering (SSR)

a document coded for selective display, you can use CSS in the print style sheet to hide navigation links in printed versions of the page.

And while we tend to focus on document design for the computer screen, and most of our document content addresses the needs of visual browsing, some elements are helpful in other contexts. In print, the page URL is helpful when you want to return to the page or cite the article. On screen, however, the page URL is readily available, so there's no need to display that information. In this case, you can use CSS to hide the URL in the screen style sheet (fig. 7.4).

FIGURE 7.3

For the best search engine visiblity, keep your most important keywords and headlines near the top of the page.

TEXT ALTERNATES

Web page design is concerned with providing both visual and nonvisual access to information and functionality. The primary reason we can meet the needs of such a broad and diverse audience in the online environment is that text can be read by software. Of course, not all of the information and functionality on the web is in text format; indeed, the web is continually enriched by other content such as images, video, and interactivity. The way to achieve universal usability in a complex and visually rich environment is to provide text equivalents for all relevant nontextual elements.

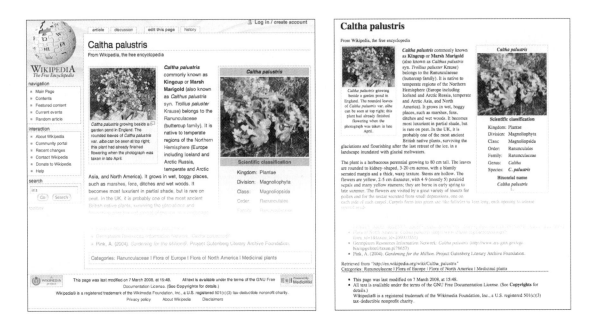

FIGURE 7.4

The print version of Wikipedia articles does not include navigation and does include the page URL in the footer.

Alternate text comes in many forms. A descriptive caption is an alternative means to convey information contained in an image. Many sites use text links in the footer of the page to provide a text-only alternative to image-based links. You can provide alternate text in the code of the page: for example, using the "alt" attribute of the <img> tag to provide alternate text for images. Audio and video presentations are often presented with captions and a text transcript. The key concept is not so much how it is provided but rather that alternate text is provided in the source code so that the essential content and functionality of the page is machine-readable and therefore accessible and universally usable (fig. 7.5).

UNDERSTAND THE MEDIUM

People experience web pages in different ways. For some, the web is a direct medium where pages are read online—on a large computer display, a small portable device, or read aloud by software. For others, the web is a delivery medium that allows access to information for offline use—downloaded to disk or printed onto paper. Your expectations about how people will typically use your site should govern your page design decisions. Documents to be read online should be written for online reading (see chapter 9, *Editorial*

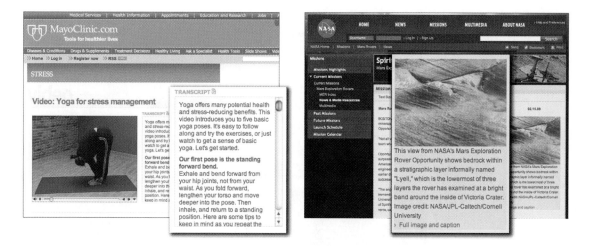

FIGURE 7.5

Text transcripts of spoken audio and descriptive image captions are methods of providing text alternates.

Style), with a page design that adapts gracefully to different screen sizes and access methods. Documents that will probably be printed and read offline should ideally appear on one page and should use print style sheets to adapt the design to an optimal layout for print, by, for example, stripping the print page of extraneous site navigation links. Documents likely to appeal to mobile users should work in the hybrid mobile environment, readable both in a stripped-down version of the page and in a regular view that works on a full-blown, albeit small, mobile browser (fig. 7.6).

VISUAL DESIGN

Some foundational ideas are so thoroughly ingrained in modern life that we hardly see them for their ubiquity and familiarity. The concept of "module and program"—regular building blocks of repeating patterns that when joined together produce an organized whole—permeates our information-age lives even more thoroughly than it did the lives of our ancestors in the industrial revolution launched by manufacturing innovators like Eli Whitney.

As the industrial world grew more complex, document designers in the mid-1800s began to adapt modular programs to newspaper, catalog, financial, and other publications, and modern page layout was born. In the early twentieth century the Bauhaus designers adopted the elements of visual logic discovered by the Gestalt perceptual psychologists, and those German and Swiss designers created modern graphic design (see Visual Design Principles sidebar, below).

Page rendered with a screen style sheet

Page as printed with
a print style sheet

FIGURE 7.6

Mobile web displays
could be a stripped-
down page or a small
representation of the
regular screen view.

The primary purposes of graphic design are to:

- Create a clear visual hierarchy of contrast, so you can see at a glance what is important and what is peripheral
- Define functional regions of the page
- Group page elements that are related, so that you can see structure in the content

A simple page grid establishes discrete functional areas, and adequate negative space defines the figure-ground relationships for the page. The page uses familiar principles of page layout, and users can easily predict the location of major content and functional elements.

The *Atlantic* home page

Functional areas

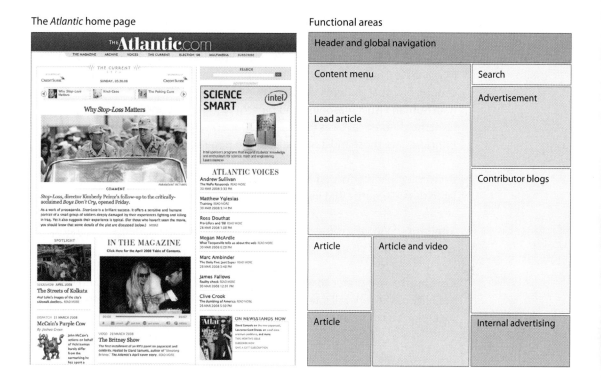

Header and global navigation	
Content menu	Search
	Advertisement
Lead article	
	Contributor blogs
Article	Article and video	
Article	Internal advertising

Crowded pages confuse the figure-ground relationships of page elements by creating an ambiguous field of visual texture, with little contrast to draw the eye and few landmarks to help the user understand content organization. Crowded elements also cause $1 + 1 = 3$ effects, adding visual confusion.

As you design the HTML and CSS for menu lists, content lists, page header graphics, and other design elements, always consider the spacing, grouping, similarity, and overall visual logic of the patterns you create on the page so that you provide easily seen structure, not confusing detail.

Proximity and uniform connectedness are the most powerful Gestalt principles in page layout; elements that are grouped within defined regions form the basis for content modularity and "chunking" web content for easy scanning. A well-organized page with clear groups of content shows the user at a glance how the content is organized and sets up modular units of content that form a predictable pattern over pages throughout the site (fig. 7.7).

FIGURE 7.7

The functional units of the *Atlantic*'s home page use the Gestalt principles of proximity and enclosure to organize a complex visual field and keep it extremely legible.

VISUAL DESIGN PRINCIPLES

The Gestalt psychologists of the early twentieth century were fascinated with the mind's ability to see unified "wholes" from the sum of complex visual parts ("Gestalt" is German for "whole" or "whole form"). Their research into the perception of visual patterns yielded a number of consistent principles that dominate human visual reasoning and pattern recognition, and these principles form the theoretical basis for much of modern graphic design. The following principles are those most relevant to web page design:

Proximity Elements that are close to each other are perceived as more related than elements that lie farther apart (*a*, below).

Similarity Viewers will associate and treat as a group elements that share consistent visual characteristics (*b*, below).

Continuity We prefer continuous, unbroken contours and paths, and the vast majority of viewers will interpret *c*, below, as two crossed lines, not four lines meeting at a common point.

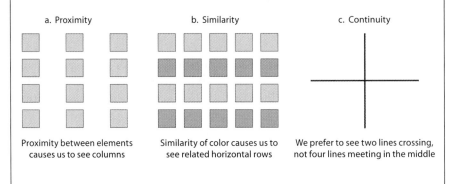

a. Proximity	b. Similarity	c. Continuity
Proximity between elements causes us to see columns	Similarity of color causes us to see related horizontal rows	We prefer to see two lines crossing, not four lines meeting in the middle

Closure We have a powerful bias to see completed figures, even when the contours of the figure are broken or ambiguous. We see a white rectangle overlying four circles (*a*, opposite), not four circles that each have a section missing.

Figure-ground relationships In figure-ground reversal the viewer's perception alternates between two possible interpretations of the same visual field: you see either a goblet or two faces, but you cannot see both at once (*b*, below). Proximity has a strong effect on figure-ground relationships: it's easier for most people to see the goblet when it's wider and the "faces" are farther apart (*c*, below). Also, visual elements that are relatively small will be seen as discrete elements against a larger field. The small element will be seen as the "figure" and the larger field as the "ground" around the figure.

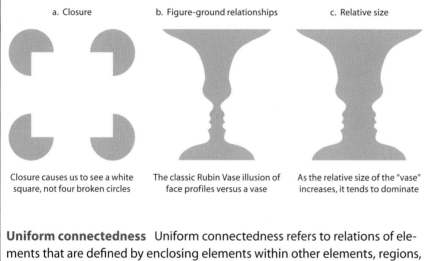

a. Closure   b. Figure-ground relationships   c. Relative size

Closure causes us to see a white The classic Rubin Vase illusion of As the relative size of the "vase"
square, not four broken circles face profiles versus a vase   increases, it tends to dominate

Uniform connectedness Uniform connectedness refers to relations of elements that are defined by enclosing elements within other elements, regions, or discrete areas of the page.

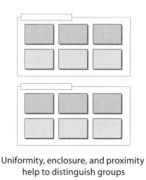

Uniformity allows us to see a Uniformity is a common Uniformity, enclosure, and proximity
blue column and a green group organizing device in interfaces help to distinguish groups

1 + 1 = 3 effects The "white space" between two visual elements forms a third visual element and becomes visually active as the elements come closer together. The well-known visual illusion below of gray "spots" appearing in the spaces between the dark squares shows the worst-case scenario for 1 + 1 = 3 effects, but this principle applies to all closely spaced elements in which the ground forms an active part of the overall design.

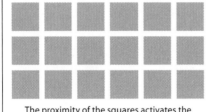

The proximity of the squares activates the white spaces between, producing shimmering

The more complex the layout, the worse the shimmering optical illusions and 1+1=3 effects

CONSISTENCY

Establish a layout grid and a style for handling your text and graphics, and then apply it consistently to build rhythm and unity across the pages of your site. Repetition is not boring; it gives your site a consistent graphic identity that creates and then reinforces a distinct sense of "place" and makes your site memorable. A consistent approach to layout and navigation allows users to adapt quickly to your design and to predict with confidence the location of information and navigation controls across the pages of your site.

If you choose a graphic theme, use it throughout your site. The Hiram College home page banner sets the graphic theme for the site and introduces distinctive typography and a set of navigation tabs. Note how the typography and the navigation theme are carried over to the interior banners. There is no confusion about whose site you are navigating through (fig. 7.8).

CONTRAST

The primary task of graphic design is to create a strong, consistent visual hierarchy in which important elements are emphasized and content is organized logically and predictably. Graphic design is visual information management, using the tools of page layout, typography, and illustration to lead the reader's eye through the page. Readers first see pages as large masses of shape

FIGURE 7.8
Consistent organizational identity across all levels of a site.

and color, with foreground elements contrasting against the background field. Then they begin to pick out specific information, first from graphics if they are present, and only after this do they start parsing the harder medium of text and begin to read individual words and phrases (fig. 7.9).

The overall graphic balance and organization of the page is crucial to drawing the user into your content. A page of solid text will repel the casual reader with a mass of undifferentiated gray, without obvious cues to the structure of your information. A page dominated by poorly designed or overly bold graphics or typography will also distract or repel users seeking substantive content. You will need to strike an appropriate balance between

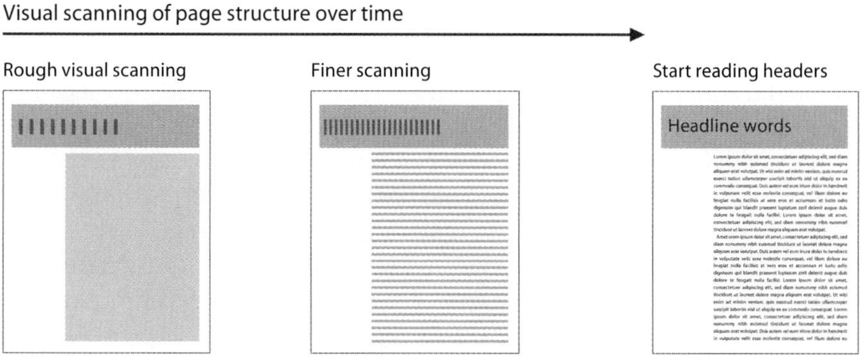

Visual scanning of page structure over time

Rough visual scanning   Finer scanning   Start reading headers

Headline words

FIGURE 7.9
The reader's visual scanning proceeds from a very general perception of contrast through finer levels of attention and finally to actual reading of the major headlines.

FIGURE 7.10
NOVA's website
achieves great
visual impact with
a careful collection
of relatively small
images coupled with
colored backgrounds
and text.

attracting the eye with visual contrast and providing a clear sense of organization, through the variations in contrast that result from proper proximities, groupings, figure-ground relationships, and headings. Visual balance and appropriateness to the intended audience are the keys to successful design decisions. The most effective designs for general audiences employ a careful balance of text and links with relatively small graphics. These pages load quickly yet have substantial graphic impact (fig. 7.10).

Color and contrast in typography

Color and contrast are key components of universal usability. Text legibility is dependent on the reader's ability to distinguish letterforms from the background field. Color differentiation depends mostly on brightness and saturation. Black text on a white background has the highest level of contrast since black has no brightness and white is all brightness. Hue is also a factor, with complementary colors, such as blue and yellow, producing the greatest contrast. Be sure your color choices do not make it hard for users to distinguish text from background. Also, never forget that almost 10 percent of male

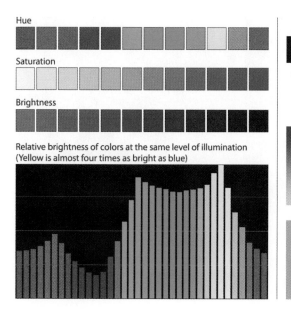

Hue

Saturation

Brightness

Relative brightness of colors at the same level of illumination
(Yellow is almost four times as bright as blue)

The optimal combination for legibility is black on white

White text on black is almost as good for legibility

Optically bright colors like yellow disappear on white

Inherently dark colors like blue or red work much better

Gradient backgrounds almost always create legibility
issues because some part of the text will suffer from
poor contrast and reduced legibility. If you must use
a gradient, stick with black text, and avoid using dark
colors in the background.

The 10 percent of males who are partially red-green
color-blind would find this paragraph almost impossible
to read, particularly because the green and red colors
are very close in brightness level. Don't depend on
color alone to produce contrast in text.

readers have some trouble distinguishing fine shades of red from shades of green (fig. 7.11).

Contrast variability

Web pages viewed on mobile devices are usually compromised by the mobile environment: small screens, tiny text, lack of optimal screen resolution and color, and sun or other lighting glare all degrade the legibility of web pages seen outside the office or home environment. Even many laptops have displays that don't do a good job of showing fine color or shade distinctions, and the colors on pages viewed via computer projector are normally washed out. Test your designs on a number of devices and laptops and in a variety of conditions, especially if you are using subtle colors to define important page functions or content. In general it's best to use a more robust, high-contrast typography color scheme.

Avoid overusing contrast

Horizontal rules, decorative graphic bullets, prominent icons, and other visual markers have their occasional uses, but apply each sparingly (if at all) to avoid a patchy and confusing layout. The tools of graphic emphasis are pow-

FIGURE 7.11
Not all colors and color combinations are created equal, especially for the 10 percent of males who have some degree of color-blindness.

FIGURE 7.12
Colors drawn
from nature are
almost inherently
harmonious and
subdued.

erful and should be used only in small doses for maximum effect. Overuse of graphic emphasis leads to a "clown's pants" effect in which everything is equally garish and nothing is emphasized.

Color palettes chosen from nature are an almost infallible guide to color harmony, particularly if you are not a trained graphic designer. Subtle, desaturated colors make the best choices for backgrounds or minor elements. Avoid bold, highly saturated primary colors except in regions of maximum emphasis, and even there use them cautiously (fig. 7.12).

WHITE SPACE

With today's larger display screens and more complex graphic interfaces, your web page is likely to be sharing the screen with many other windows and desktop elements. Use white space to avoid crowding the edges of the browser windows with important elements of your page content. In fixed-width layouts, consider floating the page in the center of the browser window. If your page width is reasonable, this should produce some visual relief for your page even on a crowded computer screen (fig. 7.13a). For "liquid" layouts, consider pages that use 90–95 percent of the screen instead of the full 100 percent, leave some background around the functional areas of the

page to provide visual relief, and avoid unfortunate "1 + 1 = 3" interactions with elements outside the browser window (fig. 7.13b).

All graphic design is ultimately the management of white space—the ground field behind all figure elements on the page. To understand graphic design, you must appreciate that the ground field around page elements is as active and important a part of the design as any figure element on the page. Filling all the white space on a page is like removing all the oxygen from a room—an efficient use of space perhaps, but decidedly difficult to inhabit.

STYLE

Don't set out to develop a "style" for your site, and be careful about simply importing the graphic elements of another web site or print publication to decorate your pages. The graphic and editorial style of your web site should evolve as a natural consequence of consistent and appropriate handling of your content and page layout. Prefer the conventional over the eccentric, never let the framing overwhelm the content, and remember that the best style is one that readers never notice—where everything feels logical, comfortable (even beautiful) but where a heavy-handed design never intrudes on the experience.

SIMPLICITY

All users benefit from clear and consistent web site design, but for some users it is critical. With a lack of spatial cues and with radically different approaches to navigation that must be relearned at every site, vision-impaired users can easily get disoriented or lost on the web. For people with cognitive disabilities, such as memory or learning disabilities, this difficulty is magni-

FIGURE 7.13
Visual relief helps isolate the page content from the "noise" of other programs and windows on the screen.

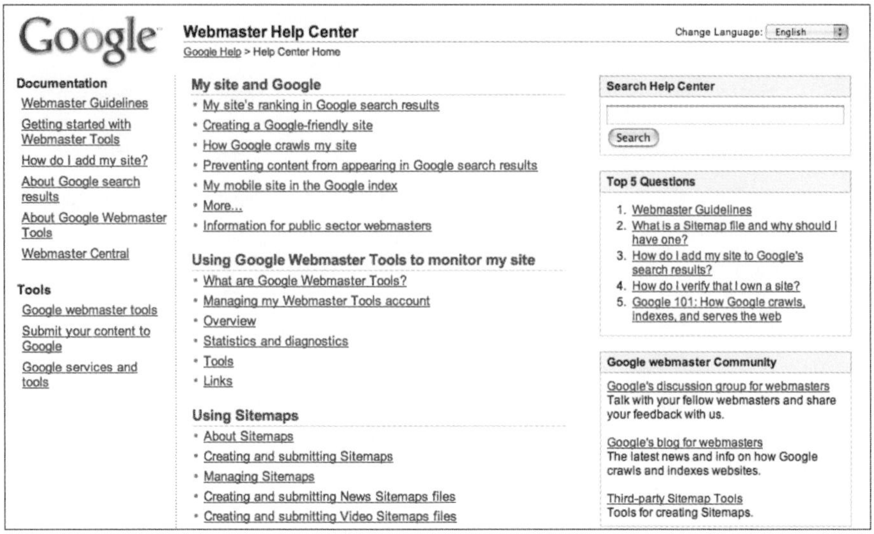

FIGURE 7.14
Google's minimal
design aesthetic
makes their
pages easy to
use and instantly
recognizable.

fied manyfold. Stick with a simple language and navigation applied consistently throughout your site, and everyone will benefit. Google's various support sites are a model of simple, clear design, with minimal but highly functional page framing and interface elements (fig. 7.14).

THE GESTALT OF VISUAL DESIGN

The fundamental principles of Gestalt perception and human visual processing form the basic toolbox of all graphic design. Web design adds the dimensions of interactivity and a wide range of possible display media, but the core principles of graphic design, document organization, editorial standards, and communication on the page have not changed. The web as it exists today is clearly an extension of print publishing, not because of any failure of imagination from designers and technologists, but because centuries of designing documents for readers have taught the world useful lessons in how humans read and absorb information.

PAGE FRAMEWORKS

Web pages are plastic in both horizontal and vertical dimensions in a way that paper pages are not. Therefore, even before you decide on a page grid, you need to decide on the fundamental page framework that suits your site best: a fixed-width page or a flexible-width page.

Deciding on page length is easier. Here the best practice is a common-sense approach that works well for your content. The old saw that "web readers don't scroll" may have been true of *new users* a decade or more ago, but it certainly isn't true now. As readers have grown used to the web as a reading medium, the design constraints on page length have lessened, and usability studies have shown that web readers certainly do scroll through web content that interests them.

FIGURE 7.15
Fixed-width designs may fall apart visually if the reader chooses to enlarge the text size.

FIXED PAGE WIDTHS

Fixed-width page designs are widely used, particularly for complex page layouts with many functional subregions of the page, such as in newspaper sites. Putting content into a fixed-width column means that your page layout will be stable whatever the size of the user's screen or browser window. Designing in a stable environment means that you can fix the position of elements on the page and control such typographic features as line length and spacing. Stable layouts also preserve the Gestalt visual and spatial logic of how various components in the page layout relate to one another.

Fixed-width layouts have several downsides. On large display screens a major portion of screen real estate goes unused, and in a narrow browser window users may need to scroll horizontally to see the full width of the page. Also, fixed-width layouts do not always respond gracefully to enlarged text (fig. 7.15).

Pages that look reasonable in a fixed layout (below, left) can fall apart when converted to a stretchy "liquid" layout (right)

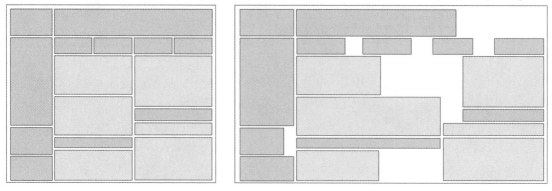

Careful planning and a hybrid approach that mixes liquid (green) and fixed-width layout elements (blue) can give you the best of both worlds: pages that adapt to a wide variety of screen sizes and media, with some areas of predictable widths

FIGURE 7.16
Careful HTML and CSS design can create "hybrid" page designs that contain both fixed and "liquid" design elements.

One common hybrid alternative is to combine one or more fixed-width columns with a flexible-width center column that has relatively simple content structure and stretches to fill the full width of the browser window (fig. 7.16).

The "safe" page width is a constantly moving target, because the average size of computer screens increases all the time. The best way to decide on an optimal page width is using web analytics to determine the average screen size of your site visitors.

Summary

Fixed layouts are optimized for the most common web viewing conditions—the desktop or laptop screen—and can be adapted to handheld devices and other forms of mobile computing with mobile style sheets. But fixed layouts will always be more brittle and prone to universal usability problems than flexible layouts. We thus strongly recommend that you consider flexible page layouts as a design solution.

FLEXIBLE PAGE WIDTHS

With the variety of sizes in display screens ranging from small cell phones to wide cinema displays, the entire notion of designing to a standard "safe" size is often impractical. The web is a flexible medium designed to accommodate different users and a variety of display devices. Unlike a printed document fixed on paper, the look of a web page depends on such elements as the display size, resolution, and color settings, the height and width of the browser window, software preferences such as link and background color settings, and available fonts. Indeed, there is no way to have complete control over the design of a web page. Often the best approach is to embrace the flexibility of the medium and design pages that are legible, adaptable to many display devices, and accessible to all users.

Flexible or "fluid" page design is in many ways more challenging than fixed design because it requires a deep understanding of HTML and its implementation across platforms and browsers. It also requires that you think outside the box of your configuration and come up with graphics and layouts that will still work under varying conditions. There are several methods for defining flexible page widths. The most common approach is to use percentages to define the width of the different elements on the page. For example, for a two-column layout, the content may occupy 75 percent of the page width and the section navigation the remaining 25 percent. The same page printed would hide the display of the navigation column since it's of little use on paper and set the page width to a measure that is comfortable for reading. And on a mobile device, where navigation is essential but the narrow screen width does not support multiple columns, we would collapse the two columns into one and maximize the space available on screen (fig. 7.17).

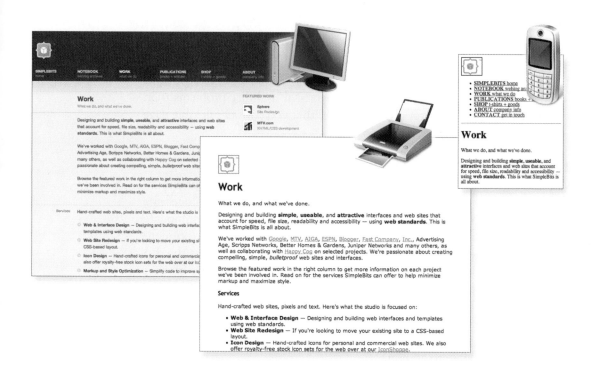

FIGURE 7.17

Strategic use of CSS and flexible HTML page coding can liberate your content to work well across many display media.

Summary

Flexible page designs have enormous advantages in adaptability across various display devices (desktop, laptop, cell phone, iPod, and so on). Flexible designs are also more universally usable because they can be easily adapted to increase text size, display color and contrast, and other viewing or reading parameters. Flexible pages may not be the best approach for complex page layouts that depend on relatively fixed visual relations among page size, typography, and graphics.

PAGE WIDTH AND LINE LENGTH

The ideal line length for text layout is based on the physiology of the human eye. The area of the retina used for tasks requiring high visual acuity is called the macula. The macula is small, typically less than 15 percent of the area of the retina. At normal reading distances the arc of the visual field covered by the macula is only a few inches wide—about the width of a well-designed column of text, or about twelve words per line. Research shows that reading

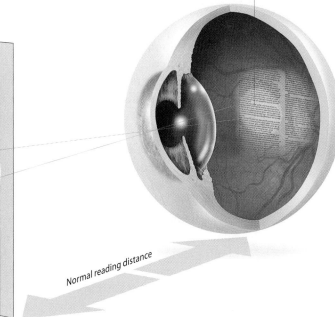

Macula area of the retina

Normal reading distance

Typical column width roughly matches the macula, the "sharp focus" part of the retina.

slows as line lengths begin to exceed the ideal width, because the reader then needs to use the muscles of the eye or neck to track from the end of one line to the beginning of the next line. If the eye must traverse great distances on a page, the reader must hunt for the beginning of the next line (fig. 7.18).

Given the user-defined nature of the web and the vagaries of technology, it's impossible to control line length in all circumstances. A line that is designed to display a comfortable sixty-six characters per line of standard text will become a narrow, twenty-character line if the user enlarges the default browser text size. A multicolumn layout with fixed column widths can easily become difficult to read with enlarged text.

Universal usability offers a great solution to the line-length problem by ensuring that the page design can fluidly adapt in page width, so that users are not locked into a single view that may not work well for them. Readers can adapt line length in fluid layouts by narrowing the browser window.

FIGURE 7.18
Columns of text work well because they complement aspects of our visual system.

PAGE LENGTH

Determining the proper length for any web page is a balance of four factors:

1. The relation between page and screen size
2. The content of your documents
3. Whether the reader is expected to browse the content online or to print or download the documents for later reading
4. The bandwidth available to your audience

Researchers have noted the disorientation that results from scrolling on computer screens. The reader's loss of context is particularly troublesome when such basic navigational elements as document titles, site identifiers, and links to other site pages disappear off-screen while scrolling. This disorientation effect argues for the creation of navigational web pages (especially home pages and menus) that contain no more than one or two screens' worth of information and that feature local navigational links at the beginning and end of the page layout. Long web pages require the user to remember too much information that scrolls off the screen; users easily lose their sense of context when the navigational buttons or major links are not visible (fig. 7.19).

FIGURE 7.19

Although average screen width increases every year, screen height in laptops increases much more slowly.

But long web pages have their advantages. They are often easier for creators to organize and for users to download. Web site managers don't have to maintain as many links and pages with longer documents, and users don't need to download multiple files to collect information on a topic. Long pages are particularly useful for providing information that you don't expect users to read online.

It makes sense to keep closely related information within the confines of a single web page, particularly when you expect the user to print or save the text. Keeping the content in one place makes printing or saving easier. But more than four screens' worth of information forces the user to scroll so much that the utility of the online version of the page begins to deteriorate. Long pages often fail to take advantage of the linkages available in the web medium.

If you wish to provide both a good online interface for a long document and easy printing or saving of its content:

- Divide the document into chunks of no more than one to two printed pages' worth of information, including in-lined graphics or figures. Use the power of hypertext links to take advantage of the web medium.
- Provide a link to a separate file that contains the full-length text combined as one page designed so the reader can print or save all the related information in one step. Don't forget to include the URL of the online version within the text of that page so users can find updates and correctly cite the source.
- Make long pages friendlier by positioning "jump to top buttons" at regular intervals down the page. That way the user will never have to scroll far to find a navigation button that quickly brings him or her back to the top of the page.

In general, you should favor shorter web pages for:

- Home pages and menu or navigation pages elsewhere in your site
- Documents to be browsed and read online
- Pages with very large graphics

In general, longer documents are:

- Easier to maintain (content is in one piece, not in linked chunks spread across many pages)
- More like the structure of their paper counterparts (not chopped up)
- Easier for users to download and print

PAGE HEADERS AND FOOTERS

Many web authors surrender to the giddy thrills of large graphics, forgetting that a web page is not just a visual experience—it has to function efficiently to retain its appeal to the user. Remember that the page builds its graphic impact gradually as it is downloaded to the user. The best measure of the ef-

FIGURE 7.20

A great example of designing page headers to create consistent site identity and global navigation.

ficiency of a page design is the number of options available for readers within the top six inches of the page. A big, bold graphic may tease casual web surfers, but if it takes the average reader several seconds to download the top of your page and there are few links to be seen until he or she scrolls down the page, then you may lose a big part of your audience before you offer them links to the rest of your site.

Page headers

Careful graphic design will give your web site a unique visual identity. A "signature" graphic and page layout allows the user to grasp immediately the purpose of the document and its relation to other pages. Graphics used within headers can also signal the relatedness of a series of web pages. Unlike designers of print documents, designers of web systems can never be sure what other pages the user has seen before linking to the current page. Pages on the Creative Commons site include a signature header graphic that includes basic navigation and search features, exactly where most users would expect to find them (fig. 7.20).

a. IBM footer

b. *Scientific American* footer

FIGURE 7.21

Simple (*a*) and complex (*b*) page footers.

Even if you choose not to use graphics on your pages, the header area of every web page should contain a prominent title at or near its top. Graphics placed above the title line should not be so large that they force the title and introductory text off the page on standard display screens. In a related series of documents there may also be subtitles, section titles, or other text elements that convey the relation of the displayed document to others in the series. To be effective, these title elements must be standardized across all the pages in your site.

Page footers

Every web page should contain basic data about the origin and age of the page, but this repetitive and prosaic information does not need to be placed at the top of the page. Remember, too, that by the time users have scrolled to the bottom of your web page the navigation links you might have provided at the top may no longer be visible. Well-designed page footers offer the user a set of links to other pages in addition to essential data about the site.

The pages in the IBM web site all carry a distinctive footer that covers the basic housekeeping functions of "about," "privacy," and other topics and provides social bookmarking links to Del.icio.us and Digg (fig. 7.21a). The much larger *Scientific American* footer forms a distinct region on each page, covering the basic informational footer functions as well as advertisements for sister publications (fig. 7.21b).

FIGURE 7.22

opposite

Vertical stratification
into multiple
functional screens of
information.

VERTICAL STRATIFICATION IN WEB PAGES

A web page can be almost any length, but you have only the area "above the fold"—at the top of your page—to capture the average user, because that is all he or she will see as the page loads. One crucial difference between web page design and print page design is that when readers turn a book or magazine page they see not only the whole next page but the whole two-page spread, all at the same time. In print design, therefore, the two-page spread is the fundamental graphic design unit.

Print design can achieve a design unity and density of information that web design cannot emulate—yet. Regardless of how large the display screen is, the reader still sees one page at a time, and even a large display screen will display only as much information as is found in a small magazine spread.

Design for screens of information

Most web page designs can be divided vertically into zones with different functions and varying levels of graphics and text complexity. As vertical scrolling progressively reveals the page, new content appears and the upper content disappears. A new graphic context is established each time the reader scrolls down the page. Web page layouts should thus be judged not by viewing the whole page as a unit but by dividing the page into visual and functional zones and judging the suitability of each screen of information. Notice the vertical structure of the *New York Times* home page. The top screen of information is much denser with links because it is the only area all users will see (fig. 7.22).

DESIGN GRIDS FOR WEB PAGES

Consistency and predictability are essential attributes of any well-designed information system. The design grids that underlie most well-designed paper publications are equally necessary in designing electronic documents and online publications, where the spatial relations among on-screen elements are constantly shifting in response to the user's input and system activity. When used inappropriately or inconsistently, the typographic controls and graphics of web pages can create a confusing visual jumble, without apparent hierarchy of importance. Haphazardly mixed graphics and text decrease usability and legibility, just as they do in paper pages. A balanced and consistently implemented design scheme will increase users' confidence in your site (fig. 7.23).

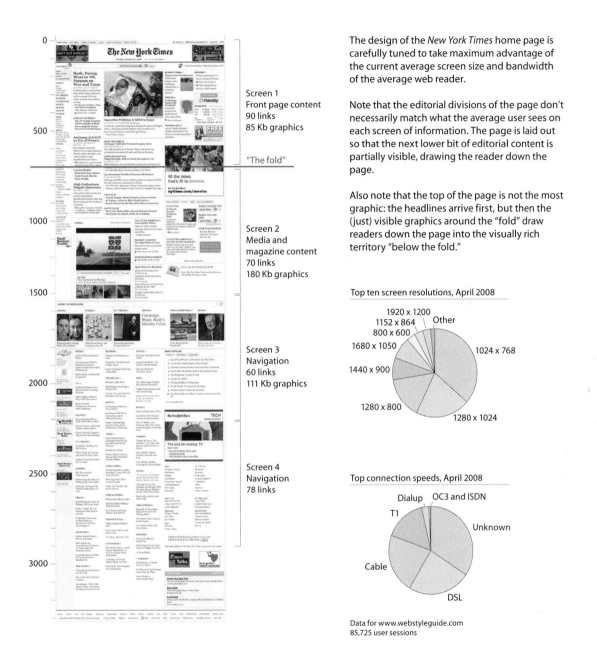

Screen 1
Front page content
90 links
85 Kb graphics

"The fold"

Screen 2
Media and
magazine content
70 links
180 Kb graphics

Screen 3
Navigation
60 links
111 Kb graphics

Screen 4
Navigation
78 links

The design of the *New York Times* home page is carefully tuned to take maximum advantage of the current average screen size and bandwidth of the average web reader.

Note that the editorial divisions of the page don't necessarily match what the average user sees on each screen of information. The page is laid out so that the next lower bit of editorial content is partially visible, drawing the reader down the page.

Also note that the top of the page is not the most graphic: the headlines arrive first, but then the (just) visible graphics around the "fold" draw readers down the page into the visually rich territory "below the fold."

Top ten screen resolutions, April 2008

1920 x 1200
1152 x 864
800 x 600   Other
1680 x 1050
                            1024 x 768
1440 x 900
1280 x 800
                    1280 x 1024

Top connection speeds, April 2008

Dialup   OC3 and ISDN
T1
                    Unknown
Cable
                    DSL

Data for www.webstyleguide.com
85,725 user sessions

FIGURE 7.23

Even when the page grid is solid, good design depends on creating a hierarchy of contrast and viewer attention, so that a few focal areas of the page become entry points and the other page materials are clearly secondary. Without contrast management the design can look like many random elements competing for the reader's attention.

Visually monotonous, no obvious entry points; reading gravity and the "Gutenberg Z" take over

Contrast creates clear primary and secondary entry points to content

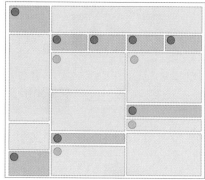

Good management and hierarchy of contrast

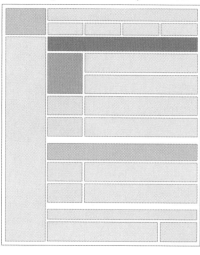

Poor contrast management creates confusion about what is important on the page

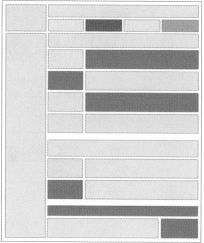

The business logic of design grids and templates

Regular page grids—and the module and program efficiency and consistency they create—are the core element of cost-effective design programs for larger enterprises. One of the most famous and successful design grid systems ever produced has been used by the National Park Service for more than thirty years. Massimo Vignelli's Unigrid design system organizes and systematizes

The basic units of the grid can be modularly expanded from a small brochure to a large fold-out map booklet.

a huge array of park service paper publications (and now online PDF documents), from single-page brochures to large park maps and posters. Thanks to the strong, consistent Unigrid design program, the National Park Service has saved many tens of millions of dollars over the decades by not reinventing brochure and map design with every new print project (fig. 7.24).

Grids and templates on the web

Grids for page templates on the web are a more complex matter because the web is a fluid medium with many possible display conditions and a constantly changing technology base. The fundamental principles of consistent modular

FIGURE 7.24

The National Park Service design grid for print publications. Thinking in a strategic, modular way about design can save a fortune in the long run.

design programs still apply, but web page grids must necessarily accommodate a wider range of visual possibilities than their print counterparts. Print design grids are driven largely by fixed positioning and paper sizes. Web templates also create a regular, repeating structure of design patterns that consistently organize identity, navigation, content, and technical functionality, but they do it in a much more fluid, flexible medium than paper printing.

A good web template program establishes not just the visual look and feel of particular pages in the site but also specifies how regular patterns of XHTML, CSS, include files, and more complex application or content functionality will all merge using well-established, well-documented, and consistent standards throughout the site. And, like Vignelli's Unigrid system, a good enterprise template system can save millions of design dollars that might otherwise be wasted in reinventing web publishing with each new corporate or enterprise site.

Templates and the enterprise

For maximum efficiency in web publishing, all large enterprises should have an existing, well-designed, well-documented set of web page templates that incorporate:

- The global identity of the enterprise as an organized part of a larger enterprise identity program across all media
- Global enterprise navigation features that tie smaller sites and programs to the larger institution
- Well-designed, carefully validated XHTML and CSS code
- Consistent semantic nomenclature for all XHTML and CSS containers and page elements
- A consistent, enterprise-wide typography program
- Accessibility standards that meet and ideally exceed requirements
- Compatibility with, at minimum, a basic web content management tool such as Adobe Contribute or, ideally, an enterprise-wide web content management system

The Yale University page grids are a system of page formats in both fixed-width and fluid page forms. The templates define a consistent set of web identity, user interface, department identification, and typography standards for major university academic and administrative sites. The pages specify the

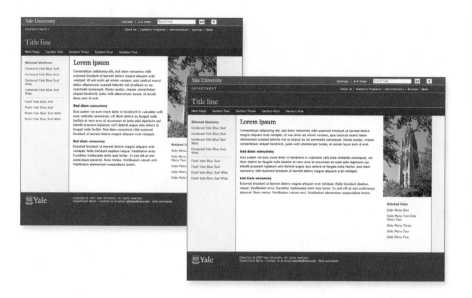

FIGURE 7.25
Theme and variation
in Yale University's
web template
system.

locations of standard identification elements, content column widths, and a system of unique page element ID nomenclature, and they provide a consistent set of typographic standards via a master set of enterprise-wide style sheets (fig. 7.25).

Typography is a key element in template design

Consistent web typography has a huge but subtle effect on establishing coherence across a wide range of enterprise web sites. In a site with a strong typographic identity, most users will never explicitly notice *why* a wide range of related sites produces a cohesive web experience. Consistent web typography can bind those disparate sites in a way that still leaves enormous design flexibility to meet many functional needs and, with css techniques that use a master enterprise-type style sheet, is technically trivial to accomplish.

Typography exists to honor content.

—Robert Bringhurst

CHAPTER 8

Typography

Typography is the balance and interplay of letterforms on the page—a verbal and visual equation that helps the reader understand the form and absorb the substance of the page content. Typography plays a dual role as both verbal and visual communication. When readers scan a page they are subconsciously aware of both functions: first they survey the overall graphic patterns of the page, and then they parse the language and read. Good typography establishes a visual hierarchy for rendering prose on the page by providing visual punctuation and graphic accents that help readers understand relations between prose and pictures, headlines and subordinate blocks of text.

CHARACTERISTICS OF TYPE ON THE WEB

Although the basic rules of typography are much the same for both web pages and conventional print documents, type on-screen and type printed on paper are different in crucial ways. The computer screen renders typefaces at a much lower resolution than is found in books, magazines, and even pages output from inexpensive printers. Most magazine and book typography is printed at 1200 dots per inch (dpi) or greater, whereas computer screens rarely show more than about 85 pixels per inch (ppi).

The current Apple Macintosh and Microsoft Windows operating systems use anti-aliased type to increase the apparent resolution of type on the computer screen. Anti-aliasing works by smoothing the edges around type, so that at normal screen reading distances the type looks much like high-resolution printed type. Anti-aliasing works: careful legibility and reading studies have long shown that it improves reading speed and accuracy. The letterforms look fuzzy when enlarged but appear sharp when viewed under normal reading conditions (fig. 8.1).

In addition to much lower type resolution, the usable area of typical computer screens is a little smaller than a typical trade book spread (particularly in height), and typical laptop displays are quite limited in their vertical

FIGURE 8.1

Comparison of
aliased and anti-
aliased typography.

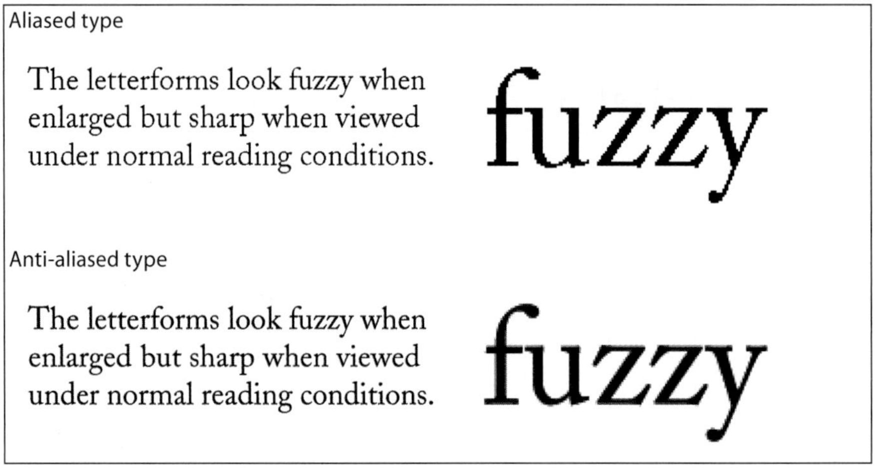

Aliased type

The letterforms look fuzzy when
enlarged but sharp when viewed
under normal reading conditions.

fuzzy

Anti-aliased type

The letterforms look fuzzy when
enlarged but sharp when viewed
under normal reading conditions.

fuzzy

dimension. These maximum-area calculations assume that the reader has maximized the browser window on the screen, but much of the time it is likely that the browser will be sharing screen space with other windows the reader has open on the screen.

ON-THE-FLY CONSTRUCTION

The most distinctive characteristic of web typography is its variability. Web pages are built on the fly each time they are loaded into a web browser. Each line of text, each headline, and each unique font and style are re-created by a complex interaction of the web browser, the web server, and the operating system of the reader's computer. The process is fraught with the unexpected: a missing font, an out-of-date browser, a peculiar set of font preferences designated by the reader. You should regard your web page layouts and typography as *suggestions* of how your pages should be rendered—you'll never know exactly how they will look on the reader's screen.

CONTENT STRUCTURE AND VISUAL LOGIC

The originators of HTML were scientists who wanted a standard means to share particle physics documents. They had little interest in the exact visual form of the document as seen on a particular computer screen. In fact, HTML was designed to enforce a clean separation of content structure and graphic design. In the early 1990s the intent was to create a "World Wide Web" of pages that both display on every system and browser available, including browsers that "read" content to visually impaired users, and can be accurately interpreted by automated search and analysis engines.

In disregarding the graphic design and editorial management traditions of publishing, the original designers of the web ignored human motivation and the desire to persuade. Early web programmers were so concerned about making web documents machine-friendly that they produced documents that only machines (or particle physicists) would want to read. In focusing solely on the structural logic of documents, they ignored the need for the visual logic of sophisticated graphic design and typography.

CASCADING STYLE SHEETS

This division between structural logic and visual logic is reconciled through the use of Cascading Style Sheets. Style sheets provide control over the exact visual style of headers, paragraphs, lists, and other page elements. For example, if you prefer <h3> headers to be set in Arial bold type, you can specify those details in a style sheet. In this way you can retain the logical use of HTML's structural tags without sacrificing graphic design flexibility.

Advantages of CSS

This book is not a manual on HTML, and covering the full design implications of Cascading Style Sheets is well beyond the scope of this chapter. If you are not using CSS to manage the graphic design of your web site, you should certainly incorporate CSS design techniques with your next site redesign.

Cascading Style Sheets offer web designers two key advantages in managing complex web sites:

- Separation of content and design. CSS gives site developers the best of both worlds: content markup that reflects the logical structure of the information, and the freedom to specify exactly how each HTML tag will look.
- Efficient control over large document sets. The most powerful implementations of CSS will allow site designers to control the graphic look and feel of thousands of pages by modifying a single master style sheet document (fig. 8.2).

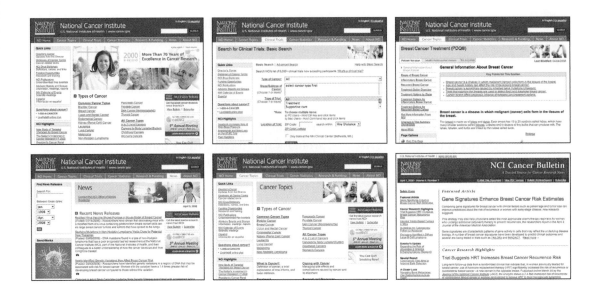

FIGURE 8.2

Multiple web page designs and typography all controlled by a single master style sheet.

Style sheets provide greater typographic control with less code. Using plain HTML, you need to define the physical properties of an element such as the `<h1>` tag each time you use it.

```
<h1 align="center"><font face="Verdana, Helvetica, Arial, sans-
    serif" size="6" color="gray">Section heading< /h1>
```

When you define these properties using CSS, that single definition, or rule, applies to every instance of the `<h1>` element in all documents that reference the style sheet.

```
h1 { text-align: center; font-size: 1.4em; font-family: Verdana,
    Helvetica, Arial, sans-serif; color: gray }
```

In addition, style sheets offer more formatting options than plain HTML tags and extensions. For example, spacing between lines of type, or leading, can be controlled using style sheets, as can such text properties as letter spacing and background color.

But the greatest advantage of CSS is that it enables universal usability by giving you the ability to control the way your site looks in very differ-

```
html, body, div, h1, h2, h3, h4, h5, h6, p,
ul, ol, table, form
{
        background: black !important;
        color: white !important;
        font: 16pt/20pt verdana !important;
}

a:link { color: white !important; }
a:visited { color: white !important; }
a:active { color: white !important; }
a:hover { color: white !important; }
```

ent display circumstances. For example, some browsers have a feature that allows users to override author-defined style sheets with their own style sheet. This means that users can define a custom style sheet that meets their viewing needs. For example, a low-vision user might define a style sheet that renders all headings and paragraphs at 32 pixels and sets the background to black and the text to white for maximum contrast. But these measures will not work, or will work in a limited fashion, on pages that are formatted using presentation markup. If the text color is set using `<font color>` and headings are set using `<font size>` and boldface `<b>` for emphasis, the user-defined style sheet will have no paragraph or heading tags to restyle. If you define formatting using style sheets, users who need to customize the page can do so. Web pages styled with old-fashioned `<font>` tags are like text soup—they have no logical structure to analyze or work with—and therefore they are both less accessible and dramatically less relevant to search engines (fig. 8.3).

FIGURE 8.3

User-defined style sheets allow users with special needs the ability to systematically change the display to suit their needs, *if* the page was designed to maximize CSS control of the visual display.

How style sheets work

Web style sheets are not new. Every graphic web browser has incorporated style sheets, even as far back as Mosaic, the earliest graphic web browser. Before CSS it just wasn't possible to *modify* the fixed styles that browsers used to determine, for example, exactly how heading 1 (`<h1>`) headers look on the screen. The fundamental idea behind CSS is to let site authors and users determine the size, style, and layout details for each standard HTML tag.

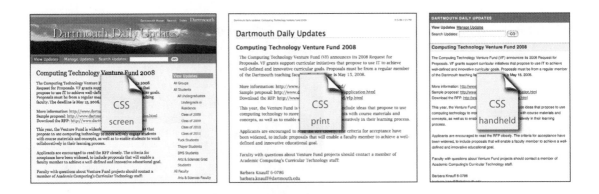

FIGURE 8.4
Media style sheets optimize the look of the page content across different display media.

If you have ever used the "styles" features of a page layout or word processing program, you'll understand the basic idea behind CSS. The styles feature of a word processor is used to determine exactly how your titles, subheadings, and body copy will look, and then the text is formatted when you apply a style to each element. Once all the text has been styled, you can change the look of each occurrence of an element simply by changing its style information: for example, setting "Heading 1" elements in Times New Roman. If you change your mind and want another font, you just change the Heading 1 style, and every Heading 1 in your whole document then changes to reflect the new font. CSS works in the same way, except that with CSS you can set up one master style sheet that will control the visual styling of *every page in your site* that is linked to the master style sheet.

Media style sheets

We can use CSS to provide formatting appropriate to a specific context. Many media are represented in the HTML and CSS specifications, but of those, "print" and "handheld" are the most widely supported. Print style sheets control formatting of pages when they are printed on paper, and handheld style sheets control formatting when pages are accessed using a mobile device. This functionality has significant implications since the qualities of good typography differ across media. For example, the characteristics that make type readable on-screen look oversized and clumsy on paper. By using media style sheets tuned to different contexts, we can deliver good typography across many media (fig. 8.4).

CONSISTENCY

As in traditional print publishing, high-quality web sites adhere to established type style settings consistently throughout the site. Consistency gives polish to a site and encourages visitors to stay by creating an expectation about the structure of a text. If sloppy, inconsistent formatting confounds this expectation you will decrease your readers' confidence in your words, and they may not return. You should decide on such settings as fonts, interparagraph spacing, the size of subheads, and so on and then create a written style guide to help you maintain these settings as you develop the site. This step is especially critical for large sites that incorporate numerous pages. And with css you will have powerful tools to maintain the consistency of styles throughout your site. This is particularly true if you use a master style sheet for your whole site via the "link" option in css.

LEGIBILITY

Good typography depends on the visual contrast between one font and another, as well as among text blocks, headlines, and the surrounding white space. Nothing attracts the eye and brain of the reader like strong contrast and distinctive patterns, and you can achieve those attributes only by carefully designing contrast and pattern into your pages. If you cram every page with dense text, readers see a wall of gray and will instinctively reject the lack of visual contrast. Just making things uniformly bigger doesn't help. Even boldface fonts quickly become monotonous: if everything is bold, then nothing stands out "boldly."

When your content is primarily text, typography is the tool you use to "paint" patterns of organization on the page. The first thing the reader sees is not the title or other details on the page but the overall pattern and contrast of the page. The regular, repeating patterns established through carefully organized pages of text and graphics help the reader to establish the location and organization of your information and increase legibility. Patchy, heterogeneous typography and text headers make it hard for the user to see repeating patterns and logical content groups. The chaos makes it difficult to predict where information is likely to be located in unfamiliar documents (fig. 8.5).

FIGURE 8.5
Use contrast and
logic to create
meaningful
repeating patterns of
contrast to help the
reader quickly make
sense of your page
layouts.

Too patchy, inconsistent   Better layout of type blocks

ALIGNMENT AND WHITE SPACE

Margins define the reading area of your page by separating the main text from the surrounding environment. Margins provide important visual relief in any document, but careful design of margins and other white space is particularly important in web page design because web content must coexist on the computer screen with the interface elements of the browser itself as well as with other windows, menus, and icons of the user interface.

Margins and space can be used to delineate the main text from the other page elements. And when used consistently, margins provide unity throughout a site by creating a consistent structure and look to the site pages. They also add visual interest by contrasting the positive space of the screen (text, graphics) from the negative (white) space. If you want any understanding of graphic design or page layout, learn to see and appreciate the power and utility of "white space," the ground field behind page elements. The spaces within the ground field are as important as any other element on the page.

ALIGNMENT OPTIONS

Text blocks have different ways of sitting within margins. Left-justified, centered, right-justified, and justified text are the alignment options available on the web.

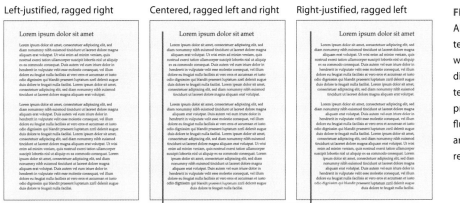

Left-justified, ragged right　　Centered, ragged left and right　　Right-justified, ragged left

Lorem ipsum dolor sit amet

A ragged left margin makes for difficult reading

FIGURE 8.6
Always use flush-left text alignment for web and other screen displays and for long text passages in print. Centered and flush-right designs are much harder to read.

Justified text

Justified text is set flush with the left and right margins. Justified blocks of text create solid rectangles, and headings are normally centered for a symmetrical, formal-looking document. In print, justification is achieved by adjusting the space between words and by using word hyphenation. Page layout programs use a hyphenation dictionary to check for and apply hyphenation at each line's end and then adjust word spacing throughout the line. But even with sophisticated page layout software, justified text blocks often suffer from poor spacing and excessive hyphenation and require manual refinement.

This level of control is not even a remote possibility on web pages. Modern browsers support justified text, but it is achieved by crude adjustments to word spacing. Fine adjustments are not possible on low-resolution computer displays and are impractical to implement in today's web browsers. Also, web browsers are unlikely to offer automatic hyphenation any time soon, another "must" for properly justified text. For the foreseeable future, the legibility of your web documents will suffer if you set your text justified.

Centered and right-justified text blocks

Centered and right-justified text blocks are difficult to read. We read from left to right, anchoring our tracking across the page at the vertical line of the left margin. The ragged-left margins produced by centering or right-justifying text make that scanning much harder, because your eye needs to search for the beginning of each new line (fig. 8.6).

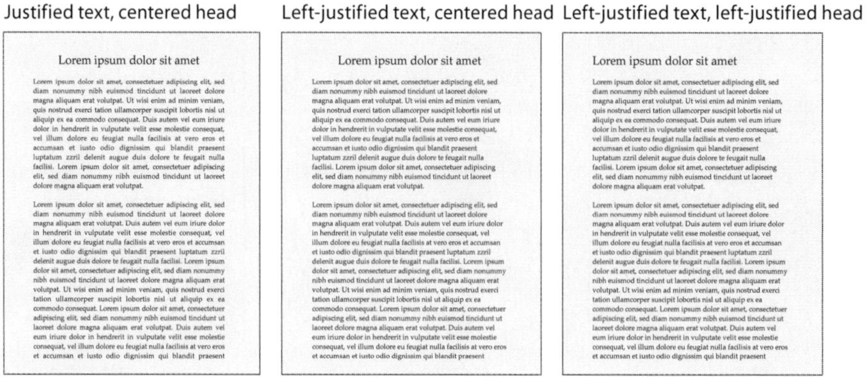

FIGURE 8.7

The best alignment
option for web
pages is left-justified
headings and left-
justified text.

Justified text, centered head   Left-justified text, centered head Left-justified text, left-justified head

Left-justified text

Left-justified text is the most legible option for web pages because the left margin is even and predictable and the right margin is irregular. Unlike justified text, left justification requires no adjustment to word spacing; the inequities in spacing fall at the end of the lines. The resulting ragged-right margin adds variety and interest to the page without reducing legibility.

Justification of headlines

Titles and headings over left-justified body text should also be flush left. Centered headings pair well with justified text, but justified text should not be used on web pages. Centered display type contrasts with the asymmetry of the ragged-right margin of left-justified body text and produces an unbalanced page. Until typographic options for web pages become more sophisticated, we recommend that you use left-justified text blocks and headlines as the best solution for most layout situations (fig. 8.7).

LINE LENGTH

Text on the computer screen is hard to read not only because of the low resolution of computer screens but also because the layout of most web pages violates a fundamental rule of book and magazine typography: the lines of text on most web pages are far too long for ideal reading. Magazine and book columns are narrow for physiological reasons: at normal reading distances, the eye's span of acute focus is only about three to four inches wide, so designers try to keep dense passages of text in columns not much wider than that comfortable eye span. Wider lines of text require readers to move their

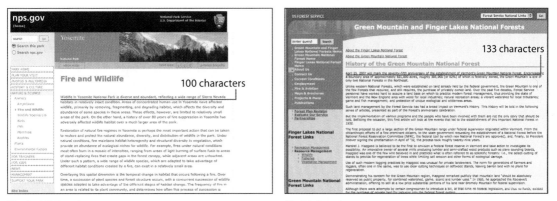

Fixed-width layout   Flexible layout

heads slightly or use their eye muscles to track over the long lines of text. Readability suffers because on the long trip back to the left margin the reader may lose track of the next line.

By using a fixed layout, you can attempt to restrict the text line length (see chapter 7, *Page width and line length*). However, the exact character count is difficult to predict because of the way different browser software and operating systems display type sizes and the variety among access devices and user-controlled browser settings. In conventional print layouts, columns of forty-five to seventy-five characters per line are considered ideal.

In the end, the decision to restrict line length is a philosophical one. From a design standpoint, a measure that is comfortable for reading is good practice. But a fundamental principle of the web is that users should be able to structure their own view. Users with a large monitor may not want their text blocks circumscribed if it means that a large portion of their screen goes unused. A low-vision user with fonts set large will not appreciate being forced to view long pages with short lines of text. So although leaving text free to fill the browser window may affect readability, following conventions may also affect the accessibility and legibility of your documents (fig. 8.8).

When designing a fixed-width layout, set text columns to no wider than 365 pixels. With standard text, this yields a line of about fifty characters, averaging about nine to ten words per line. If you choose a flexible layout approach, use css leading controls to increase line spacing (see *Leading*, below). Additional line spacing permits a slightly longer line length without sacrificing legibility.

FIGURE 8.8

Fixed-width layouts (left) offer some control over line length, whereas flexible layouts (right) expand to fill the browser window.

TYPE COLOR

When typographers speak of "type color," they are speaking about the various ways of manipulating fonts, line spacing, and paragraphs to optimize the overall look and legibility of type on the page.

Leading

Leading is the vertical space in a text block, the distance from one baseline of text to the next. Leading strongly affects the legibility of text blocks: too much leading makes it hard for the eye to locate the start of the next line, whereas too little leading confuses the lines of type, because the ascenders of one line get jumbled with the descenders of the line above. In plain HTML it is not possible to implement true leading, but CSS offers leading control ("line-height"). In print the general rule is to set the leading of text blocks at about 2 points above the size of the type: for example, 12-point type with 14 points of leading. On the web we suggest more generous leading to compensate for longer line lengths and the lower resolution of the computer screen. Use relative measures, such as ems or percentages, to set leading relative to text size:

```
body { font: 1em/1.3em Georgia, "Times New Roman", serif; }
```

Indenting paragraphs

There are two major schools of thought on denoting paragraphs. The classic typographic method uses indents to signal the beginning of a new paragraph (as in this book). However, many technical, reference, and trade publications use a blank line of white space to separate paragraphs. Indented paragraphs work especially well for longer blocks of prose, where the indents signal new paragraphs with minimal disruption to the flow of text. Blank line spacing between paragraphs, in contrast, makes a page easy to scan and provides extra white space for visual relief. Either approach is valid as long as the paragraph style is implemented consistently throughout the site.

To separate paragraphs using indents, use the "text-indent" property of paragraphs:

```
<p style="text-indent: 2em">To separate paragraphs using
    indents...</p>
```

To separate paragraphs with blank lines, apply the margin property to your paragraphs:

```
<p style="margin-bottom: 1.2em">To separate paragraphs with blank
   lines…</p>
```

TYPEFACES

Each typeface has a unique tone that should produce a harmonious fit between the verbal and visual flow of your content. With the first versions of HTML, web authors had no control over typefaces ("fonts" in personal computer terminology). Fonts were set by the browser, so pages were viewed in whatever font the user specified in his or her browser preferences. Modern versions of HTML and CSS allow designers to specify typeface. This is useful not only for aesthetic reasons but also because of the differing dimensions of typefaces. A layout that is carefully designed using one typeface may not format correctly in another.

In specifying typefaces you should choose from the resident default fonts for most operating systems. If you specify a font that is not on the user's machine, the browser will display your pages using the user-specified default font. Bear in mind, too, that users can set their browser preferences to display all pages in their favorite font.

Legibility on-screen

Some typefaces are more legible than others on the screen. A traditional typeface such as Times Roman is considered one of the most legible on paper, but at screen resolution its size is too small and its shapes look irregular. Screen legibility is most influenced by the x-height (the height of a lowercase "x") and the overall size of the typeface.

Adapted traditional typeface

Times New Roman is a good example of a traditional typeface that has been adapted for use on computer screens. A serif typeface like Times New Roman is about average in legibility on the computer screen and has a moderate x-height. Times New Roman is a good font to use in text-heavy documents that will probably be printed by readers rather than read from the screen. The compact letter size of Times New Roman also makes it a good choice if you need to pack a lot of words into a small space.

Designed for the screen

Typefaces such as Georgia and Verdana were designed specifically for legibility on the computer screen; they have exaggerated x-heights and are very robust compared to more traditional typefaces in the same point size. These screen fonts offer excellent legibility for web pages designed to be read directly from the screen. However, the exaggerated x-heights and heavy letterforms of Georgia and Verdana sometimes look massive when transferred to the high-resolution medium of paper.

Typefaces for other media

Much of our attention is focused on the screen version of our pages, but we also have control over how a page looks when printed on paper. Print offers a far richer palette of options when it comes to selecting a typeface; many more typefaces look good on paper than the relatively few that are readable and attractive on-screen. In contrast, there is no point specifying a typeface for handheld styling since most devices have only one font.

CHOOSING TYPEFACES

The most conventional scheme for using typefaces is to use a serif face such as Times New Roman or Georgia for body text and a sans serif face such as Verdana or Arial as a contrast for headlines. Various studies purport to show that serif type is more legible than sans serif type, and vice versa. You can truly judge type legibility only within the context of the situation—on the screen, on paper—as users will see your web page.

You may use either a variation of the serif font or a contrasting sans serif face for the display type. It is safest to use a single typographic family and vary its weight and size for display type and emphasis. If you choose to combine serif and sans serif faces, select fonts that are compatible, and don't use more than two typefaces (one serif, one sans serif) on a page.

The most useful fonts that ship with the Apple Macintosh and Microsoft Windows operating systems are reproduced here, differentiated by their effectiveness on-screen and on paper. Remember that many Macintosh users who have installed Microsoft Office will have Windows fonts installed on their systems (fig. 8.9).

Common screen fonts

Georgia

Each typeface has a unique tone that should produce a harmonious fit between the verbal and visual flow of your content.

Lucida Bright

Each typeface has a unique tone that should produce a harmonious fit between the verbal and visual flow of your

Verdana

Each typeface has a unique tone that should produce a harmonious fit between the verbal and visual flow of your content.

Trebuchet

Each typeface has a unique tone that should produce a harmonious fit between the verbal and visual flow of your content.

Common print fonts

Times New Roman

Each typeface has a unique tone that should produce a harmonious fit between the verbal and visual flow of your content.

Times

Each typeface has a unique tone that should produce a harmonious fit between the verbal and visual flow of your content.

Arial

Each typeface has a unique tone that should produce a harmonious fit between the verbal and visual flow of your content.

Helvetica

Each typeface has a unique tone that should produce a harmonious fit between the verbal and visual flow of your content.

FIGURE 8.9
Common Apple Macintosh and Microsoft Windows screen and print fonts.

Specifying typefaces

You can specify any typeface for your web pages, but many computers have only the default operating system fonts installed. If the typeface you specify is not available on the user's computer, the browser will switch to the default font (generally Times New Roman or Times). To increase the chances that the reader will see your preferred typeface, you can specify multiple fonts for each style. The browser will check for the presence of each font (in the order given), so you can specify three or four alternates before the browser applies the default font, for example, "Verdana, Geneva, Arial, Helvetica." As a last-ditch effort you can end your font declaration with a generic font designation such as "serif." That way, if the browser cannot find any of the listed fonts, it will display the text in an available serif font:

```
p { font-family: "Times New Roman", Georgia, Times, serif }
```

Notice that multiword font names such as Times New Roman must appear within quotation marks in your specification. Also note in the font example below that although "Trebuchet" and "Trebuchet MS" are the same typeface, the *exact name* you specify in the font list matters. If you want both Macintosh and Windows users to see the typeface Trebuchet, then use both names in your font declaration:

```
p { font-family: "Trebuchet MS", Trebuchet, Verdana, Arial, sans-
    serif }
```

A good way to make sure that your type settings are functioning correctly is to set your browser's default proportional font setting to something that is obviously different from your intended font. For example, set your browser's default font to Courier if you are not using Courier in your document. When you view your page, anything that appears in Courier must not be marked up properly.

TYPE SIZE

Scalable text is essential to the goals of universal usability. To ensure scalability, use relative units to control the typography—type size, margins and indents, leading—on the page. Use graphic text sparingly, and always offer a text equivalent. Text rendered to graphic form is no longer text but im-

Fixed-width layout with enlarged text   Flexible layout with enlarged text

age and thus cannot be manipulated—enlarged, colored—as plain text can. Graphic text is also invisible to search engines, so without alternate text the most important words on your page may be invisible to search.

With css, designers have many methods for setting type size. We recommend setting the body text to the default text size defined in users' browser settings and setting all text variants (such as headings, captions, and links) using relative units, such as ems or percentages. An em in the web context is the same as the font height, which makes it a relative unit and therefore flexible. For example, if the user-set default is 16 pixels, than a two-em text indent would be double, or 32 pixels. But if the user used the text zoom feature of the browser to change the text size to 18 pixels, the indent would change to 36 pixels to reflect the larger type size:

```
p { font-size: 1em; text-indent: 2em; }
```

As you might imagine, this flexibility can send page layouts into disarray. Most web page layouts are not designed with large type in mind. For example, fixed layouts that limit the text column to a specified width are typically designed to accommodate standard or small type. Indeed, at large type sizes a fixed-width column may contain only a few words, which makes the text awkward to read. For best results with resizable text, use a flexible layout that transforms gracefully to accommodate larger type sizes (fig. 8.10). (For more on fixed and flexible layouts, see chapter 7, *Page Frameworks*.)

FIGURE 8.10

Enlarged text can send fixed-width layouts into disarray (left). Flexible "liquid" layouts (right) respond more gracefully when users enlarge text.

TYPE FOR COMFORTABLE READING

Most studies of reading and typography have been done using paper documents, with higher-resolution type than computer screens currently display. Nonetheless, with today's improved computer monitors and the benefits of anti-aliased type, we can draw some useful lessons from print reading studies:

1. Readers like large type more than most designers do. It's not just the taste for graphic subtlety that drives the dichotomy: web designers are usually under great pressure to "cram in as much as possible," and smaller type means more words per inch.
2. Generous leading (line spacing) is a key to legibility. Larger type helps, but the data suggests that a moderate type size—11 points—and a standard 13 points of leading yields the best balance of type size and overall reading comfort.

On the web type size is controllable through the web browser, as it should be for universal usability. Studies of web browser users also show, however, that the overwhelming majority of users never change the default type settings in their browsers, so choose a type size comfortable for sustained reading or risk losing many older members of your audience.

Different operating systems display type differently, even when the same typefaces are being used. In general, type displayed on Windows web browsers will look slightly larger and sometimes lighter in weight than the equivalent face on the Macintosh. This difference in font rendering can affect your page layouts and the overall "type color" of your page.

EMPHASIS

A web page of solid body text is hard to scan for content structure and will not engage the eye. Adding display type to a document will provide landmarks to direct the reader through your content. Display type establishes an information structure and adds visual variety to draw the reader into your material. The key to effective display type is the careful and economic use of typographic emphasis.

There are time-honored typographical devices for adding emphasis to a block of text, but be sure to use them sparingly. If you make everything bold,

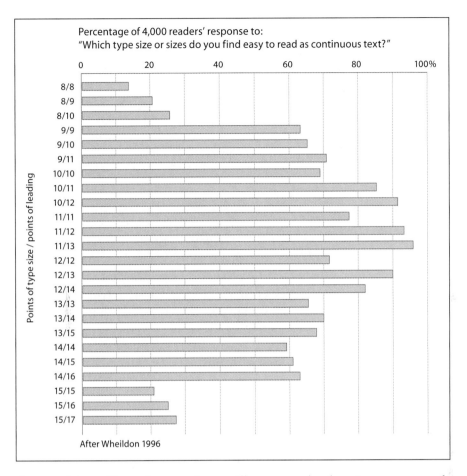

After Wheildon 1996

then nothing will stand out and you will appear to be shouting at your readers. A good rule of thumb when working with type is to add emphasis using one parameter at a time. If you want to draw attention to the section heads in your document, don't set them large, bold, and all uppercase. If you want them to be larger, increase their size by one measure. If you prefer bold, leave the heads the same size as your body text and make them bold. You will soon discover that only a small variation is required to establish visual contrast.

Italics
Italicized text attracts the eye because it contrasts in shape from body text. Use italics for convention—for example, when listing book or magazine

titles—or within text for stressed or foreign words and phrases. Avoid setting large blocks of text in italics because the readability of italicized text, particularly at screen resolutions, is much lower than in comparably sized roman ("plain") text.

Bold

Boldface text gives emphasis because it contrasts in weight from the body text. Section subheads work well set in bold. Boldface text is readable on-screen, though large blocks of text set in bold lack contrast and therefore lose effectiveness.

Underlining

Underlined text is a carryover from the days of the typewriter, when such options as italics and boldface were unavailable. In addition to its aesthetic shortcomings (too heavy, interferes with letter shapes), underlining has a special functional meaning in web documents. Most readers have their browser preferences set to underline links. This default browser setting ensures that people with monochromatic monitors or people who are color-blind can identify links within text blocks. If you include underlined text on your web page, it will certainly be confused with a hypertext link.

Color

Although the use of color is another option for differentiating type, colored text, like underlining, has a special functional meaning in web documents. You should avoid putting colored text within text blocks because readers will assume that the colored text is a hypertext link and click on it. Colored text does work well as a subtle means to distinguish section heads, however. Choose dark shades of color that contrast with the page background, and avoid using colors close to the default web link colors of blue and violet.

Bear in mind that some users cannot distinguish colors. To emphasize text—for example, in headings or key phrases within text—so that it won't be overlooked, use bold formatting as well as color. Also be sure that there is sufficient contrast between the background and text on your page. Although contrast is particularly important for vision-impaired users, all users will benefit from greater readability.

Capitals

Capitalized text is one of the most common and least effective methods for adding typographical emphasis. Whether you choose capital or lowercase letters has a strong effect on the legibility of your text. Indeed, words set in all capitals should generally be avoided—except perhaps for short headings—because they are hard to scan.

We read primarily by recognizing the overall shape of words, not by parsing each letter and then assembling a recognizable word. Words formed with capital letters are monotonous rectangles that offer few distinctive shapes to catch the eye (fig. 8.11).

We recommend down-style typing (capitalize only the first word and any proper nouns) for your headlines, subheads, and text. Down style is more legible because as we read we primarily scan the tops of words (fig 8.12a). Notice how much harder it is to read the bottom half of the same sentence (fig. 8.12b). If you use initial capital letters in your headlines, you disrupt the reader's scanning of the word forms (fig. 8.12c).

a. Legibility depends on the tops of

b. Legibility depends on the tops of

c. Initial Caps Cause Pointless Bumps

FIGURE 8.12
The tops of words (*a*) are much more important to legibility than the bottoms (*b*). Initial caps disrupt and slow the scanning process (*c*).

To read a block of text set in all capital letters we must read the text letter by letter, which is uncomfortable and significantly slows reading. As you read the following paragraph, notice how tiring the process is:

THE DESIGN OF THE SITE WILL DETERMINE THE ORGA-NIZATIONAL FRAMEWORK OF YOUR WEB SITE. AT THIS STAGE YOU WILL MAKE THE ESSENTIAL DECISIONS ABOUT WHAT YOUR AUDIENCE WANTS FROM YOU, WHAT YOU WISH TO SAY, AND HOW TO ARRANGE THE CONTENT TO BEST MEET YOUR AUDIENCE'S NEEDS.

ALTHOUGH PEOPLE WILL INSTANTLY NOTICE THE GRAPHIC DESIGN OF YOUR WEB PAGES, THE ORGANIZA-TION OF THE SITE WILL HAVE THE GREATEST IMPACT ON THEIR EXPERIENCE.

Spacing and indentation

One of the most effective and subtle ways to vary the visual contrast and relative importance of a piece of text is to isolate it or treat it differently from the surrounding text. If you want your major headings to stand out more without making them larger, add space before the heading to separate it from any previous copy. Indentation is another effective means of distinguishing bulleted lists, quotations, or example text (such as the capitalization example, above). You can define margins and indents using css.

Semantic emphasis

Always consider the semantic meaning of any visual styles you apply to your words. Using Cascading Style Sheets you can style the semantic emphasis (`<em>`) and strong emphasis (`<strong>`) HTML tags to look any way you choose. If a word you wish to mark with boldface really reflects a strong semantic emphasis, then by all means mark it with a `<strong>` tag, and use css to style all `<strong>` tags to use a bold visual weight. Similarly, you can use css to control all aspects of the size, color, and font weight of other semantic HTML tags like `<acronym>`, `<cite>`, and `<blockquote>` (table 8.1). With semantic techniques and css you can add context and meaning to your words and visually style them at the same time.

		TABLE 8.1 Semantic elements of HTML markup.
Abbreviation	`<abbr>`	
Acronym	`<acronym>`	
Address	`<address>`	
Block quotation	`<blockquote>`	
Citation	`<cite>`	
Computer code	`<code>`	
Defined term	`<dfn>`	
Emphasis	`<em>`	
Headings	`<h1>`, `<h2>`, `<h3>`, `<h4>`, `<h5>`, `<h6>`	
Lists	`<ol>`, `<ul>`, `<dl>`, `<menu>`, `<dir>`	
Strong emphasis	`<strong>`	

DISPLAY TYPOGRAPHY WITH GRAPHICS

Plain HTML text is best for typography because it provides the most flexibility across many display media, allows quick editorial changes, improves search engine visibility, and facilitates universal access. There are instances, however, where display typography using graphics is important. In enterprises with strong and consistent identity programs, you should always use the recommended "company" typefaces and logo treatments according to the corporate identity program, and usually that will mean rendering header-area logos and display typography within a graphics program like Adobe Photoshop (fig. 8.13).

FIGURE 8.13
Canonical header designs include the organizational logo graphic in the upper left. Quick recognition of a familiar graphic logo is key.

SIGNAL TO NOISE RATIO

The concept of signal-to-noise ratio began as an abstract electrical engineering equation but has since evolved into a useful metaphor for many kinds of communication. All communication is a chain of creation, transmission, and reception of information. At each step along the way, the useful information—the signal—is degraded by extraneous or irrelevant information: the noise. Good communication thus maximizes what's important while minimizing the things that distract from the message.

Data ink versus "chartjunk" The classic graphic metaphor in signal-to-noise ratio is Edward Tufte's concept of "data ink," the ratio of ink in a data graphic devoted to useful information, versus the amount used by distracting visual noise, which Tufte memorably labeled "chartjunk." Thanks to critics like Tufte, most people who care anything about high-quality communication are now well aware that they shouldn't use loud polka-dot patterns in their graphs and charts. On web pages three factors combine to produce "webjunk":

- The desire for attention at any cost. Flash is aptly named: it's a measure of the attention span you get for gratuitous web animation. That animated splash page or cool home page graphic isn't going to buy you more than an instant of retinal response from a reader.
- The restricted space of the screen. Even with today's larger monitors, the web page is a small space, especially when you have a lot to pack in, as on home pages. Crowding inevitably increases visual noise because it increases accidental associations among page elements and reduces the white space so crucial to visual organization.
- Lack of control over the elements of a page. Today's home pages are often complex combinations of content from many sources; databases, RSS feeds, and text from content management systems must all coexist on the page in an organized way. This argues for rigorous use of a few enterprise style sheets that harmonize page displays from many sources.

> **The "cliff of complexity"** Every data display has a zone of optimal density beyond which the increase in visual complexity rapidly tends toward noise. The lessons of Gestalt visual psychology and the visual engineering of careful information design can help you maximize the signal ratio in your pages. We *like* some complexity in data displays: the "high signal" is what makes well-designed pages interesting. But push the degree of complexity too far and you go past a point of rapidly diminishing viewer interest: the "cliff of complexity."

When using graphics for text, always provide the equivalent text using the "alt" attribute of the `<img>` tag so that the text is available to nonvisual users, users with images disabled, and software such as search engines:

```
<img src="page-headline.gif" alt="The major headline" width="300"
    height="90" />
```

CREATING DISPLAY TYPOGRAPHY

Most designers use Adobe Photoshop to create and finalize display typography for the web. Photoshop allows you to use any font installed in your computer's operating system. Virtually all conventional display typography is done using Photoshop's options for anti-aliasing type (sharp, crisp, strong, or smooth). In most instances we prefer the "sharp" option for rendering type, but you should explore the other smoothing options for your graphics. The heavier smoothing options can be useful in creating "demi-bold" weights of fonts in between the regular and bold weights.

Small labels within diagrams and illustrations

Type in sizes smaller than 10 points or 10 pixels is common in diagrams and illustrations prepared for the web. In instances where your type sizes are small, you may want to experiment with turning off anti-aliasing (the "none" option in Photoshop) to achieve crisper typography.

How do I know what I think until I see what I say?

— E. M. Forster

CHAPTER 9

Editorial Style

P eople read differently on the web, and a new writing genre designed to accommodate the reading habits of online users has emerged. Given the low resolution of the computer screen and the awkwardness of the scrolling page, many users find reading on-screen uncomfortable, and so they scan on-screen text and print pages for reading. Web reading is also not a stationary activity. Users roam from page to page, collecting salient bits of information from a variety of sources. They scan the contents of a page, get the information, and move on. Web reading may also be disorienting because web pages, unlike book or magazine pages, can be accessed directly without preamble. Too often web pages end up as isolated fragments of information, divorced from the larger context of their parent sites through the lack of essential links and the failure to inform the user of their contents.

Web authors use hypertext links to create or supplement concepts: a list of related links can reinforce their content or even serve as the focus of their site. The problem posed by links has little to do with the web but is rooted in the concept of hypertext: Can the quick juxtaposition of two separate but conceptually related pieces of information encourage a better understanding of the message? A collection of links cannot create or sustain an argument or deliver a collection of facts as efficiently or legibly as conventional linear prose. When there is no sustained narrative, users are sent aimlessly wandering in their quest for information. Links also become a maintenance issue, because most web pages are ephemeral. Broken links shake the user's confidence in the validity and timeliness of content. Links should be used sparingly and never as a substitute for real content.

STRUCTURING YOUR PROSE
Documents written to be read online should be concise and structured for scanning. Most online readers are at some point "scanners" who skim web pages rather than read them word by word. Even methodical readers will appreciate your efforts to accommodate online reading patterns rather than

forcing readers to slow down and pick their way through your pages in order to glean information. That said, keep in mind that much content is not well suited to the telegraphic style that works well for online documents. Web authors often cut so much out of their presentations that what remains would barely fill a printed pamphlet. Concise writing is always better, but don't dumb down what you have to say. Simply make printing easy for those who prefer to read offline, and you can use the web to deliver content without cutting the heart out of what you have to say.

SITE STRUCTURE

The first accommodation for online reading is in how you structure your site. Rather than provide a single page with all the information on a topic, break up a body of information into logical "chunks," each on its own page, and connect the pages using links. This approach accommodates online reading by providing direct access to subcategories of specific information rather than combining all information about a topic on a single page.

Only use chunking where it makes sense (see chapter 3, *Chunking information*). Don't break up a long document arbitrarily; users will have to download each page and will have difficulty printing or saving the entire piece. The key to good chunking is to divide your information into comprehensive segments. That way users will have direct and complete access to the topics they are interested in without having to wade through irrelevant material or follow a series of links to get the whole picture.

As you review content for your new or revised site, always look for opportunities to develop and use modular, consistent means of approaching content topics. A consistent, repeatable, well-specified content structure makes it much easier for writers and editors to understand what is expected of them. Modular structure is also easier on users, since they can quickly predict how to scan chunks of content that share the same structure (fig. 9.1).

PAGE STRUCTURE

The page level is where web writing really differs from other genres. Web readers often approach a web page with a quick skim in order to form an overview of the page and determine whether the information they are seeking is likely to be found there. Some users then read through the page, while others print the page for offline reading. The following guidelines support both the skimming and reading behaviors of online readers.

FIGURE 9.1
Recipes allow
for the modular
organization
of content into
logical "chunks"—
description,
ingredients, and
preparation.

patrick lynch
artist | author | photographer | web designer

home | recipes

home
about
portfolios
publications
library
links
painting
recipes

herb sweet pepper bread

A basic French bread recipe, moistened with a bit of oil and egg, and with herbs and garlic added. This bread is especially appropriate for late summer meals with salad, when the garden herbs are at their peak and you're looking for things to do with them.

related links
epicurious
mark bittman
mario batali

Makes: 3 baguettes, or the equivalent
Time: About 3.5 hours, largely unattended

4 cups King Arthur or other unbleached bread flour
3 teaspoons Fleishman's jarred yeast
2 teaspoons sea salt
2 teaspoons brown sugar
5 twists of fresh ground pepper from a mill
1 teaspoon dried or fresh oregano
1 tablespoon canola oil
2 large eggs
1 tablespoon chopped garlic
3 tablespoons finely grated Parmesan cheese
4-5 large basil leaves, loosely chopped
3 tablespoons finely diced sweet red pepper
2 tablespoons sun-dried tomatoes in oil
3 tablespoons canned artichokes, chopped
1 tablespoon fresh chives, loosely chopped
1.5 cups lager beer (1 12-ounce bottle)
2 tablespoons of red wine vinegar

1. Mix all ingredients and place in a heavy kitchen mixer to start the kneading. With the right amount of water the flour should form a moist and sticky ball with some dough sticking to the mixer bowl, but the dough should not be very runny like a batter.
2. Use mixer or bread machine until the dough is thoroughly mixed. Transfer the dough to a greased bowl and set aside for at least 2 hours for first rise.
3. Gently knead down the risen dough and form into your preferred shapes.
4. Use the Dutch oven baking method for the best results.

See my general notes on yeast bread baking for more information on what brands of ingredients and equipment I use. Also, I have notes on the Dutch-oven bread baking method that I usually use for this bread.

> ## INVERTED PYRAMID
>
> The inverted pyramid is a method for presenting information where the most important information, represented by the base of the pyramid, is presented first and the least important (the tip) is presented last. Information designed using this model begins with a lead that summarizes the information, followed by the body, where the information presented in the lead is elaborated on and substantiated, in descending order of importance. Thanks to its long use in journalism the inverted pyramid style has a number of well-established advantages:
>
> - Important information comes first, where it is more likely to be seen and remembered
> - This front-loading of content permits efficient scanning for information
> - The initial major facts establish a context for later secondary information
> - The structure places facts and keywords at the head of the page, where they carry more weight in search engine relevance analysis
>
> In crowded home pages, it's often good practice to provide only the lead and perhaps a "teaser" sentence, with the body of the article available through a "learn more" link to another page.

Segment the text for easy scanning

Browsing a page is easier when the text is broken into segments topped by headings that describe the subject of each segment. This often means breaking up long paragraphs, and using more subheadings than you would for print publication. Remember that in the restricted world of the computer screen, a long paragraph may fill the screen with a visually monotonous block of text.

Use descriptive headings

Avoid catchy but meaningless headings. Don't force readers to read a text segment to determine its topic. Highlighting or linking meaningless or ambiguous phrases will not help you with optimizing your content for search engines and may even harm the overall search visibility of your page by adding confusing keywords into the mix.

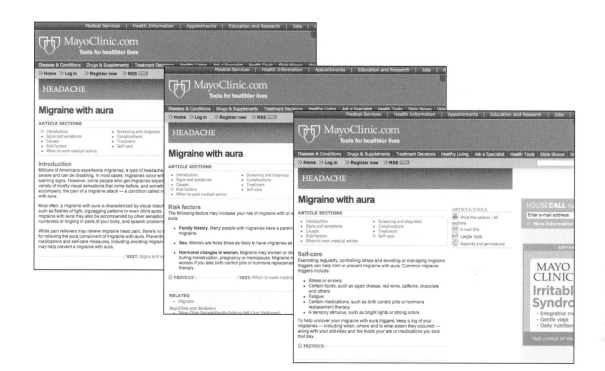

Highlight important words and sections

Within sections, use lists and typographical emphasis for words or sections you wish to highlight; these and headings are the elements that will grab the user's attention during a scan.

Use the inverted pyramid

The inverted pyramid style used in journalism works well on web pages, with the conclusion appearing at the beginning of a text. Place the important facts near the top of the first paragraph where users can find them quickly (fig. 9.2).

Structural markup

HTML is a markup language that adds a layer of structural meaning to documents. It works by wrapping elements, such as titles, headings, paragraphs, lists, tables, addresses, and citations, in defining tags. The result is a machine-friendly document that can be read and interpreted by software. Tags

FIGURE 9.2

Put the important words and phrases at the top of the page, where the reader (or search engine) will scan them first.

tell software, for example, that the text from here to here is a heading, and the following text block is a paragraph, and so on. For example, when a web author defines a block of text as the page title, web browser software can display the page title in the browser title bar, in the browser history, and as a bookmark.

On the surface, a structured document looks no different from one that uses font size and other visual formatting to distinguish elements such as headings. When it comes to functionality, however, structure gives power and utility to the web. Take, for example, the heading of this section. `<b>Structural markup</b>` is visually identifiable as a heading because it is bold and sits directly above plain text. But software cannot infer that it is the primary subheading of this section because `<b>` means nothing more than bold. If the chapter title is marked as `<h1>Structural markup</h1>`, software knows that the page is *about* structural markup, and that in turn facilitates all kinds of functions, such as returning the page on searches for structural markup or adding the page to compilations about structural markup.

When marking up text, think about what each text element *is* and not what it should look like. Tag each element with the appropriate HTML structural tag, and then use CSS to manage its visual properties (see chapter 8, *Semantic emphasis*).

ONLINE STYLE

Online writing is best presented using short segments of texts written in a clear, concise style and with ample use of editorial landmarks. This style supports the scanning style used by many web readers. But online prose does not have to be stripped down to a few headlines and bullet points to be effective: many readers will engage directly with longer written material online or print long articles to read offline.

CONTRAST AND EMPHASIS

On the web, more than any other prose medium, the look of text layout strongly affects how readers relate to written content. The contrast produced by headlines, subheads, lists, and illustrations give users visual "entry points," drawing their eyes down the page and into the content. Although the heading and list markup might look excessive in print form, on the web this markup has two big advantages:

UNIFORM CONNECTEDNESS

We use the Gestalt principles of perception to decode the structure of a document visually. One task in making sense of a document is determining which elements are related and which are not. Uniform connectedness defines groups of related information, frequently using "common regions," in which elements are grouped within a bounding box or uniform background.

Structural markup provides the means to use uniform connectedness to group elements in a nonvisual and machine-readable way. A list tag in essence draws a line around several items and asserts that they are related. The `<table>` tag connects data in rows and cells into a single expression of a concept. Even the `<cite>` tag surrounds a phrase and declares its relatedness as a book, magazine, or article title. Using uniform connectedness both on the surface in the visual design and in the structural markup in underlying page code allows both visual and nonvisual users to make sense of the structure of a document.

- Frequent headings and lists of items favor both scanning and methodical readers by adding visible structure to the online reading experience. Compared to large, high-resolution print pages, web pages usually lack the room to use the more subtle white space and typography of print publications.
- The added structure of heading and list markup aids in search engine optimization and online searches for content, because the additional markup provides explicit semantic emphasis, heading keywords, and context cues that listed items are strongly related to one another.

PROSE STYLE

For general advice on clear, concise writing, it is hard to beat George Orwell's rules for writing:

- Never use a metaphor, simile, or other figure of speech that you are used to seeing in print.
- Never use a long word where a short one will do.
- If it is possible to cut a word out, always cut it out.
- Never use the passive where you can use the active.
- Never use a foreign phrase, a scientific word, or a jargon word if you can think of an everyday English equivalent.
- Break any of these rules sooner than say anything outright barbarous.

OTHER STYLISTIC CONSIDERATIONS

Front-load your content

Make sure the text you present is of immediate value. Avoid empty chatter such as "welcome" messages from unit managers or instructions on how to use the site. Don't use the first paragraph of each page to tell users what information they'll find on the page. Start with the information, written in a concise and factual inverted pyramid style.

Stick to the point

Write in easily understood sentences, and keep the subject matter of each page focused. This topical focus helps the reader evaluate the page content quickly and has many advantages for search engine visibility, where a clear and quickly identifiable content theme is important to search ranking.

Cultivate a particular voice

Use active verbs and first-person language. Web readers welcome a measure of individuality from their information sources. With so many competing sources, a unique voice may distinguish your pages, but beware of going over the top. There is a fine line between engaging and annoying.

Think globally

Remember that you are designing documents for the *World Wide* Web and that your audience may not understand conventions specific to your corner of the world. For example, when including dates, use the international date format of day/month/year (14 March 2009). Also, consider that the metaphors, puns, and popular culture references that you use may make sense only in the context of your language and culture.

Use numerals for specific numbers whenever possible

Write "2,402" instead of "twenty-four hundred and two." The numerals stand out on the page and attract users scanning for facts. Don't use numerals for general estimates. Write "thousands of protesters," not "1,000s of protesters."

KEYWORDS

Online readers generally skim text to get an overview of a page before settling into full-fledged reading. Positioning keywords at the beginnings of sentences, headings, and links makes skimming more effective. Initial keywords also help with link and heading lists. These features of software such as screen readers give users a list of links or a list of page headings. Such features are more usable when links and headings begin with keywords than if every link or heading begins with "The." In addition, search engines give more relevance weight to keywords that appear early in titles, paragraph text, and linked text (see chapter 5, *Optimizing your pages for search*).

Keywords and SEO

When readers use web search engines, they generally use words or short phrases that describe what they are seeking. Along with the text of the page title, these keywords (the term covers both individual words and short phrases) become the crucial determinants of your page's relevance rank in the search engine's indexes. For search engine optimization, a good keyword

RHETORIC AND WEB DESIGN

Rhetoric is the art and technique of persuasion, through oral, written, or visual media. The contemporary World Wide Web is a unique combination of all three media, but audience reaction to your high-tech web site is still governed by aspects of rhetoric that the Greek philosopher Aristotle identified almost 2,400 years ago. In *The Art of Rhetoric,* Aristotle outlined three major elements of rhetorical persuasion that can easily be understood in relation to web design.

Ethos Ethos establishes the credibility of an information source. Does the speaker have the credentials and seriousness of purpose to be believed? Many otherwise distinguished and credible institutions still present a painfully amateurish web presence—government and higher education sites being especially notorious offenders here—in spite of the damage poor presentation does to the credibility of the web site and the host institution. Even small lapses can erode the ethos of a site: broken links, missing graphics, outdated content, and misspelled words all damage the overall trustworthiness of a site. Ironically, with attention to editorial detail, ethos can also be easily spoofed on the web. Many email scams depend on carefully crafted forgeries of real sites like eBay, PayPal, and personal banking sites. Beware of cheap thieves in expensive suits.

Pathos Pathos is the art of developing a positive emotional response in the viewer. Most sites don't develop high emotional responses in users, but a well-designed home page with attractive graphics and interesting articles and links makes users more likely to explore your site. A strong appeal to pathos is central to many marketing web sites, particularly where the user's identification with an upscale brand image is crucial.

Logos Logos uses reason, logic, statistics, convincing examples, and depth of information to persuade an audience. A newspaper front page or home page isn't just about packing the maximum amount of news into a given space. Over weeks, months, and years, a news source builds credibility with an audience through the sheer depth and breadth of information, carefully presented news photography, and information graphics, now augmented on the web with audiovisual media.

Review your rhetoric Go to your home page and do your best to see the site anew, the way a stranger might, who knows you only through your web presence. Does the rhetoric of your site support or erode the user's sense of the credibility, trustworthiness, and humanity of your enterprise?

strategy is to make sure that key page elements are working in concert to portray the page content accurately. Ideally there is one key word or phrase for your page, and it is mentioned in most or all of the following elements:

- Page title
- Major `<h1>`, `<h2>`, or `<h3>` headings
- The words that appear early in titles, and near the beginnings of the top five paragraphs of text
- The alternate ("alt") text of all content images
- The `<meta>` tags (if any) in the header section of the page HTML code
- The words in the HTML file name, separated with hyphens: "files-names-also-matter.html"

One thing you should *never do* is pack in gratuitous repetitions of keywords or use sophomoric tricks like creating white text on a white background to hide keywords. All the major search engines know that even in well-written and edited text, keywords and phrases will make up only 5–8 percent of the number of words on the average page of text. Pages with a suspiciously high keyword rate will lose search engine ranking, and pages that use hidden word repetition tricks may be banned from mainstream search engines.

The best keyword advice for good search visibility is simple: write clear, well-edited, interesting prose, and check your page titles and the other elements above to make sure the key descriptive words or phrases are featured.

TITLES AND SUBTITLES

Editorial landmarks such as titles and headings are the fundamental human interface device in web pages, just as they are in any print publication. A consistent approach to titles, headings, and subheadings in your documents will help your users navigate through a complex set of web pages.

The text styles we recommend are below. Choose one style or the other but not both:

Headline style: bold, capitalize initial letters of words
- Document titles
- References to other web sites
- Titles of documents mentioned in the text
- Proper names, product names, trade names

Down style: bold, capitalize first word only
- Subheads
- References to other sections within the site
- Figure titles
- Lists

PAGE TITLES

Web page titles are designated in the HTML document head section with the `<title>` tag. The title is crucial for several reasons. The title is the first thing users see (particularly those with slower Internet connections) and the first thing users of screen readers hear. It also becomes the text for any bookmarks the reader makes to your pages. In addition, most search engines regard the page title as the primary descriptor of page content, so a descriptive title increases the chance that a page will appear as the result of a related search query.

The page title should:

- Contain carefully chosen keywords and themes for the page
- Form a concise, plainly worded description of the page contents
- Be unique, if possible

Some enterprises make it a policy to incorporate the company or organization name as the initial part of the page title. Although this practice is often useful, you should always consider the length of your page title. The page title also becomes the bookmark text, and many web browsers truncate long page titles (more than sixty-five characters, including spaces) in a way that makes them less legible. If your page title starts with a long company name, the most relevant part of the page title may not be visible in a reader's bookmark for that page. Always consider what your page title will look like in a long list of bookmarks or in a list of search results. Will the title remind the user of what he or she found interesting about your pages? Will it tell the searcher enough about the contents of the page to elicit a click?

TEXT FORMATTING FOR WEB DOCUMENTS

Keep the following in mind when formatting text copy for the web, bearing in mind that web markup is not just about how the text looks on the page. The most important aspect of text formatting is providing the structural markup that underlies the formatted page.

Avoid excessive links

Too many links will destroy the homogeneous, even "type color" that characterizes good typesetting, and the links will become a constant distraction to the reader. Consider adding a list of parenthetic or reference links to the bottom of the article, where they are freely available but not distracting.

If you include links in the body of your text, choose custom link colors that harmonize with your text color in order to minimize their distraction. Always underline inline links so that users who cannot distinguish colors will be able to differentiate links from regular text.

Avoid excessive or purely visual typographic markup

Develop a careful heading hierarchy and use it consistently throughout your web site. Develop at least a simple style sheet that tells everyone on the team when and where to use `<h1>`, `<h2>`, and `<h3>` headings, list styles, and other semantic markup. Avoid using purely visual markup like italics or bold (`<i>` or `<b>` tags). These tags add nothing to semantic content. Whenever possible, use semantically meaningful tags like "emphasis" and "strong emphasis" (`<em>` and `<strong>`). Use a master linked style sheet to establish the typography for your whole site.

Use the best tool

Write your text in a good word-processing program with spell-checking and search features. Transfer your text to HTML only after it has been proofread.

Style sheets in word processors

Don't use the word processor's style sheets to produce "All capitals" or other visual formatting effects for text or headings. You will lose those special formats when you convert to HTML.

Special text characters

When composing text in a word-processing program like Microsoft Word, leave the "smart quotes" and other special characters in place in the manuscript, but be aware that special characters, math and science symbols, diacritical marks, typographer's ligatures, and international punctuation will need to be replaced with the HTML code for each character. With the special characters in place in the Word file, this conversion to web special characters can easily be accomplished with the search-and-replace feature of a web text editor or with web design software like Adobe Dreamweaver.

Consult a good HTML guidebook (we recommend several in the References section) for a full listing of special and international characters supported through HTML's extended character formatting.

Avoid the auto-hyphenation feature of word processors for text destined for the web. This may add nonstandard "optional hyphen" characters that will not display properly in web browsers, and you'll just have to scrub them out of the web text with search-and-replace techniques.

LINKS

Two types of links are used in web sites: navigational links that connect pages within a site, and the classic "embedded" hypertext links within the content that offer parenthetical material, footnotes, digressions, or parallel themes that the author believes will enrich the main content of the page. Although navigational links can cause problems in site design, more disruptive is the overuse or poor placement of embedded hypertext links.

Embedded hypertext links pose two fundamental design problems. They disrupt the flow of content in your site by inviting the user to leave your site. They can also radically alter the context of information by dumping the users into unfamiliar territory without preamble or explanation when they follow the embedded links to new pages—particularly when those new pages are outside your site.

The primary design strategy in thoughtful hypertext is to use links to reinforce your message, not to distract users or send them off chasing a minor

FIGURE 9.3
Provide context along with links so that users know whether the links are to pages within the same section, elsewhere in your site, or in external resources.

footnote in some other web site. Most links in a web site should point to other resources within your site, pages that share the same graphic design, navigational controls, and overall content theme. Whenever possible, integrate related visual or text materials into your site so that users do not have the sense that you have dumped them outside your site's framework. If you must send your reader away, make sure the material around the link makes it clear that the user will be leaving your web site and entering another site by following the link. Provide a description of the linked site along with the link so that users understand the relevance of the linked material (fig. 9.3).

When placing links on the page, put only the most salient links within the body of your text, and group all minor, illustrative, parenthetic, or footnote links at the bottom of the document where they are available but not distracting.

DESCRIPTIVE LINKS

Most of your web visitors are passing through on their way to some other destination and will appreciate your efforts to make the trip as straightforward and predictable as possible, with few meaningless side trips or dead ends. Key to the success of any trip is the clarity of the signage along the way, which in the web context comes in the form of links.

Links are the signposts that help users know which route is most likely to get them to their destination. Good link text gives users a description of the page that will load, allowing them to make informed decisions about which path to take. Bad link text, such as nondescriptive "click here" links or catchy but meaningless phrases, forces the user to follow the link to learn its destination. Nondescriptive links often lead to dead ends, requiring users to retrace their steps and waste time.

When writing links, never construct a sentence around a link phrase, such as "click here for more information." Write the sentence as you normally would, and place the link anchor on the keyword or phrase that best describes the additional content you are linking to.

- Poor: <u>Click here</u> for more information on link underlines.
- Better: For universal usability, use <u>link underlines</u> to ensure that all users can identify links.

Links and search

Web links aren't just a convenience for the user; they also add semantic meaning to the page. By choosing to link a particular word or phrase you have signaled to both users and search engines that it is potentially important as a search keyword.

LINK UNDERLINES

Underlining is a carryover from the days of handwriting and the typewriter, when options such as bold and italics were not readily available as ways to distinguish elements such as headings and emphasized words or phrases. Typographically, underlining is undesirable, since it interferes with the legibility of letterforms. However, link underlines ensure that users who cannot see colors can distinguish links from other text—users with color vision issues, and users who access the web on devices that do not display color. For universal usability, links must be visually identifiable with or without

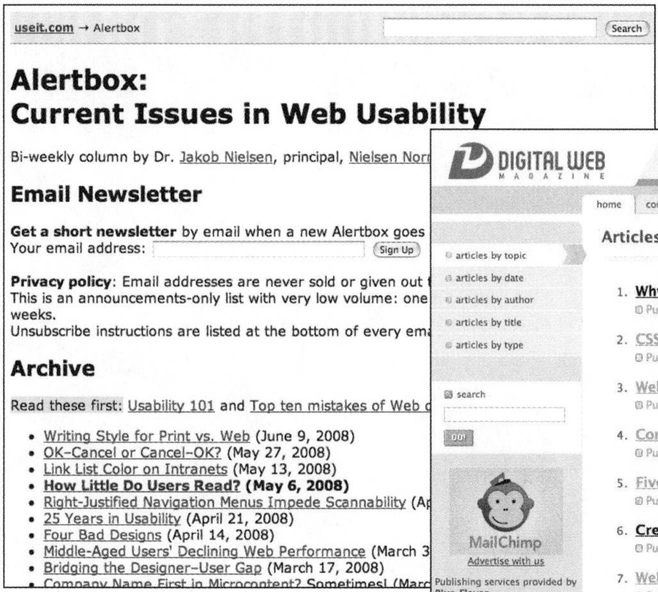

useit.com → Alertbox

Search

Alertbox:
Current Issues in Web Usability

Bi-weekly column by Dr. Jakob Nielsen, principal, Nielsen Norr

Email Newsletter

Get a short newsletter by email when a new Alertbox goes
Your email address: [   ] Sign Up

Privacy policy: Email addresses are never sold or given out
This is an announcements-only list with very low volume: one
weeks.
Unsubscribe instructions are listed at the bottom of every em

Archive

Read these first: Usability 101 and Top ten mistakes of Web

- Writing Style for Print vs. Web (June 9, 2008)
- OK–Cancel or Cancel–OK? (May 27, 2008)
- Link List Color on Intranets (May 13, 2008)
- **How Little Do Users Read? (May 6, 2008)**
- Right-Justified Navigation Menus Impede Scannability (Ap
- 25 Years in Usability (April 21, 2008)
- Four Bad Designs (April 14, 2008)
- Middle-Aged Users' Declining Web Performance (March 3
- Bridging the Designer–User Gap (March 17, 2008)
- Company Name First in Microcontent? Sometimes! (Marc

DIGITAL WEB
MAGAZINE

The web professional's online magazine of choice.
(mt) mediatemple

home   contribute   subscribe   contact   about   events

articles by topic
articles by date
articles by author
articles by title
articles by type

search

MailChimp
Advertise with us

Publishing services provided by
Blue Flavor

Photos provided courtesy of
iStockPhoto.com

Publication managed with the
help of Basecamp

Newsletter powered by
Campaign Monitor

Articles by Topic: CSS

1. **Why Opera?**
   Published on January 7, 2008

2. CSS Not([hacks])
   Published on January 7, 2008

3. Web Design 101: Floats
   Published on September 10, 2007

4. Corporate Web Standards
   Published on July 16, 2007

5. Five Pertinent Questions for Andy Budd
   Published on June 18, 2007

6. **Creative Use of PNG Transparency in Web Design**
   Published on May 28, 2007

7. Web Design 101: Backgrounds
   Published on May 21, 2007

8. Coding for Content
   Published on April 23, 2007

9. Web Design 101: Positioning
   Published on April 16, 2007

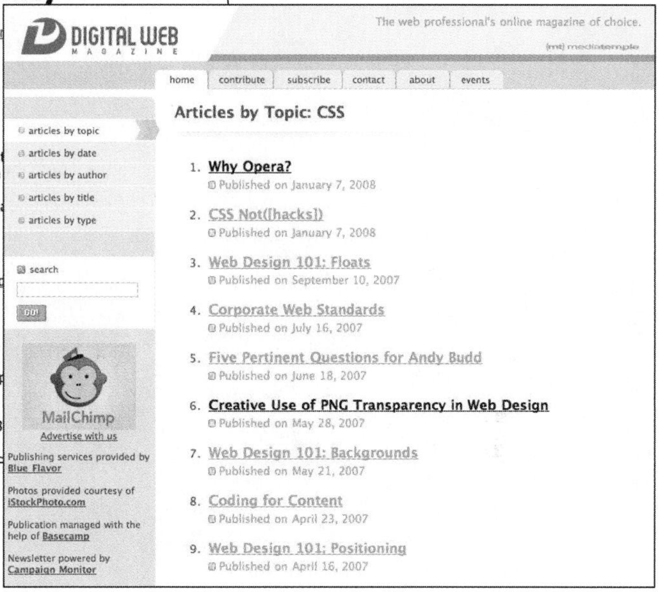

color. Links that display within a navigation column or button bar are clearly links and do not necessarily need underlining. However, links that appear within body text should be underlined to set them off from the surrounding text.

VISITED AND UNVISITED LINKS

Most web sessions involve trial and error. For example, finding a phone number or a price or location may involve multiple rounds of searching and following unproductive paths. The process can become circuitous if there is no way to tell where you have already looked, with repeat visits to pages that did not prove fruitful. By providing different link colors for visited and unvisited links, you allow users to identify the paths they have already taken (fig 9.4).

FIGURE 9.4

Link color allows readers to differentiate visited and unvisited pages. Link colors can be standard browser colors (left) or custom colors set using CSS (right).

Everything should be made as simple as possible,
but not simpler.

—Albert Einstein

Forms and Applications

Web interaction today has moved beyond clicking hyperlinks and completing form fields to working with full-blown web applications that provide a range of interactivity, including inline editing and drag-and-drop file management. The web has become a two-way street, with users as both consumers and active participants. And as users take a more active role in web interactions, so demand increases for more dynamic graphical user interfaces. In some ways, we are in the same phase with web interaction as we were with visual design a few years ago: working around the limitations of the web environment by introducing new technologies and practices that, though not universally supported and usable, allow for better methods for designing more usable interfaces. And users have come to expect a certain level of sophistication in web interaction, greeting simple, link-driven interaction designs with the same scorn as with first-generation, text-only web pages.

We hope the coming years will bring the same technology growth and stabilization as we have enjoyed in the area of visual design, which produced web standards, accessibility, and the separation of content and presentation through the introduction and support of Cascading Style Sheets. In the meantime, we continue to favor well-supported technologies for designing web forms and applications, with more advanced scripting serving only as an enhancement to standard modes of interaction.

TECHNOLOGIES THAT SUPPORT INTERACTION

With web interaction at its most basic, users interact with pages by clicking on links and submitting forms. This interaction initiates a dialog between the client, usually a web browser, and the server, where the client sends data and page requests to the server, and the server collects data and returns pages. Once the server delivers a page, all dialog is suspended until the client makes another request. What the user does with the page is immaterial, unless another link is clicked or another form submitted.

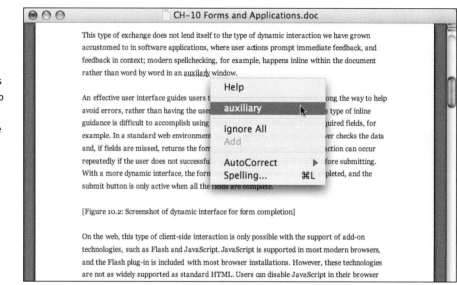

This type of exchange does not lend itself to the type of dynamic interaction we have grown accustomed to in software applications, in which user actions prompt immediate feedback, and feedback in context; modern spell-checking, for example, happens inline within the document rather than word by word in an auxiliary window (fig. 10.1).

An effective user interface guides users through a task, providing feedback along the way to help avoid errors, rather than having the user correct errors after completion. This type of inline guidance is difficult to accomplish using standard web technologies. Take required fields, for example. In a standard web environment, the user submits the form, then the server checks the data and, if fields are missed, returns the form to the user to complete. This transaction can occur repeatedly if the user does not locate all of the required fields before submitting. With a more dynamic interface, the form fields are validated as they are completed, and the submit button is active only when all the fields are complete (fig. 10.2).

On the web, this type of client-side interaction is possible only with the support of add-on technologies, such as Flash and JavaScript. JavaScript is supported in most modern browsers, and the Flash plug-in is included with most browser installations. However, these technologies are not as widely supported as standard HTML. Users can disable JavaScript in their browser

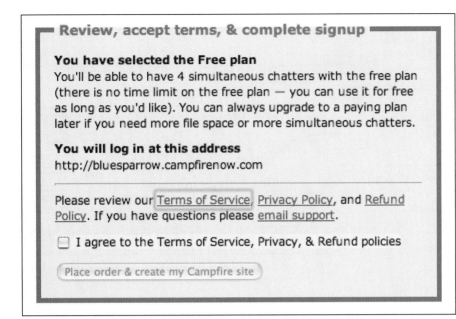

preferences, and some devices do not offer support for JavaScript and Flash; others offer support but with different implementations. Although client-side scripting offers many benefits to interaction, it cannot be relied on exclusively to provide necessary interaction. For universal usability, a web application that makes use of client-side scripting must also function when these technologies are unavailable or disabled.

AJAX

Ajax, which stands for Asynchronous JavaScript and XML, is a technique for providing both dynamic interface elements and dynamic page content, and it is frequently used for building web applications. With Ajax, the page sends requests for small bits of data in response to user actions—for example, zooming in on a map—and the data is displayed in an area of the page without requiring the entire page to reload. Ajax has performance benefits because each user action doesn't require a full page reload. Ajax also provides much more in the way of interactivity by allowing for dynamic and responsive user interfaces (fig. 10.3).

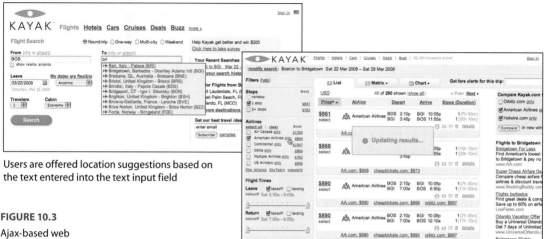

Users are offered location suggestions based on the text entered into the text input field

FIGURE 10.3

Ajax-based web applications and forms are beginning to rival conventional software applications in the complexity of interactivity they can offer the user.

The list of flights updates dynamically when the user changes a filter, such as number of stops, airline, or flight time

The shortcomings of Ajax have to do with its reliance on JavaScript, which we have already identified as risky since there's no guarantee that it will be running on the client's browser. Also, implementations of JavaScript vary among browsers, making extensive cross-platform checking a key component of any Ajax project. In addition, search engines cannot accurately index pages with dynamic content, because content that is hidden from the user is also hidden from search engine software. Last, Ajax, and dynamic interfaces more generally, present challenges to accessibility.

ACCESSIBILITY

When we moved from text-based web pages to graphical web pages in the early days of the web, we improved usability but sacrificed universal usability. Because text is machine-readable, it can be accessed by a wide range of users and devices. Graphics are not machine-readable, and a page that employs graphics and complex layouts is harder to make accessible. Now we are seeing a similar trend with interaction, as we move from simple links and forms to complex and dynamic interfaces. Although these interfaces can be much more usable and efficient, they are also more difficult to make accessible to all users. Users of screen readers may not know when dynamic content has loaded onto the page. Keyboard users may not be able to work interface widgets. Some "thin" clients, such as PDAs and cell phones, do not have horse-power to run these technologies. And HTML and other W3C technologies are designed to support accessible designs, with such features as text equivalents and fallbacks, whereas many of the add-on technologies were not designed with accessibility in mind.

The good news is that the W3C is working to create standards to support the development of interfaces that are both dynamic and accessible. The ARIA (Accessible Rich Internet Applications) initiative is developing a specification for marking up application interfaces in such a way that clients of all kinds—from standard browsers to screen magnifiers to screen readers—can help users access and manipulate dynamic interface elements. Developments such as ARIA and Adobe's work to make accessible Flash, along with the ongoing work on HTML and XHTML, will produce tools that we can use to build accessible dynamic interfaces. In the meantime, we have standard tools at the ready that will allow us to create accessible and effective web applications.

DESIGNING WEB APPLICATIONS
Because web applications place greater demands on the user, it is particularly important to focus on system requirements, avoiding scope creep at all costs. In designing your application, use recognizable interface conventions and provide guidance to help your users be successful.

RESTRAINT AND SIMPLICITY
Good interface design arises from restraint. All too often, applications are cluttered and complicated by the enthusiasm of their developers, who add in features and functionality because they can and because they might be useful to some users. Users also often get carried away in their requests for features, thinking, Wouldn't it be great if the application did this, that, and the other thing, and not taking into account the complexity that inevitably results. In the end, users benefit more from simple designs than from a wealth of features. The cost of adding features that benefit a few users is too high to justify the negative effect on overall usability and ease of use. You are better off focusing on the most critical functions of an application and avoiding all nice-to-have or easy-to-add features. Address those critical features with a design that is uncluttered by unnecessary elements.

FIGURE 10.4
Common design
patterns for sign-in
boxes.

DESIGN PATTERNS

Design patterns are recognizable patterns for interaction, such as drop-down menus for accessing subsection pages and paging navigation for moving through a sequence of pages. Design patterns are designs that have been introduced and proven effective and then are widely adopted until they become conventions. After widespread adoption, the approach becomes a pattern that is readily recognizable by users, which improves usability. Users can leverage what they know and don't have to create a new mental model for interaction at each site.

Design patterns for interface elements do not have to look the same, but they do need to share the same interaction model and features. Don't employ a design pattern but change the way it works. Modifying an existing design pattern is worse than adopting a new approach because it conflicts with the users' mental model for how the pattern works, and users will have to unlearn and learn how to work with your site (fig. 10.4).

CONTROLS

HTML form controls have their basis in the graphical user interface that is used in most modern operating systems. Since these elements are widely used and readily recognizable, users know how to work them, as long as you use them according to convention.

Menus

Menus are helpful for collecting information in a standard format. They work with information where the possible responses are known, such as dates. Using a menu makes for cleaner data collection since the responses can be standardized in both substance and format, whereas users can enter the wrong information, or the right information in the wrong format, in a text input field.

- Select menus have the benefit of providing many choices in a small space, but they can be hard to use. In particular, menus with many options, such as to choose your state or country, are challenging to scan. It's easier to enter a state or country code than to choose it from a select menu.
- Radio buttons are easy to scan because the options display on the page. However, because a long list takes up screen space, and because long lists are hard for readers to parse, limit your radio button groups to four to six options.
- Checkboxes allow users to make multiple selections. Single checkboxes are also the right control for binary choices, such as yes or no, in which checked means "yes."

Always set menus to nonactionable defaults to keep users from submitting information that is incorrect simply by neglecting to choose from the menu. For example, make the checkbox default unchecked, and the first item of a select menu a null value, such as "None" or "Select an item" (fig. 10.5).

Input fields and text areas

Form fill-in using input fields and scrolling text areas allows users to type information directly into a field rather than choosing from a predefined menu of choices. Fields are required when the information is open-ended and therefore cannot be represented in a menu. Fields are sometime preferable for information that is easier to enter into a field than to choose from a menu. For example, even though dates are predefined, it may be easier to enter the information into a form field than to choose it from a set of menus. "Year of birth" menus, for instance, need to be enormous and can be awkward to manipulate. A simple input field is the easier choice.

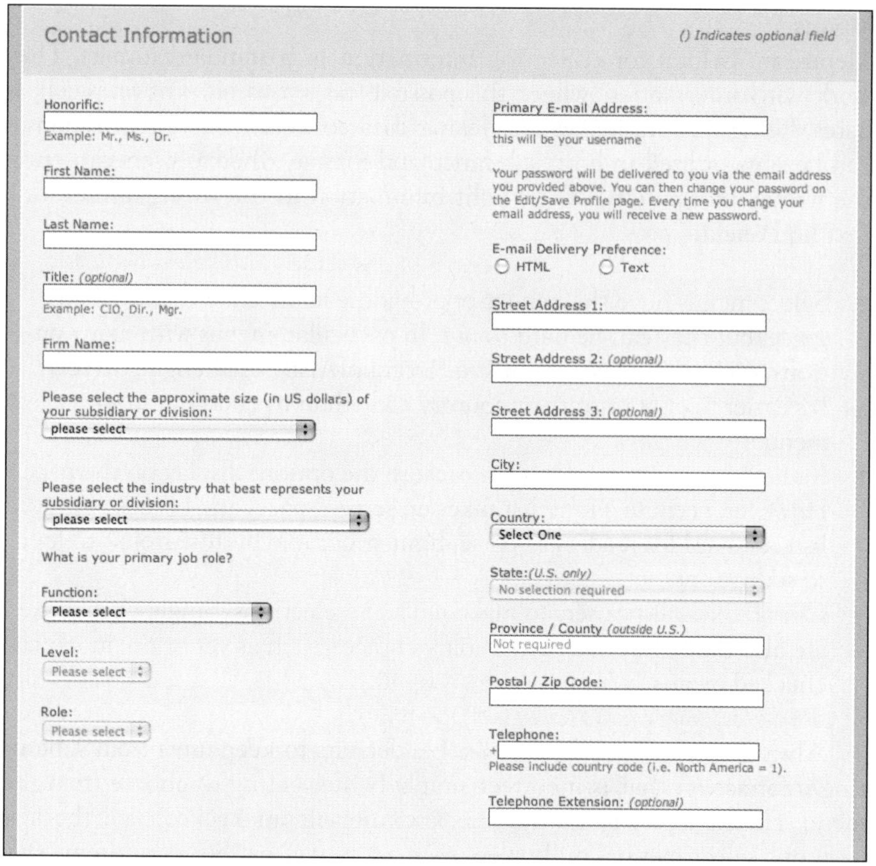

FIGURE 10.5
The Gartner
signup form offers
instructions through
field labels and
example text, and
clearly indicates
which fields are
optional in the field
label. The select
menus offer a null
value as the default
option.

Contact Information   *() Indicates optional field*

Honorific:
[   ]
Example: Mr., Ms., Dr.

First Name:
[   ]

Last Name:
[   ]

Title: *(optional)*
[   ]
Example: CIO, Dir., Mgr.

Firm Name:
[   ]

Please select the approximate size (in US dollars) of
your subsidiary or division:
[please select   ▼]

Please select the industry that best represents your
subsidiary or division:
[please select   ▼]

What is your primary job role?

Function:
[Please select   ▼]

Level:
[Please select ▼]

Role:
[Please select ▼]

Primary E-mail Address:
[   ]
this will be your username

Your password will be delivered to you via the email address
you provided above. You can then change your password on
the Edit/Save Profile page. Every time you change your
email address, you will receive a new password.

E-mail Delivery Preference:
○ HTML   ○ Text

Street Address 1:
[   ]

Street Address 2: *(optional)*
[   ]

Street Address 3: *(optional)*
[   ]

City:
[   ]

Country:
[Select One   ▼]

State:*(U.S. only)*
[No selection required   ▼]

Province / County *(outside U.S.)*
[Not required   ]

Postal / Zip Code:
[   ]

Telephone:
+[   ]
Please include country code (i.e. North America = 1).

Telephone Extension: *(optional)*
[   ]

Keyboard accessibility

Many users work at the computer using a keyboard without a mouse or by using other input methods, such as a switch device or voice commands, which activate keyboard commands. Some devices, such as cell phones, have only a keyboard. Interfaces that require direct manipulation using a pointing device are inaccessible to these users. For universal usability, all actionable elements must be workable using keyboard commands: directional arrows, the tab key, the return or enter key. Push aside your mouse and work through your web applications and forms using the keyboard only to make sure you are not building in obstacles for keyboard users.

GUIDING INTERACTION

A central goal of any design is to be self-explanatory—to tell people how to interact with functional elements. In web forms and applications, the design of the user interface guides users through the functional elements of the page and, using instructions, labels, prompts, and design patterns, explains what is expected and how the page works. The designer's role of benevolent guide is critical to user success—more important in many ways than designing the functional elements themselves. With gentle guidance, users can recover from mishaps better than when they have to puzzle out a confusing interface on their own.

Field labels

Form labels are essential guides, telling us what information to provide in form fields. HTML provides a means to attach form labels to form fields, so there is never any mystery about what information is being requested. The <label for> tag associates a label with its element using the "id" attribute:

```
<label for="departdate">Departing (YY/MM/DD):</label><input
    type="text" id="departdate" />
```

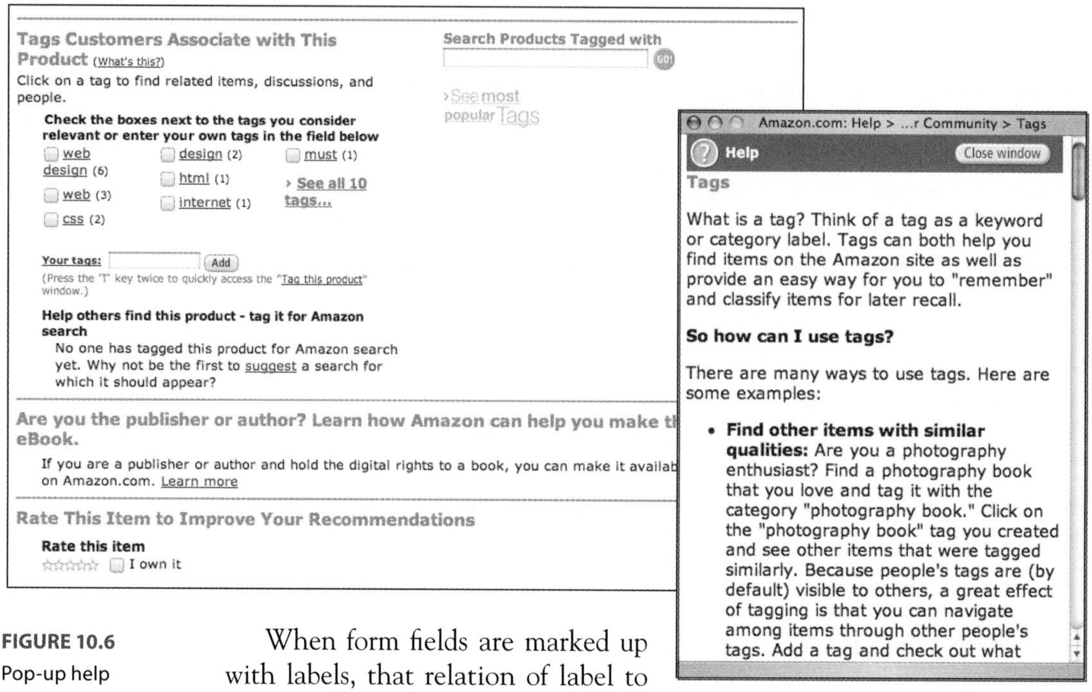

Tags Customers Associate with This Product (What's this?)

Click on a tag to find related items, discussions, and people.

Check the boxes next to the tags you consider relevant or enter your own tags in the field below

- [ ] web design (6)
- [ ] web (3)
- [ ] css (2)
- [ ] design (2)
- [ ] html (1)
- [ ] internet (1)
- [ ] must (1)

› See all 10 tags...

Your tags: [_____] [Add]
(Press the 'T' key twice to quickly access the "Tag this product" window.)

Help others find this product - tag it for Amazon search

No one has tagged this product for Amazon search yet. Why not be the first to suggest a search for which it should appear?

Are you the publisher or author? Learn how Amazon can help you make th eBook.

If you are a publisher or author and hold the digital rights to a book, you can make it availab on Amazon.com. Learn more

Rate This Item to Improve Your Recommendations

Rate this item
☆☆☆☆☆ [ ] I own it

Search Products Tagged with
[_____] [GO!]

› See most popular Tags

Amazon.com: Help > ...r Community > Tags

Help   [Close window]

Tags

What is a tag? Think of a tag as a keyword or category label. Tags can both help you find items on the Amazon site as well as provide an easy way for you to "remember" and classify items for later recall.

So how can I use tags?

There are many ways to use tags. Here are some examples:

- **Find other items with similar qualities:** Are you a photography enthusiast? Find a photography book that you love and tag it with the category "photography book." Click on the "photography book" tag you created and see other items that were tagged similarly. Because people's tags are (by default) visible to others, a great effect of tagging is that you can navigate among items through other people's tags. Add a tag and check out what

FIGURE 10.6

Pop-up help windows allow users to maintain content and focus on a task while they get the help that they need.

When form fields are marked up with labels, that relation of label to field is available to software. For example, users of screen readers can enter a form field and hear its label, along with any instructions contained within the label. Without the label, that information must be gleaned from browsing the surrounding text.

Help and instructions

Contextual help offers answers and guidance within the context of the page. A common implementation of this is the "(What's this?)" concept used by Amazon to explain new and potentially confusing features. Contextual help is often offered in a second, auxiliary window. This method allows users to get help without having to deviate from the task at hand (fig. 10.6).

A web form often needs to provide instructions beyond simple form labels. Some types of information, such as dates and credit card numbers, for example, need to share a standard format. Ideally, the user can enter the information in a variety of formats, and the system will be smart enough to reconfigure the information to the required format. In reality, however, not all our systems are that smart, in which case we need to ask the user to enter

FIGURE 10.7
Always make it clear to users which elements of the form are required and which are optional.

the information in the required format. A date, for example, can be entered in a variety of formats, but your backend system architecture may require a specific format, such as year, month, and day. Provide an example in the field label, for example, "Departing (YY/MM/DD)." Also, be sure to note which fields are required, and use a universally accessible method. Don't rely on color, because not all users can distinguish colors. One convention is to use an asterisk ("*") to denote required fields. To avoid ambiguity, include the word "required" in the form label (fig. 10.7).

Do not use field default text for essential instructions. Default text displays within an input field and can provide help and instructions without

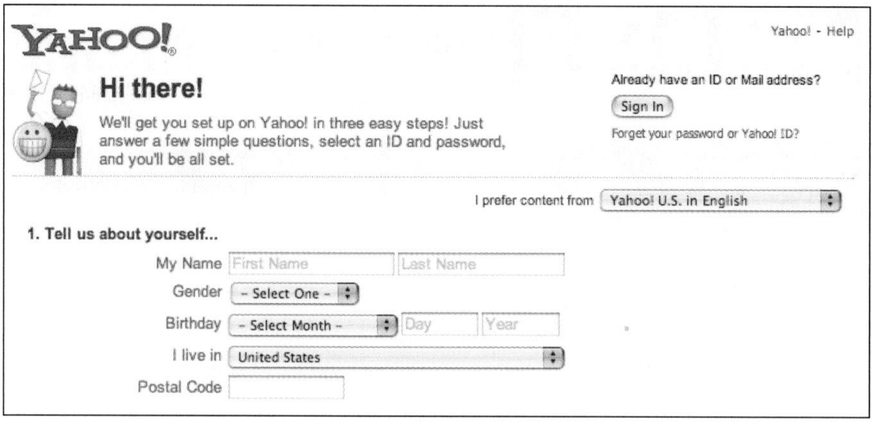

FIGURE 10.8
Default field text
is not the best
option for providing
instructions because
the default text
disappears when the
field is activated.

using precious screen space. However, default text disappears when the user activates the field to enter information, which is just when the instructions are needed most (*Was that year, month, day, or day, month, year?*). The best location for instructions is on the screen, alongside the corresponding form element (fig. 10.8).

RESPONDING TO ERRORS

The best way to handle errors is to keep them from happening, which often means adding functionality to web applications. For example, an email application must address that fact that users may unintentionally delete files. One way to prevent this is to ask users to confirm their choice every time they ask to delete a file, which can quickly turn into nagging. A better approach is to allow users to go ahead and delete but to save all deleted messages in a location where they can be readily retrieved.

Not all errors can be prevented, however, and web application design involves responding to errors in a way that is informative and helps users get back on track.

Providing feedback

Client-side scripting provides effective methods for preventing and responding to errors. These methods are worth exploring, but keep in mind that some users may not enjoy their benefits. Provide other methods—for example, also validate data when a form is submitted—to make sure you respond to all errors.

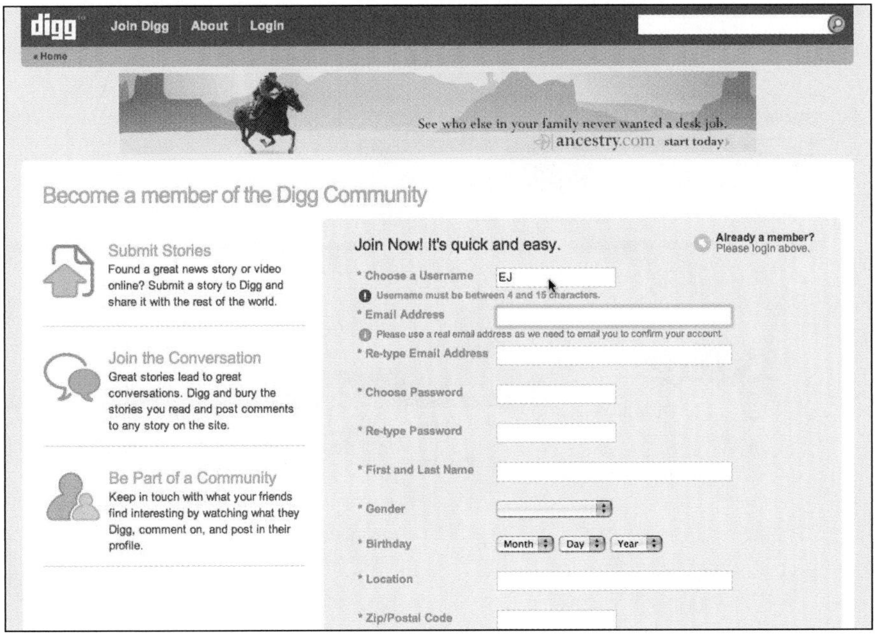

FIGURE 10.9
The best forms
actively monitor user
input and correct
errors as they occur.

Form completion is more usable when users get feedback as they work through a form rather than after the fact, on submission. For example, a form that has required fields will be completed successfully the first time if the fields are monitored and the submit button is enabled only when all the required fields have been completed (fig. 10.9).

When an error occurs, let the user know. This may seem obvious, but many lazy applications simply return the same page when a user submits a form with an error. For example, some login screens simply display the login again when the login fails. Instead, return the page with feedback right at the top of the page, indicating that an error occurred. An alert icon can be helpful in drawing attention to an error message, but be sure to include alternate text with the image (alt="Alert!") so that nonvisual users know that the icon and text comprise an error message. Provide specifics about what happened: "Your password is incorrect" rather than "Your username and password do not match." Provide this explanation next to the field in question—in this case, next to the password field (fig. 10.10).

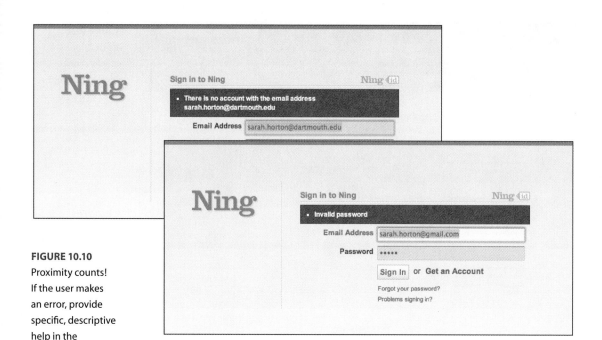

FIGURE 10.10
Proximity counts!
If the user makes
an error, provide
specific, descriptive
help in the
immediate area of
the problem.

Explaining errors

In responding to errors, make sure your error messages are tuned to users' needs. Error messages are too often written in programmer speak, either too detailed and specific or too vague, offering little in the way of explanation and guidance on where to go next ("Operation failed: try again"). Give users just enough information about what happened. They don't need to know that the error number is "404," but they do need to know that the page they requested cannot be found on the server. Provide guidance about what to do in response to the error. If the page cannot be found, offer search and a site map to help the user find it, along with links to the main sections of your site (fig. 10.11).

On the subject of missing pages, use server logs to track failed requests— that is, pages that are being requested but are not on the server. If an important page moves, send users to the new location with a redirect. If a page or section is receiving numerous failed requests, consider adding a link to the section on your custom error page. Be sure to check your links periodically to make sure they are functioning properly.

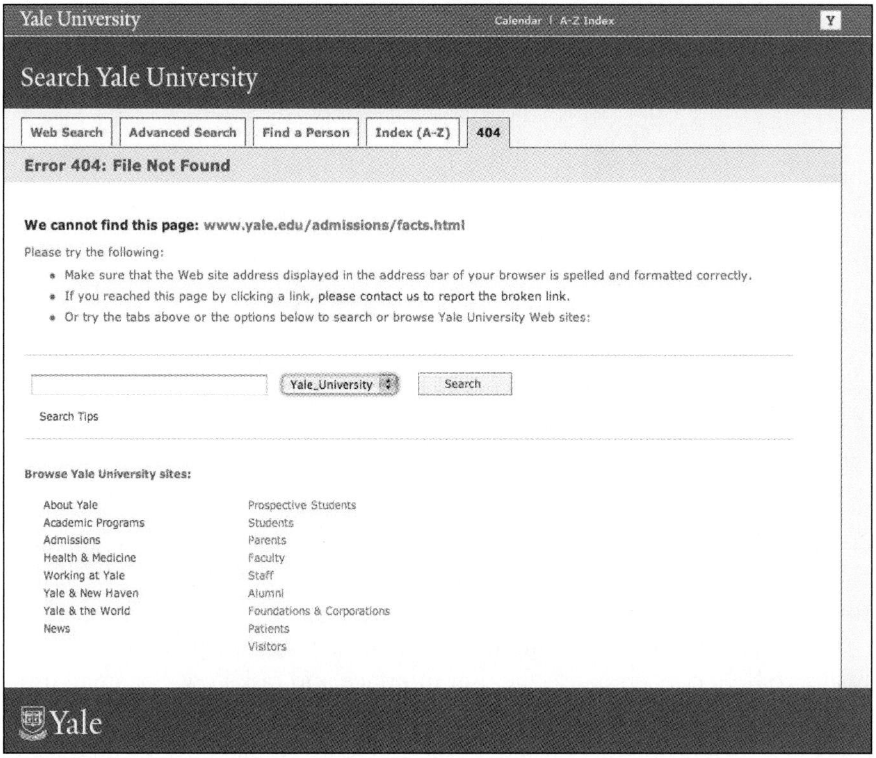

FIGURE 10.11
Typing errors, broken links, and missing pages are inevitable. Don't just point out the "Error 404." Provide as much help as you can to the user in your "error" screens, with search, navigation, and suggestions.

THE DESIGN PROCESS

Web applications ask more of the user than when web browsing and searching; as a result, they demand a rigorous, user-centered design process for successful designs. In particular, web applications benefit from iterative design, with many cycles of modeling, testing, and refinement before the design is finalized.

WIREFRAMES

Wireframes provide low-cost and highly effective support for iterative design. Wireframes are easy to create and, most important, easy to change—far easier to change than a coded web application. The wireframe phase of a web application project should provide a conceptual screen design and task flow and, through testing, evolve into a solid interface and task flow to hand off to programmers.

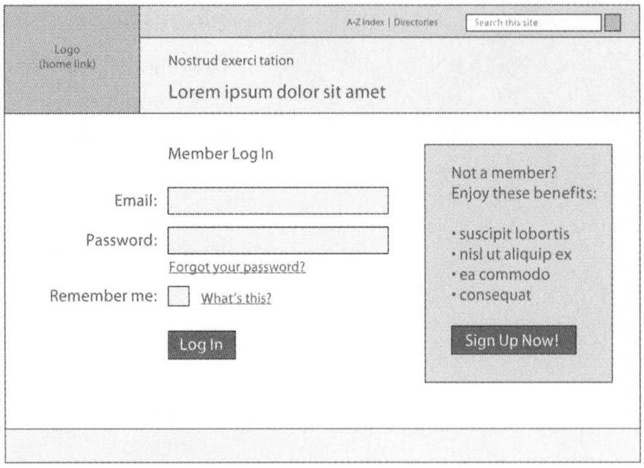

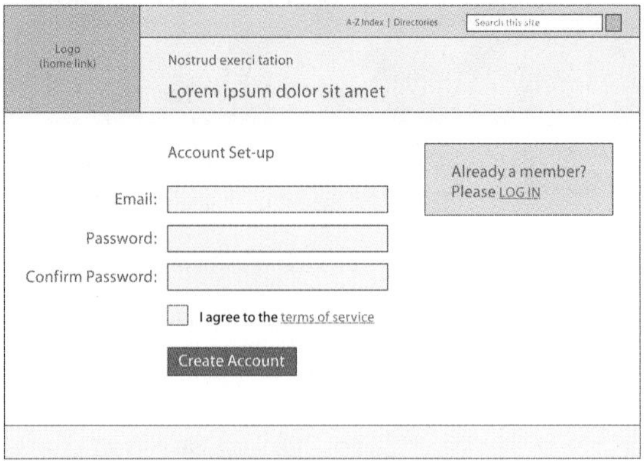

FIGURE 10.12
Wireframe designs
for a web application.

Spend ample time creating and testing wireframes. By virtue of their malleability, they are your best defense against poorly conceived, ineffective designs. Once you move your web application into development, changes to the user interface and task flows become more costly and are therefore less likely to be implemented.

Your initial wireframes might be simple sketches on paper or a whiteboard, to help conceptualize the user interface and task flow. For small projects, these may be sufficient to move a project from concept to development. Most projects, however, will move from sketches to diagrams created using software such as Adobe Illustrator, Visio, or OmniGraffle. These wireframes are best for complex projects with many design cycles because they are easier to modify and easier to share and distribute among the design team. Create a wireframe to represent each screen in your web application (fig. 10.12).

PROTOTYPES

A prototype is a set of wireframes used to simulate a functioning application. The prototype models the purpose of the application, its flow, and its patterns for interaction. With this model, you create an environment for walking a user through a task and identifying points of confusion or difficulty. You can then produce new wireframes to address any problems and test the prototype again (and again and again).

Paper prototypes consist of a set of wireframes, each on its own page (or index card), and can be used to conceptualize the flow of an application. Paper prototypes can be used for usability testing early in the design process,

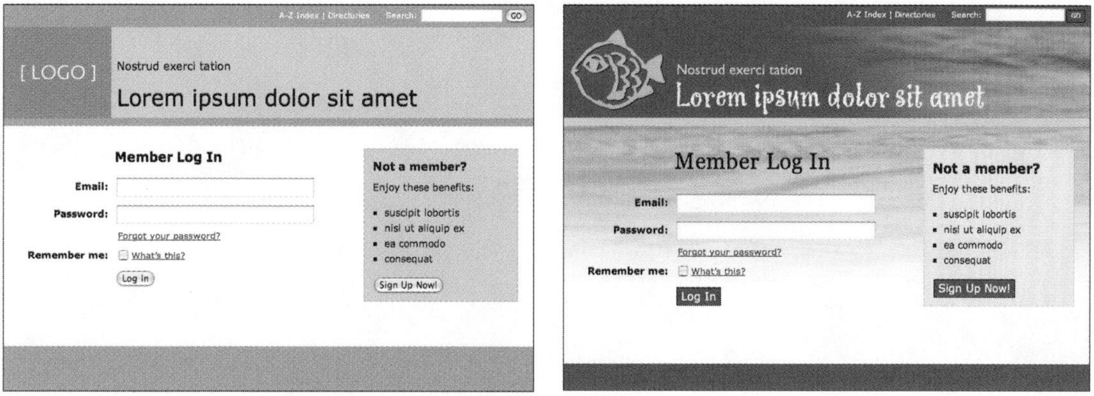

FIGURE 10.13
A functional
wireframe (left) and
the corresponding
finished design
(right).

before any screens are built or code is written. To test a paper prototype, place the first screen of an application—say, the login screen—in front of the user and ask for feedback—what action would you take? Then replace the first screen with the one that would result from the user's action, and continue working through the various stages of the interaction. Ask for feedback all along the way, and spend time after the session collecting additional feedback and suggestions.

A "functional" prototype provides an intermediate step between a rough sketch and a fully designed web application and can provide a framework for moving from the conceptual to the design phase of a project. HTML wireframes form the basis of this high-fidelity prototype, with the essential elements of the application represented on separate web pages (see chapter 3, *Wireframes*). The "functional" features of the application are simulated using basic links among and between pages, allowing users to experience and respond to the flow of the application. The HTML prototype can be refined in response to user feedback and then retested and further refined. Once the functionality and back-end systems are fully developed and thoroughly tested, the visual design and website interface can be "poured" into the wireframe to produce a finished design (fig. 10.13).

Good design is clear thinking made visible.

—Edward Tufte

CHAPTER 11

Graphics

Good diagrams and interesting illustrations are visually arresting and create documents that are distinct and memorable. Illustrations can convey complex quantitative or spatial information quickly, transcending language barriers, and combine with text to complement many styles of information gathering and learning. Personal computing and the rise of the Internet as a publishing medium have liberated information publishing from physical constraints: new tools have increased our ability to create information graphics, and the web provides a full-color multimedia medium unbounded by the costs of publishing and distributing paper. Our limits are now fewer and our tools are more powerful, but we still have to answer the same questions communicators have always asked: What are the most effective uses of graphics, and what's the best way to integrate words and images into an understandable story for the user?

THE ROLE OF WEB GRAPHICS

First and foremost, consistent interface and identity graphics across a collection of web pages define the boundaries of a web "site." Although web designers could build a site without graphics, most users would not readily recognize a collection of bare pages as a cohesive "site," and such a site would seem unpleasantly odd, well outside of design norms and user expectations. Site-defining identity graphics do not need to be elaborate, but they do need to be consistent across the range of pages in a site for the user to establish a sense that your pages are a discrete region—related perhaps to a larger whole if you work in a major enterprise—but in some ways distinct as a "place" (fig. 11.1).

GRAPHICS AS CONTENT

Graphics serve a number of purposes as elements of content—along with and complementary to text content:

FIGURE 11.1
Site graphics are the
most powerful tools
for defining a distinct
sense of "place"
across all the pages
of the site.

- Illustrations: Graphics can show you things, bringing pieces of the world into your document
- Diagrams: Quantitative graphics and process diagrams can explain concepts visually
- Quantitative data: Numeric charts can help explain financial, scientific, or other data
- Analysis and causality: Graphics can help take apart a topic or show what caused it
- Integration: Graphics can combine words, numbers, and images in a comprehensive explanation

THE ORIGINS OF INFORMATION GRAPHICS

Diagrams and information graphics arose in the nineteenth century from mapmaking, early scientific publishing, and industrial-scale engineering and finance. In the hundred years from 1850 to 1950, mechanical reproduction and mass publishing created our current expectation that publishing media will present a mix of words, diagrams, data graphics, and photographs in a seamless multimedia narrative. Although such venerable magazines as *National Geographic* rightly deserve recognition for raising the standard of diagrammatic communications, the credit for creating the genre of elaborate explanatory diagrams and complex story visualizations actually goes to such early twentieth-century popular publishers as Joseph Pulitzer. In an age when publishers had powerful new tools of mass print communication but the "masses" were still largely illiterate, elaborate graphics gave a preliterate public the means to understand the increasingly complex industrial age.

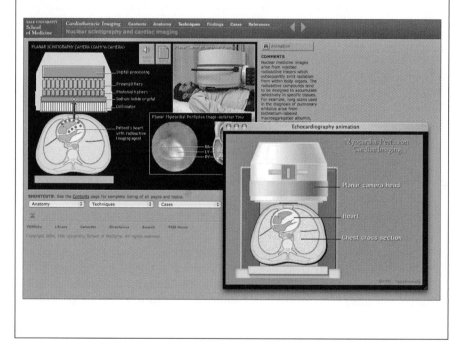

ILLUSTRATIONS

Photographs and illustrations bring the world into your document in a concise and unforgettable way that saves that proverbial "thousand words" of explanation. Why describe something when you can simply—and more memorably—show it? The web is a color medium with an enormous range of display colors, and color graphics on web pages are almost the equal of fine printing on paper, especially when graphics are reproduced at roughly the same size as they might appear in print.

DIAGRAMS AND QUANTITATIVE DATA

The resolution limitations of the computer screen (72–90 pixels per inch) versus print (300+ dots per inch) begin to show when you create complex charts and diagrams for the computer page. Most chart graphics work as well on the screen as on paper, but the label typography in charts and diagrams must be optimized for display on web screens. The visual detail of complex diagrams converted from print uses is often surprisingly good, but always plan to redo the labels or they will likely be illegible.

INTEGRATED VISUAL PRESENTATIONS

Multifaceted information graphics often integrate quantitative charts, three-dimensional illustrations, and extensive captioning in free-form layouts that become visual narratives capable of explaining complex concepts and natural phenomena (fig. 11.2).

GRAPHIC COMMUNICATION ON THE WEB

A chart or diagram is an implicit promise to the user that you'll make a complex world easier to understand. Our advice on graphic communications is the same as on written communications:

- Trust the reader's intelligence. Don't dumb down your material on the supposition that web users are somehow fundamentally different kinds of people from print readers and have no interest in complexity. Regular readers of web sites may once have been distinguishable from other publishing audiences, but now everyone reads the web.
- Respect the medium. The readers are the same as in print media, but the web has a different profile of strengths and weaknesses. Take advan-

Lunge Feeding

Scientists tracking fin whales have created the first detailed model of how they feed. After gliding to depths of more than 600 feet in search of krill, a fin whale will repeatedly accelerate and open its mouth wide, engulfing about 20 pounds of krill and more than its own weight in water as it grinds to a halt.

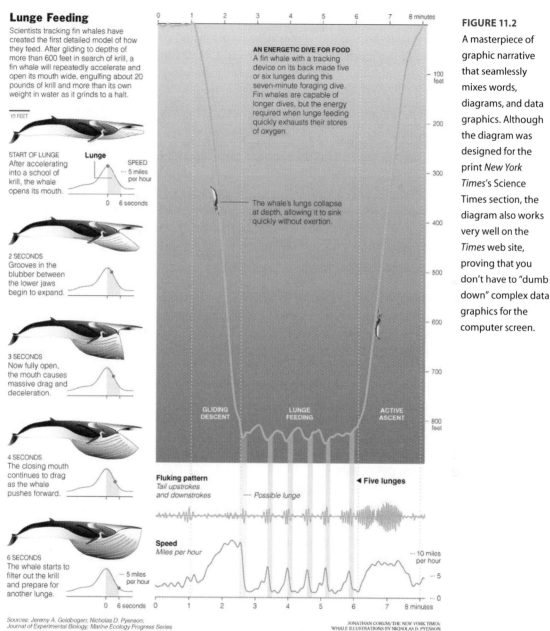

10 FEET

START OF LUNGE
After accelerating into a school of krill, the whale opens its mouth.

Lunge

SPEED
··· 5 miles per hour

0   6 seconds

2 SECONDS
Grooves in the blubber between the lower jaws begin to expand.

3 SECONDS
Now fully open, the mouth causes massive drag and deceleration.

4 SECONDS
The closing mouth continues to drag as the whale pushes forward.

6 SECONDS
The whale starts to filter out the krill and prepare for another lunge.

··· 5 miles per hour

0   6 seconds

AN ENERGETIC DIVE FOR FOOD
A fin whale with a tracking device on its back made five or six lunges during this seven-minute foraging dive. Fin whales are capable of longer dives, but the energy required when lunge feeding quickly exhausts their stores of oxygen.

The whale's lungs collapse at depth, allowing it to sink quickly without exertion.

GLIDING DESCENT   LUNGE FEEDING   ACTIVE ASCENT

0   1   2   3   4   5   6   7   8 minutes
100 feet
200
300
400
500
600
700
800 feet

Fluking pattern
Tail upstrokes and downstrokes
— Possible lunge

◄ Five lunges

Speed
Miles per hour

··· 10 miles per hour
··· 5
··· 0

0   1   2   3   4   5   6   7   8 minutes

Sources: Jeremy A. Goldbogen; Nicholas D. Pyenson; Journal of Experimental Biology; Marine Ecology Progress Series

JONATHAN CORUM/THE NEW YORK TIMES; WHALE ILLUSTRATIONS BY NICHOLAS D. PYENSON

FIGURE 11.2

A masterpiece of graphic narrative that seamlessly mixes words, diagrams, and data graphics. Although the diagram was designed for the print *New York Times*'s Science Times section, the diagram also works very well on the *Times* web site, proving that you don't have to "dumb down" complex data graphics for the computer screen.

tage of the web's enormous capabilities to communicate complex color visuals without the expense of printing and physical distribution.

- Tell the truth as you understand it. Distorting quantitative data isn't just a failure to communicate; it's a betrayal of the reader's trust.
- Don't cherry-pick your data. If you are making a case with visual evidence, don't process and edit your visuals so heavily that the audience has no choice but to accept your point of view. Trust your audience enough to give them the data: let them look at the same higher-resolution images or ambiguous results that you saw and decide the issue for themselves.
- Be bold and substantial. A serious interest in visual communication doesn't require that you use only small, mousy graphics in pale colors. Visual evidence can't become persuasive if no one ever notices it. Just don't ever try to wow an audience with bright graphics to make up for thin content.

CHARACTERISTICS OF WEB GRAPHICS

The parameters that influence the display of web graphics are the user's display monitor and bandwidth capacity. Some web users access the Internet via modem, slow wireless connection, or cell phone network, and others view pages on the small display of a handheld device such as a cell phone or an iPod Touch. This reality imposes limits on the file size and physical dimensions of web graphics. In addition, quality and contrast of display screens vary a good deal, and a poor display could ruin whatever visual effect you had in mind.

COLOR DISPLAYS

Color monitors are based on cathode ray tubes or backlighted flat-screen technologies. Because monitors transmit light, displays use the red-green-blue (RGB) additive color model. The RGB model is called "additive" because a combination of the three pure colors—red, green, and blue—"adds up" to white light.

The vast majority of computer screens in use today can display the full 16.8 million colors that are theoretically possible in a 24-bit or 32-bit display screen. This truly photographic range of colors helps compensate for the relatively low resolution of the computer screen when compared to print, so that color photographs and complex illustrations on the web can convey almost the full range of impact and visual information of comparably sized print images. The computer's operating system organizes the display screen into a grid of x and y coordinates, like a checkerboard. Each little box on the screen is called a "pixel" (short for "picture element"), with 24 or 32 bits of display memory dedicated to each pixel.

SCREEN RESOLUTION

Screen resolution refers to the number of pixels a screen can display within a given area. Screen resolution is usually expressed in pixels per linear inch of screen. Most standard computer displays have resolutions that vary from 72 to 96 pixels per inch (ppi), depending on how the monitor and display card are configured.

Images destined for print can be created at various resolutions, but images for web pages are always limited by the resolution of the computer screen. Thus a square GIF graphic of 72 by 72 pixels will be approximately one inch square on a 72-ppi display monitor. When you are creating graphics for web pages you should always use the 1:1 display ratio (one pixel in the image equals one pixel on the screen), because this is how big the image will display on the web page. Images that are too large should be reduced in size with an image editor such as Adobe Photoshop to display at proper size at a resolution of 72 ppi.

GAMMA

In computer imaging and display screens, gamma refers to the degree of contrast between the midlevel gray values of an image. The technical explanations of gamma are irrelevant here—the visual effect of changing gamma values is easy to see by looking at an image displayed on both Windows and Macintosh monitors (fig. 11.3).

The default gamma settings for Macintosh (1.8 target gamma) and Windows (2.2 target gamma) monitors are quite different, and this can lead to unpleasant surprises when you first see your images displayed on "the other" platform. Mac users will see darker and more contrasting images on Windows displays; Windows users will see images that seem more flat and washed-out when seen on Mac displays. Most web designers opt for a middle-ground solution, lightening images slightly if they work on the Macintosh; darkening images slightly and adding a little contrast if they work in Windows. Web images processed with Adobe Photoshop's "Save for Web" option will au-

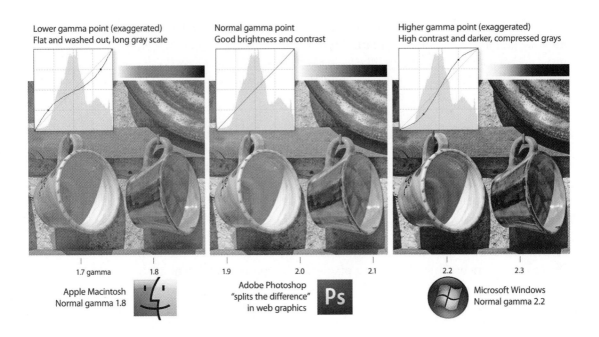

Lower gamma point (exaggerated)
Flat and washed out, long gray scale

Normal gamma point
Good brightness and contrast

Higher gamma point (exaggerated)
High contrast and darker, compressed grays

| 1.7 gamma | 1.8 | 1.9 | 2.0 | 2.1 | 2.2 | 2.3 |

Apple Macintosh
Normal gamma 1.8

Adobe Photoshop
"splits the difference"
in web graphics

Ps

Microsoft Windows
Normal gamma 2.2

FIGURE 11.3
Juggling the differing display gamma settings of the Macintosh and Windows operating systems.

tomatically adjust the gamma to an intermediate level appropriate for both Mac and Windows monitors.

Gamma considerations are particularly important when displaying images with very long gray scales (such as fine black-and-white photography) or images in which the exact color values are critical (such as works of art). If you are working with critical images, use Adobe Photoshop's color proofing options to find the middle ground between too light and too dark images, and view your work on a representative selection of Mac and Windows machines.

GRAPHICS AND BANDWIDTH

Although Internet access speeds have improved greatly in the past years, bandwidth continues to be a consideration for web designs, particularly with regards to graphics and multimedia on mobile web devices. Regardless of connection speed, the more graphics you incorporate, the longer the user will wait to see your page.

GRAPHIC FILE FORMATS

The primary web file formats are GIF (pronounced "jiff"), JPEG ("jay-peg"), and, to a much lesser extent, PNG ("ping") files. All three common web graphic formats are so-called bitmap graphics, made up of a checkerboard grid of thousands of tiny colored square picture elements, or pixels. Bitmap files are the familiar types of files produced by cell phone and digital cameras, and are easily created, edited, resized, and optimized for web use with such widely available tools as Adobe's Photoshop or Elements, Corel's Paint Shop Pro and Painter, and other photo editing programs.

For efficient delivery over the Internet, virtually all web graphics are compressed to keep file sizes as small as possible. Most web sites use both GIF and JPEG images. Choosing between these file types is largely a matter of assessing:

- The nature of the image (is the image a "photographic" collection of smooth tonal transitions or a diagrammatic image with hard edges and lines?)
- The effect of various kinds of file compression on image quality
- The efficiency of a compression technique in producing the smallest file size that looks good

GIF GRAPHICS

The CompuServe Information Service popularized the Graphic Interchange Format (GIF) in the 1980s as an efficient means to transmit images across data

FIGURE 11.4
The LZW compression built into the GIF graphic format is very good at efficiently saving diagrammatic graphics (right) but poor at compressing more complex photographic images (left).

networks. In the early 1990s the original designers of the World Wide Web adopted GIF for its efficiency and widespread familiarity. Many images on the web are in GIF format, and virtually all web browsers that support graphics can display GIF files. GIF files incorporate a "lossless" compression scheme to keep file sizes at a minimum without compromising quality. However, GIF files are 8-bit graphics and thus can only accommodate 256 colors.

GIF FILE COMPRESSION

The GIF file format uses a relatively basic form of file compression (Lempel Zev Welch, or LZW) that squeezes out inefficiencies in data storage without losing data or distorting the image. The LZW compression scheme is best at compressing images with large fields of homogeneous color, such as logos and diagrams. It is much less efficient at compressing complicated "photographic" pictures with many colors and complex textures (fig. 11.4).

DITHERING

Full-color photographs can contain an almost infinite range of color values; GIF images can contain no more than 256 colors. The process of reducing many colors to 256 or fewer is called dithering. With dithering, pixels of two colors are juxtaposed to create the illusion that a third color is present. Dithering a photographic image down to 256 colors produces an unpleasantly grainy image (fig. 11.5). In the past this technique was necessary to create images that would look acceptable on 256-color computer screens, but with today's full-color displays there is seldom any need to dither an

image. If you need a wider range of colors than the GIF format can handle, try using your image editor to save the image in both JPEG and PNG formats (described below), compare the resulting file sizes and image qualities, and pick the best balance of file size and image quality.

IMPROVING GIF COMPRESSION

You can take advantage of the characteristics of LZW compression to improve its efficiency and thereby reduce the size of your GIF graphics. The strategy is to reduce the number of colors in your GIF image to the minimum number necessary and to remove colors that are not required to represent the image. A GIF graphic cannot have more than 256 colors, but it can have fewer. Images with fewer colors will compress more efficiently under LZW compression. For example, when creating GIF graphics in Photoshop, don't save every file automatically with 256 colors. A simple GIF image may look fine at 8, 16, or 32 colors, and the file size savings can be substantial. For maximum efficiency in GIF graphics, use the minimum number of colors that gives you a good result.

INTERLACED GIF

The conventional (noninterlaced) GIF graphic downloads one line of pixels at a time from top to bottom, and browsers display each line of the image as it gradually builds on the screen. In interlaced GIF files the image data is stored in a format that allows browsers that support this feature to build a low-resolution version of the full-sized GIF picture on the screen while the file is downloading. Many people find the "fuzzy-to-sharp" animated effect of interlacing visually appealing, but the most important benefit of interlacing is that it gives the user a preview of the full picture while the picture downloads into the browser.

Interlacing is best for larger GIF images such as illustrations of 200 × 100 pixels or greater. Interlacing is a poor choice for small GIF graphics such as navigation bars, buttons, and icons. These small graphics will load onto the screen much faster if you keep them in conventional (noninterlaced) GIF format. In general, interlacing has no significant effect on the file size of average GIF graphics.

TRANSPARENT GIF

The GIF format allows you to pick colors from the color lookup table of the GIF to be transparent. You can use image-editing software such as Photoshop (and many shareware utility programs) to select colors in a GIF graphic's color palette to become transparent. Usually the color selected for transparency is the background color in the graphic. Unfortunately, the transparent property is not selective; if you make a color transparent, every pixel in the graphic that shares that color will also become transparent, which can cause unexpected results.

Adding transparency to a GIF graphic can produce disappointing results when the image contains anti-aliasing. If you use an image-editing program like Photoshop to create a shape set against a background color, Photoshop will smooth the shape by inserting pixels of intermediate colors along the shape's boundary edges. This smoothing, or anti-aliasing, improves the look of screen images by softening what would otherwise look like jagged edges. The trouble comes when you set the background color to transparent and then use the image on a Web page against a different background color. The anti-aliased pixels in the image will still correspond to the original background color. In the example below, when we change the background color from white to transparent (letting the gray web page background show through), an ugly white halo appears around the graphic (fig. 11.6).

The same problem exists with printing. Most browsers do not print background colors, and a transparent GIF anti-aliased against a colored background will not blend smoothly into the white of the printed page.

Transparent GIF set against a white background

The same graphic shows a white halo when set against a colored background

FIGURE 11.6
The dreaded "white halo" in transparent GIF graphics.

JPEG GRAPHICS

The other graphic file format commonly used on the web to minimize graphics file sizes is the Joint Photographic Experts Group (JPEG) compression scheme. Unlike GIF graphics, JPEG images are full-color images that dedicate at least 24 bits of memory to each pixel, resulting in images that can incorporate 16.8 million colors.

JPEG images are used extensively among photographers, artists, graphic designers, medical imaging specialists, art historians, and other groups for whom image quality and color fidelity is important. A form of JPEG file called "progressive JPEG" gives JPEG graphics the same gradually built display seen in interlaced GIFs. Like interlaced GIFs, progressive JPEG images often take longer to load onto the page than standard JPEGs, but they do offer the user a quicker preview.

JPEG compression uses a sophisticated mathematical technique called a discrete cosine transformation to produce a sliding scale of graphics compression. You can choose the degree of compression you wish to apply to an image in JPEG format, but in doing so you also determine the image's quality. The more you squeeze a picture with JPEG compression, the more you degrade its quality. JPEG can achieve incredible compression ratios, squeezing graphics down to as much as one hundred times smaller than the original file. This is possible because the JPEG algorithm discards "unnecessary" data as it compresses the image, and it is thus called a "lossy" compression technique.

FIGURE 11.7
JPEG compression
comes at a cost: a
big increase in visual
noise and other
compression artifacts
that degrade the
image quality if over-
used.

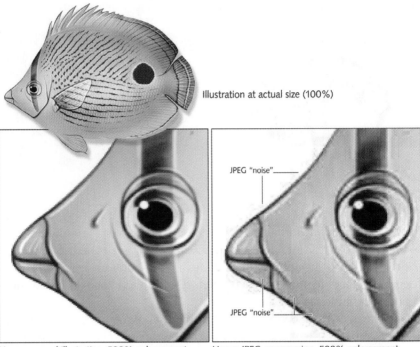

Illustration at actual size (100%)

Uncompressed illustration, 500% enlargement   Heavy JPEG compression, 500% enlargement

Notice in figure 11.7 how increasing the JPEG compression progressively de-grades the details of the image. The checkered pattern and the dark "noise" pixels in the compressed image are classic JPEG compression artifacts. Note the extensive compression noise and distortion present in the image at the right, particularly around the type labels.

Save your original uncompressed images!

Once an image is compressed using JPEG compression, data is lost and you cannot recover it from that image file. Always save an uncompressed original file of your graphics or photographs as backup. If your digital camera pro-duces JPEG images, set aside the "camera original" JPEG files and work with copies when you edit the files for web use. Each time you save or resave an image in JPEG format, the image is compressed further and the artifacts and noise in the image increase.

PNG GRAPHICS

Portable Network Graphic (PNG) is an image format developed by a consortium of graphic software developers as a nonproprietary alternative to the GIF image format. As mentioned above, CompuServe developed the GIF format, and GIF uses the proprietary LZW compression scheme, which was patented by Unisys Corporation, meaning that any graphics tool developer making software that saved in GIF format had to pay a royalty to Unisys and CompuServe. The patent has since expired, and software developers can use the GIF format freely.

PNG graphics were designed specifically for use on web pages, and they offer a range of attractive features, including a full range of color depths, support for sophisticated image transparency, better interlacing, and automatic corrections for display monitor gamma. PNG images can also hold a short text description of the image's content, which allows Internet search engines to search for images based on these embedded text descriptions.

PNG supports full-color images and can be used for photographic images. However, because it uses lossless compression, the resulting file is much larger than with lossy JPEG compression. Like GIF, PNG does best with line art, text, and logos—images that contain large areas of homogenous color with sharp transitions between colors. Images of this type saved in the PNG format look good and have a similar or even smaller file size than when saved as GIFs. However, widespread adoption of the PNG format has been slow. This is due in part to inconsistent support in web browsers. In particular, Internet Explorer does not fully support all the features of PNG graphics. As a result, most images that would be suitable for PNG compression use the GIF format instead, which has the benefit of full and consistent browser support.

IMAGING STRATEGIES

INTERFACE ELEMENTS

Small page navigation graphics, buttons, and graphic design elements such as logos and icons should be handled as noninterlaced GIF or PNG graphics.

PHOTOGRAPHS AS GIFS

When you convert a full-color image to a 256-color GIF file, Photoshop will choose the 256 colors that best fit that particular image. This results

GIF image, **428 Kb** file size
Poor image quality due to dithering

PNG image, **968 Kb** file size
Excellent quality, lossless compression

JPEG image, **280 Kb** (quality = high-8)
Very good quality and file size

FIGURE 11.8
Image format choices, and the resulting file sizes. JPEG would be the overwhelming favorite for this kind of image, with very good image quality and a reasonable file size.

in the optimal GIF image quality. Some images will look almost as good as their full-color originals, but most photographic images look best when compressed using the JPEG file format.

The image compression in the GIF file format is less efficient than JPEG compression. However, the compression advantages of JPEG are not as significant with small to medium-size images (say, up to 200 × 200 pixels). At these sizes GIF images may be only slightly larger than JPEG files. With images larger than 200 × 200, the compression advantages of the JPEG format become more obvious (fig. 11.8).

PHOTOGRAPHS AS JPEGS

JPEG files are inherently full-color (24-bit) images, so preserving the correct colors in the files is not an issue. You should standardize on the JPEG format for any photographic or other full-color or grayscale image suitable for JPEG compression.

DIAGRAMS AND ILLUSTRATIONS AS VECTOR GRAPHICS

Most web page graphics are bitmap images composed of a grid of colored pixels. Complex diagrams or illustrations, however, should be created as vector graphics and then converted to raster formats like GIF or PNG for the web. Vector graphics (also known as PostScript graphics) are composed of mathematical descriptions of lines and shapes. Although these graphics cannot be used directly to illustrate web pages without requiring users to have a special browser plug-in, there are three major reasons for producing complex diagrams in vector graphics programs:

1   Illustrations are easier to draw and modify using vector-based illustration programs such as Adobe Illustrator;
2   Vector graphics can be easily resized without loss of image quality; and
3   Complex artwork created in such vector-based programs is a better investment of your illustration budget, because vector graphics also produce high-resolution images suitable for print.

Vector graphics can be viewed directly in the browser. Adobe's Flash format supports both vector and raster images. Several viewers support Scalable Vector Graphics, a file format developed by the World Wide Web Consortium. However, support for these formats is not native to the browser, requiring users to install plug-ins to view the images. Your best bet is to create illustrations and diagrams using vector-based illustration software and then convert to GIF or PNG for use on the web.

ARCHIVING YOUR WEB SITE GRAPHICS
Always save a copy of your original graphics files, and make it a standard practice to create separate new files each time you make significant changes to an image, such as resizing it or changing the file format. After the close of a project all photos and artwork should be kept and stored at their full original resolution and in a format that does not compromise the image quality of the files through lossy image compression, as in JPEG. We prefer to archive every image generated in a project. Many small 8-bit GIF or JPEG illustrations on the finished web page start out as much larger high-resolution files in Photoshop format. We save all the intermediate pieces, not just the original and final files. This will save you a lot of time later if you change your mind about the best file format for a graphic or need to modify it. If you have archived the full-color Photoshop or camera-original JPEG version of the graphic, you can easily create a new version in a different format. If you save only the final GIFs, you will have lost your full-color version. If you save only the final JPEGs, you will no longer have images without compression ar-

GIF—Diagrams and illustrations with simple color fields and no subtle shading are ideal for the GIF graphics file format

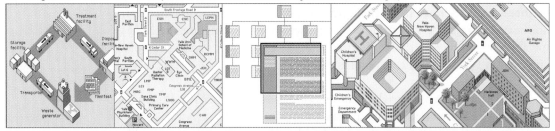

JPEG—Photographic images, complex icons, and realistic illustrations are ideal for the JPEG graphics file format

tifacts, and recompressing an image that already contains JPEG compression noise usually yields poor results.

SUMMARY: FILE FORMATS

All major browsers have native support for GIF and JPEG graphics, as well as the basic features of PNG graphics. Browsers with the Adobe Flash plug-in support Flash vector graphics. In theory, you can use any of these graphic formats for the visual elements of your web pages. In practice, however, most web developers will continue to favor the GIF format for most page design elements, diagrams, and images and will choose the JPEG format for photographs, complex "photographic" illustrations, medical images, and other types of images in which the compression artifacts of the JPEG process do not severely compromise image quality (fig. 11.9).

Advantages of GIF files

- GIF is the most widely supported graphics format on the web
- GIFs of diagrammatic images look better than JPEGs
- GIF supports transparency and interlacing

Advantages of JPEG images
- JPEG achieves huge compression ratios, which mean faster downloads
- JPEG produces excellent results for most photographs and complex images
- JPEG supports full-color (24-bit, true-color) images

IMAGES ON THE SCREEN

The primary challenge in creating images for web pages is the relatively low resolution of the computer screen. But today's computer screens typically display millions of colors, and this wealth of color minimizes the limitations of screen resolution. Complex graphics or color photographs often look surprisingly good on web pages for two reasons:

1   True-color (24- or 32-bit) displays show enough colors to reproduce photographs and complex art accurately, in as many as 16.8 millions colors; and
2   The light transmitted from display monitors shows more dynamic range and color intensity than light reflected from printed pages.

Digital publishing is color publishing: on the web there is no economic penalty for publishing in color. Web pages may in fact be the best current means of distributing color photography—it's a lot cheaper than color printing, and it's more consistent and reliable than all but the most expert (and costly) color printing.

THE SCREEN VERSUS PRINTED COLOR ARTWORK

Relative to printed pages the computer screen is a low-resolution medium. When you look at illustrations, photographs, and other sophisticated imagery, however, the differences in quality between conventional four-color printing and the computer screen are not as great as you might expect.

In terms of resolution, the computer screen is limited to about 72 to 92 dots per inch of resolution. But most four-color magazine printing is done at 150 dpi, or only about four times the resolution of the computer screen (150 dpi is four times the resolution of 75 dpi because resolution is measured over area, 150×150 per square inch) (fig. 11.10).

Four-color printed images are separated into four subtractive printing colors (cyan, magenta, yellow, and black). These four inks combined pro-

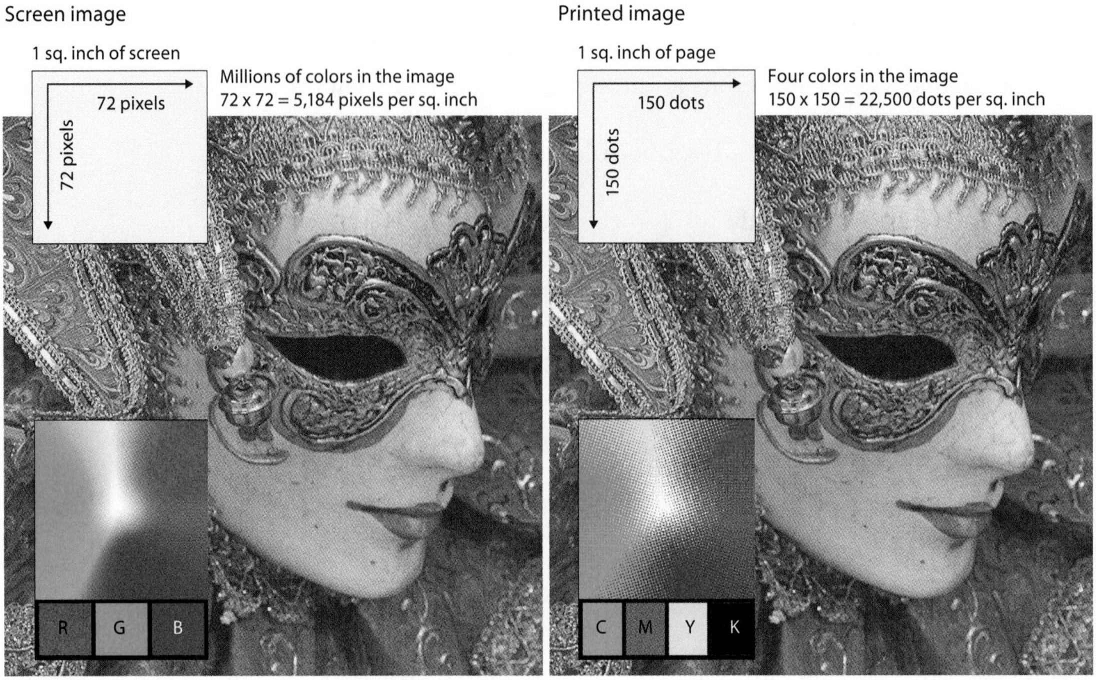

Screen image

1 sq. inch of screen

72 pixels

72 pixels

Millions of colors in the image
72 x 72 = 5,184 pixels per sq. inch

R G B

Printed image

1 sq. inch of page

150 dots

150 dots

Four colors in the image
150 x 150 = 22,500 dots per sq. inch

C M Y K

FIGURE 11.10
Although the computer screen has much less resolution than color printing, the millions of colors available on the computer screen help make the screen image very comparable to print quality.

duce the illusion of a full range of colors on the printed page, but ultimately the typical magazine or textbook image is composed of only four colors. By comparison, today's computer monitors can display millions of colors, producing a richness of color that easily rivals the best quality color printing. Also, computer screens display transilluminated images: the colored light shines out from the screen. Transilluminated images deliver a much greater range of contrast and color intensity than images printed on opaque paper, which depend on reflected light. Finally, computer displays show color images using the additive RGB color system, which can display a much broader and subtler range of colors than conventional four-color printing.

The bottom line: the computer screen is lower in resolution, but because of the other advantages of computer displays, images on web pages can easily rival color images printed on paper at equivalent size.

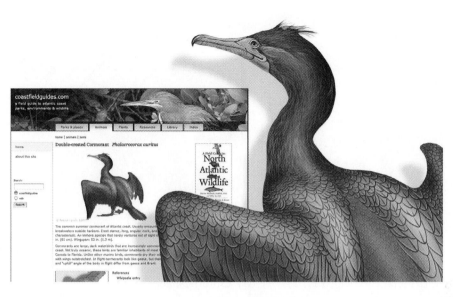

FIGURE 11.11
Get the maximum
flexibility for your
media investments.
Generate your
custom artwork
and photos at print
resolution, then use
Photoshop to bring
them down to web
resolution.

COMPLEX ILLUSTRATIONS OR PHOTOGRAPHS

The graphic above (fig. 11.11) was originally painted at much higher resolution in Adobe Photoshop (1000 × 2000 pixels, 24-bit RGB file). We then reduced a copy to the size above and used Photoshop's "Unsharp Mask" filter (at 60 percent) to restore sharpness. Although this small version of the painting has lost some resolution and color detail, it still shows the detail and subtle nuances represented in the original. We chose the JPEG file format for the graphic because the artwork is relatively large for a web page graphic.

DIAGRAMS FOR THE COMPUTER SCREEN

Basic diagrams also work well on the computer screen if they are carefully designed to match the grid of pixels on the screen. Graphics built with orthogonal lines (straight horizontal or vertical lines) or diagonal lines at 45-degree angles work best for the screen. Complex icons are hard to interpret, and they look mushy and confusing on the screen. Keep icons and navigation graphics as simple as possible. Simple isometric perspective graphics also work well because they depend on straight lines and 45-degree diagonals. Although the restrictions of working within fixed line angles make the technique unsuitable for many diagrammatic graphics, it is possible to build complex illustrations using this technique. The regularity of the isometric

FIGURE 11.12
Embrace the
limitations of GIF.
Carefully designed
graphics aimed at
optimizing the LZW
compression allow
you to put very large
images on the screen
without slowing the
page download too
much.

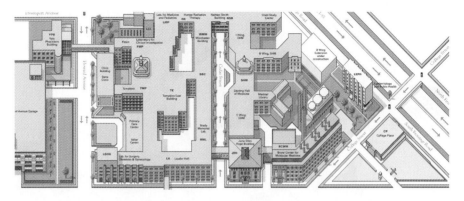

line work and the absence of the complexities of perspective bring order to graphics that might otherwise be too complex for web page presentation. Another benefit of keeping diagrammatic art and maps simple is that graphic simplicity is ideally suited to the LZW encoding compression algorithm used in GIF graphics (fig. 11.12). See GIF Graphics, above.

Be careful about choosing the proper sizes for this type of illustration. Graphics carefully built to match the pixel grid cannot be resized in

FIGURE 11.13
Pixel graphics
carefully designed
for a particular
screen size are not
flexible. If you resize
the graphic, you lose
image quality.

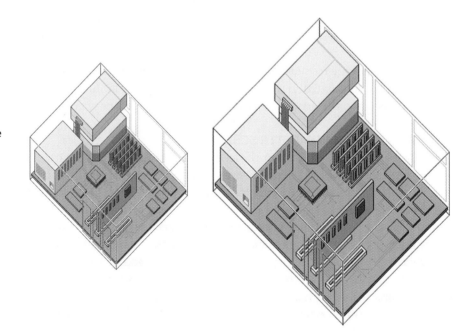

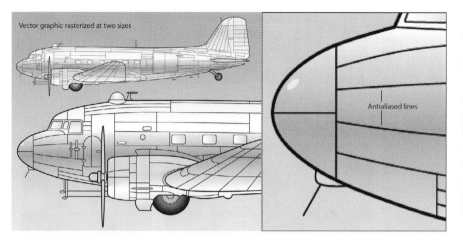

Vector graphic rasterized at two sizes

Antialiased lines

FIGURE 11.14
Vector graphics (like Adobe Illustrator files) are a much better graphics investment. The same diagram can be rendered in many sizes without losing quality, and you can print your Illustrator graphics at high resolution.

Photoshop because Photoshop will anti-alias the lines. They must be re-drawn by hand to larger or smaller sizes to avoid a mushy, fuzzy look that destroys their effectiveness (fig. 11.13).

For diagrams that do not follow the pixel grid and incorporate many curves or angles, use anti-aliasing to smooth the boundaries. At great magnification anti-aliased graphics may have fuzzy boundaries, but at normal magnification anti-aliasing produces smooth, natural-looking line work (fig. 11.14).

GRAPHIC TEXT

Graphic typography in GIF and JPEG graphics is invisible to screen readers. Search engines don't load graphics as they scan and index web pages, but even if they did, a web graphic is merely a collection of differently colored pixels arranged over an area of the screen, and text that is contained in a graphic is simply differently colored pixels. As a result, software cannot make intelligent use of those graphics by, for example, reading the text aloud. Additionally, browsers cannot enlarge graphic text as elegantly as with regular text. The only option is to enlarge the image, which results in pixilated, fuzzy text that is difficult to read. In addition, graphic text cannot be recolored or styled by the user's browser to make reading easier.

In general, the best approach is to use plain HTML text for text, particularly for essential functional elements of the interface, such as navigation links. Graphic text becomes an insurmountable barrier if it means that us-

FIGURE 11.15
Sometimes you
have to splurge on
graphics size, even
if it means a slower
page download.

ers cannot navigate your site. Graphic text is acceptable, however, for page elements whose purpose is purely visual, such as a banner graphic or logo, as long as other page elements contain the equivalent information, such as the page title and the graphic's alternate text.

WORKING WITH LARGE IMAGES

One of the most effective methods for controlling the file size is reducing image dimensions: the fewer pixels in the image, the smaller the file size, and the faster the image loads. But clearly there are times when large images are necessary. An obvious example is the Photo of the Day feature on the National Geographic web site (fig. 11.15).

The image is the featured content on the page and therefore cannot be reduced to a postage-stamp sized thumbnail. However, the interface is designed to display a modest-sized version of the photo, with links to the full-size or wallpaper version. The preview lets users decide whether they are interested enough in the image to take the time to load the large version.

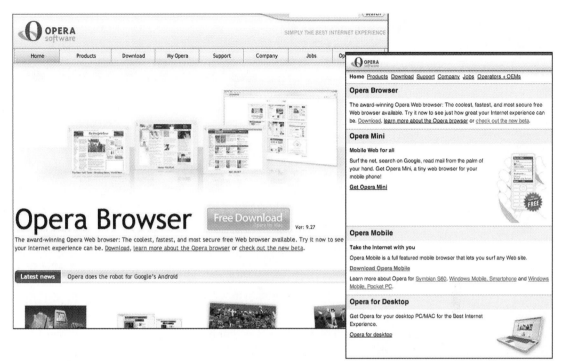

HIDING GRAPHICS

In some contexts, graphics are unnecessary and potentially costly. Graphics on mobile devices do not display well when scaled to fit the small screen, and are time-consuming for users to download. In these contexts, the best approach is to use media style sheets to hide unnecessary graphics, and replace necessary graphics, such as navigation links, with text. Cascading Style Sheets make it easy to show and hide elements in different contexts, but you will need to anticipate what is needed in the document source to adapt to different contexts and make sure everything you need is in the page code (fig. 11.16).

FIGURE 11.16
Opera uses style sheets to display appropriate graphics for screen (left) and mobile (right) contexts.

GRAPHICS MARKUP

HEIGHT AND WIDTH TAGS

All your page graphics source tags (even small button or icon graphics) should include height and width tags. These tags tell the browser how much space to devote to a graphic on a page, and they instruct the browser to lay

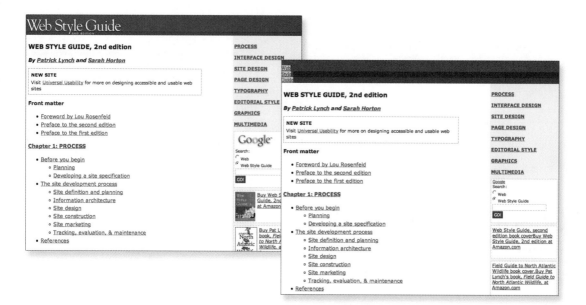

FIGURE 11.17

Page with images on (left) and off (right). Always check to see if your pages make sense even without the images in place.

out your web page even before the graphics files have begun to download. Although this does not speed up downloading (only a faster data connection can do that), it does allow the user to see the page layout more quickly. The text blocks will fill out first and then the graphics files will "pour" into the allotted spaces. This means that the user can start to read your page while the graphics are downloading.

ALT-TEXT

HTML has several built-in fallbacks designed to allow web pages to work under different conditions. One of these is the "alt" attribute of the `<img>` tag. The alt attribute allows you to supply an alternate text description with any images you place on your page. Users who cannot see your images will see or hear the text you supply using the alt attribute:

```
<img src="banner.gif" height="30" width="535" alt="Web Style
    Guide">
```

In the above example, users accessing the *Web Style Guide* site with graphic loading turned off would see the alternate text "Web Style Guide" in place of the banner graphic. Visually impaired users using screen readers to access web pages would hear the phrase "Web Style Guide" read aloud. Google Images would use the alternate text to catalog the image (fig. 11.17).

Writing good alt-text is an epigrammatic art, challenging your ability to describe the content and function of an image in just a few words. The w3c offers this helpful guidance: "A good test to determine if a text equivalent is useful is to imagine reading the document aloud over the telephone. What would you say upon encountering this image to make the page comprehensible to the listener?" Notice that the goal is to make the *page* comprehensible, not the image. The point is not to use words to express the details and nuances of an image but rather to describe the image within the context of the page. This distinction is critical in deciding how much, or how little, to say about an image.

For functional images, such as buttons, logos, and icons, the alt-text should say in words the same thing that the image says visually. A banner graphic that identifies the company should do the same with alt-text: "Acme Carpet Cleaners." Navigation graphics labeling the major site sections should include the same labels in the alt-text: "Home," "Services," "Prices," "Location," "Contact Us." Interface icons should describe the functionality represented by the icon:

```
<img src="up.gif" height="10" width="10" alt="Go to top of page">
```

Informational graphics, such as product photographs, convey information that may be difficult to encapsulate in one short phrase. One approach is to provide alt-text that tells what the image represents: "Acme Carpet Cleaners storefront." If the purpose of the image is to help guide people to the store, the alt-text might read differently: "Acme Carpet Cleaners, the red brick building on the corner of Carpenter and Main." For complex images that convey a good deal of information, the best approach is to use an image caption to describe fully in words the information conveyed in the image.

At times alt-text is not useful—for example, for interface images like custom bullets or icons—and in those cases you should include an empty alt attribute (alt="") in your <img> tag. An empty alt attribute hides the graphic from text-only browsers and assistive technologies like screen readers. If you leave out the alt-text altogether, screen reader users might hear

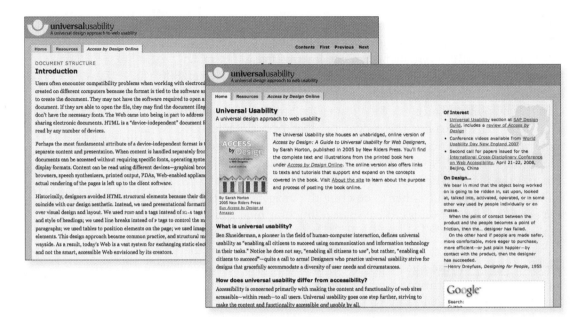

FIGURE 11.18

Graphic impact with minimal GIF or JPEG graphics. Large color fields produced with pure CSS can add great visual impact without adding large images to download.

the words "image, image, image, image" because most software is designed to let users know when there is an undescribed image on the page. If you include an empty alt attribute to indicate that the image is purely decorative, the software will skip the image.

COLORED BACKGROUNDS

Web colors offer a zero-bandwidth means to change the look of your pages without adding graphics. They also allow you to increase the legibility of your pages, tune the background color to complement foreground art, and signal a broad change in context from one part of your site to another. Universalusability.com uses background colors as an easy way to enliven the visual impact of their otherwise low-bandwidth pages (fig. 11.18).

Picking the background color is easy in WYSIWYG (what you see is what you get) web page layout programs such as Adobe Dreamweaver. Unfortunately, picking a color without one of these programs is a procedure only a propeller-head could enjoy. The color is specified in the tag in hexadecimal code, in which the six elements give the red, green, and blue values that blend to make the color. In the tag, the hex code is always preceded by a "#" sign: (#RRGGBB). Because this whole business is now handled visually by

Contrast is the key to legibility, regardless of what color scheme you choose

Never use red and green to differentiate areas—almost 10 percent of males can't tell the difference between them

Loud, fully saturated colors are tiring on the eye—it's like constantly shouting at the reader

The interface should be a quiet, effective frame—the *content* is what should stand out

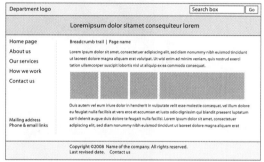

the new generation of WYSIWYG page editors and image editors like Adobe Photoshop, we will not delve further into the arcana of hexadecimal RGB color selection.

Background colors and legibility

A primary factor affecting legibility is the contrast between text and background. Low-contrast type diminishes the reader's ability to differentiate between the color of the background and the text, which in turn makes it difficult to distinguish letterforms. The web is rife with pages whose legibility is marginal because of poorly chosen background and text color combinations. Text that is hard to read is tiring for a fully sighted reader, and certain color combinations make pages unreadable for colorblind users (10 percent of males are partially colorblind) (fig. 11.19).

FIGURE 11.19

Use a light touch when creating background colors. The background should stay in the *background* and should never compete for attention with the actual page content.

COLOR TERMINOLOGY

Color is the response of our eye and brain to various wavelengths of light. Readers with normal vision can sense wavelengths of light from 400 nanometers (near ultraviolet) to 700 nm (near infrared). Computer screens use an additive color system that combines phosphors of red, green, and blue primary colors, which, when added together in various proportions, produce the more than 16 million colors possible on RGB screens. The maximum brightness of all three RGB primaries produces white light on the screen.

The visible light spectrum

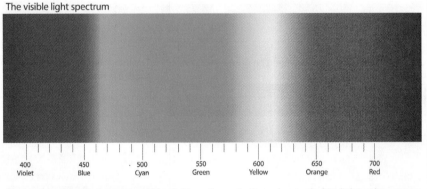

| 400 | 450 | 500 | 550 | 600 | 650 | 700 |
| Violet | Blue | Cyan | Green | Yellow | Orange | Red |

The combination of red, green, and blue light produces all other colors, and white light at the center

In computer graphics you'll see these common terms used to describe the characteristics of colors, known as the HSB system (for hue, saturation, and brightness), commonly used in graphics programs like Adobe Photoshop.

Hue

Hue is the wavelength of color along the spectrum of visible light. An easy way to think about hue is as a color name: "yellow," "orange," or "red."

Hue

Saturation

Brightness

Saturation

Saturation describes the intensity of a color, ranging from pure high-chroma colors to near-gray versions. Saturation is useful to signal depth in displays. In daily life we expect faraway objects to look desaturated and gray because of atmospheric effects (atmospheric perspective) and foreground objects to be more intensely colored. Thus in design we often use desaturated colors for backgrounds and draw attention by using full-saturated colors (sparingly!).

Brightness

The lightness or darkness of a color or how close to either black or white a given color is.

Color harmonies

Four classic formulas for combining colors are used in all forms of design.

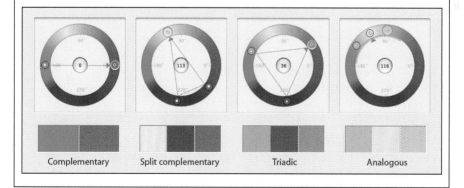

Complementary   Split complementary   Triadic   Analogous

Contrast has the most influence on color differentiation—specifically brightness, or light-dark, contrast. Black text on a white (or slightly tinted) background yields the best overall type contrast and legibility. Black backgrounds are significantly less legible than white backgrounds, even when white type is used for maximum contrast. Colored backgrounds can work as an alternative to white if the colors are kept in muted tones and are low in overall color saturation (pastels, light grays, and light earth tones work best). Complementary colors, such as yellow and blue, produce more contrast than adjacent colors, such as orange and green.

BACKGROUND GRAPHICS

Cascading Style Sheets offer powerful tools for designing layouts that include background graphics. With css, you can set a background graphic and define where it displays, whether it repeats, and, if so, in what direction, whether the image is fixed in place or scrolls with the page, and more. Background graphics can be attached to the entire page or to individual elements, such as the banner, navigation, or content area (fig. 11.20).

Your use of background graphics depends entirely on your goals for your web site. It is foolish to use large or visually complex background textures on any page that is heavily used by busy people looking for work-related information—the long download times, amateurish aesthetics, and poor legibility will simply annoy your users. That said, in the hands of a skilled graphic designer who is creating web pages designed for impact, the option to use background graphics opens up many interesting visual design possibilities.

FIGURE 11.20
Background graphics can add depth, texture, and interest to the page as well as help delineate page elements.

If you want a golden rule that will fit everybody, this is it:
Have nothing in your houses that you do not know to be useful,
or believe to be beautiful.

—William Morris

CHAPTER 12

Multimedia

A powerful aspect of computing technology is the ability to combine text, graphics, sounds, and moving images in meaningful ways. The promise of multimedia has been slow to reach the web, primarily because of bandwidth limitations. But in today's web environment, multimedia is firmly established as a viable means for delivering content. Although there are many methods for delivering web multimedia, we recommend using stable technology that works for the great majority of client machines. You risk losing your audience if they have to jump through hoops to access your content.

CONSIDERATIONS FOR MULTIMEDIA

Multimedia comes with a relatively high price tag, for both preparation and delivery, and should be used purposefully. Too often web authors include visual or moving elements on the page to grab the user's attention. This approach is based on the assumption that web users have short attention spans, which in many cases may be true. However, the solution is not to add gratuitous eye candy to your web presentation, which may, in fact, command too much of your users' attention and detract attention from the main content of your page. Use images, animations, video, and sound only when they are relevant to your message (fig. 12.1).

Bear in mind, too, that there are technical limitations to the delivery of audiovisual content via the web. For example, both long-duration video and video that requires smooth motion or clear details require large amounts of bandwidth to deliver and may tax the capacity of the user's machine. A significant amount of downsampling and compression is required to create a file that is small enough to be delivered via the web. In some cases, these compromises may be too significant to warrant the effort. When you are considering adding multimedia to your pages, make sure the technology can meet the demands of your content.

FIGURE 12.1
Multimedia is
powerful. Use it
carefully to support
the central themes
and content topics of
your site.

And finally, be aware that whenever you put multimedia content on your web pages you potentially shut out users. For example, vision-impaired users cannot see content such as graphics, video, or animations. To access visual content, they need a text alternative that can be spoken by a screen reader. Hearing-impaired users rely on content they can see and need a visual alternative to any audible materials. Initiatives such as Section 508 and the Web Accessibility Initiative have produced guidelines and mandates requiring that nontext content be rendered in an alternate format that is accessible to disabled users, such as text captions for audible content and text descriptions of visual content. When planning for multimedia content, take into account the needs of users with disabilities: both technology-disabled users who are connecting to the Internet via modem, cell phone network, or slow wireless or are using "thin" mobile devices or outdated machines, and physically disabled users for whom multimedia content may be out of reach.

WEB MULTIMEDIA STRATEGIES

Simply because we can stream hours of video out over the web doesn't mean that we should. The value of having the text of *Paradise Lost* online is not in making it available for reading—most people prefer to read the work in print. We digitize texts in order to use the strengths of computing, such as searching and linking, to enhance our understanding of the material. This holds true for multimedia, too: we need to consider how best to use the computer and not simply translate video and audio content to the computer screen. The key to successful web multimedia is to tailor your content for web delivery.

AUDIO

Audio is an extremely efficient way to deliver information. Consider a training video on measuring and weighing chemical compounds. Which track—audio or video—would be the most important in conveying information? In the soundtrack a narrator explains the procedure, and in the video track someone is measuring and weighing compounds. Which track would you remove if necessary? Which could stand alone? The audio track. Consider enhancing your presentation with an audio component. Audio can be captured and optimized fairly easily, and it compresses well.

When recording original audio, take the time to do it right. Low-frequency background noises, such as the hum of a ventilation system, will be inseparable from your audio track; no amount of tweaking will eliminate it. Remember, too, that the downsampling and compression you will have to perform to make your audio web deliverable will emphasize any flaws in your recording.

SLIDE SHOWS

Slide shows are another method for delivering multimedia on the web. In a slide show, you synchronize audio with still images. Through this approach you provide information via audio and add visual emphasis with still images. As an example, to present the training video mentioned above as a slide show, you would use video editing software to synchronize the narration with still images of the weighing and measuring procedure. Still images compress much more efficiently than video, and because slide shows do not require smooth motion, the movie frame rate can be low. This in turn means that you can devote more data to image quality and size.

VIDEO

Video is the most challenging multimedia content to deliver via the web. Part of the reason is sheer size: one second of uncompressed, full-quality video requires approximately 27 megabytes of disk storage space. The amount of scaling and compression required to turn this quantity of data into something that can be used on a network is significant, sometimes rendering the material useless. Whenever possible, tailor your video content for the web.

- Shoot original video. That way you can take steps to create video that will compress efficiently and still look good at low resolution and frame rates.
- Shoot close-ups. Wide shots have too much detail to make sense at low resolution.
- Shoot against a simple monochromatic background whenever possible. This will make small video images easier to understand and will increase the efficiency of compression.
- Use a tripod to minimize camera movement. A camera locked in one position will minimize the differences between frames and greatly improve video compression.
- Avoid zooming and panning. These can make low frame-rate movies confusing to view and interpret and can also cause them to compress poorly.
- When editing your video, favor hard cuts between shots. Use the transitional effects offered by video editing software sparingly. Dissolves, elaborate wipes, or the "Ken Burns" effect of panning across still images will not compress efficiently and may not play smoothly on the web in larger display sizes.
- If you are digitizing material that was originally recorded for video or film, choose your material carefully. Look for clips that contain minimal motion and lack essential but small details. Motion and detail are the most obvious shortcomings of low-resolution video.

ANIMATION

When used solely as an attention-getting device, the value of web animation is questionable. If you place animation alongside primary content, you will simply disrupt your users' concentration and keep them from the objective of your site. If you require users to sit through your Flash intro every time they visit your site, you are effectively turning them away at the door.

That said, there is a place for the purposeful use of animation on the web. A simple animation on a web site's main home page can add the right

amount of visual
interest to invite
users to explore your materials (fig. 12.2).
There, the essential content is typically
a menu of links, so the threat of distraction is less than it would be on an internal content page. Animation is also useful in illustrating concepts or procedures, or changes over time. Always provide accessible controls for starting and stopping the animation.

TEXT ALTERNATES

The best way to ensure that your multimedia materials are accessible is to provide alternate versions designed to accommodate different users. QuickTime reference movies provide a good illustration of the concept of alternates. When creating web video using QuickTime, it is customary to create several versions of a movie, each tuned to a different connection speed through varying levels of quality and compression, and link those versions using a reference movie. Then, when a user requests the movie via a web page, QuickTime sends the version that the user's network connection can best accommodate. This approach supports divisions in technology resources, but alternate views also benefit those who are excluded from multimedia for other reasons. By providing alternate views of your multimedia content, your information becomes accessible to people who cannot appreciate it in its native format.

Text is the most widely accessible content. For low-vision users, text can be magnified. Blind users can have text read by special software or rendered by a Braille reader. For those with technology limitations, text loads quickly

FIGURE 12.2
A well-targeted
animation is
a powerful
inducement to stay
on a site and hear the
message.

FIGURE 12.3
Captions are a way
to supply equivalent
text for the spoken
audio elements of
your site.

and can be viewed on nongraphical browsers. Another strength of text over media content is that it can be read and indexed by search engines and translated into other languages. The best alternate for multimedia content is the written word.

For instance, if you are providing video content on your site, the simplest alternate to include is a text transcript of the audio track for hearing-impaired users. The same text transcript is useful for indexing with search engines and enabling video search. An even better approach would be to use the text as captions synchronized with the video (fig. 12.3). To address the needs of visually impaired users, you could also include a text description of the video track, either as a separate audio track or as text. Or simplify the materials by reducing the video track to a series of still images synchronized with the audio for users with reduced vision or cognitive difficulties.

At a minimum, you can use basic HTML to provide information about multimedia content. For example, you can use the alt attribute to include a short description of the animation in your applet or animated GIF HTML code. Because almost all browsing devices can handle text, if you include this basic descriptive text, users who have their web pages read to them will at least be able to understand the function of the visual content.

PREPARING MULTIMEDIA

Multimedia places high demands on the network, the computer, and the user. The challenge thus lies in preparing files that are small enough to be accessible to the broadest possible audience yet are of sufficient quality to be worth the effort. To balance quality against accessibility you'll need to understand both the characteristics of different media formats and the limitations of delivering media in a networked environment, and you must be ready to compromise.

PROCESSING

In preparing media for web delivery, you should aim for files that can be managed by the average network connection and desktop machine of your target audience. The key measure is the data rate, normally measured in kilobytes per second (kbps), which is the amount of data used to represent one second of movie playback. For users to play your files in real time without hiccups or delays, you need to set a data transmission rate that is slightly lower than the throughput of your users' connections. The way to reduce data rate is through downsampling and compression.

Audio and video generally comes with certain established characteristics. For example, CD-quality audio is sampled at 44.1 kiloHertz (kHz), 16-bit stereo sound, and standard NTSC video is 640 × 480 pixels in dimension and plays at 30 frames per second (fps). However, full resolution audio and video requires enormous amounts of disk storage and is far too large to be used on a network. One way to prepare media for network delivery is to reduce the data by, for example, downsampling the audio material to 11.025 kHz, 8-bit mono sound or reducing the frame rate to 15 fps. This reduces file size as well as quality.

Compression first eliminates redundant data from a file and then removes less important data to shrink file size still further. This process is achieved using algorithms, or "codecs" (short for compressors-decompressors), that handle the media compression and the decompression when it is played. The codecs that are used for web delivery use lossy compression: the process removes data from the original source material. You should never compress material multiple times, because each process will lower the quality.

DELIVERY

The technology of networked media consists of four main components: the server, the network, the client computer, and the web browser and browser plug-ins in use. These components must work in tandem to deliver good web multimedia to the desktop. The bandwidth available between you and the viewer is the least predictable part of the equation. If your media files are served from a high-end media server, you can expect a high level of performance. You can predict playback performance on desktop machines. But unless you are working with a dedicated network, bandwidth will be hugely variable and difficult to predict in all possible conditions across the Internet. Issues regarding bandwidth run from the basic configuration of your connection to the network to the amount of network traffic at any given time.

Given these variables, the parameters for creating and delivering web multimedia are not easily defined. They will vary depending on the scope and content of your project. If you are creating a web site for a corporate intranet, for example, your media can be more technologically demanding than if you send it worldwide over the Internet. The key is to be well acquainted with the configuration of your client base, study your web server logs so that you know what your typical user's connection speed is, and prepare your multimedia content accordingly.

Streaming

Streaming technology sends data to the desktop continuously but does not download the entire file. In the optimal scenario, the content is stored on a streaming media server, which maintains a constant conversation with the client to determine how much data the user can support. Based on this information, the server adjusts the data stream accordingly and sends just enough data to the client.

Streaming offers many benefits, the first of which is random access. Streaming technology permits movies to be viewed at any point in the video stream. If your user is accessing an hour's worth of video and wishes to view only the last five minutes, he or she can use the controls to move forward to the desired starting point. Another benefit is a lower storage demand on the client machine. Streaming media plays directly to the display; it is not stored in memory or on the user's hard drive.

The strengths of streaming are also its shortcomings. To play a movie in real time the player software needs to keep up with the incoming data sent from the server. As a result, if there are glitches in the network or if the client machine cannot handle playback, the media data may simply be lost. Streaming playback requires significant processing power, so playback may be suboptimal if the viewer's computer processor has to drop video frames to keep pace with the incoming stream.

Downloading

Downloadable media is stored on the client machine in memory or on the viewer's hard drive. Most downloadable media is progressive, which means that the information necessary for playback is stored at the beginning of the file. Progressive download allows the viewer to start watching the video before the entire file has downloaded. Downloadable media is sent to the client using the same HTTP protocol as a web page, so no special server is required. As long as the download speed stays above the data rate of the movie, playback will be uninterrupted.

The quality of downloadable media is generally higher than that of streaming media. Because the data rate is not forced to remain low enough to play the material in real time, more data can be devoted to image quality and motion. Downloadable media also has integrity: all the data in the original movie is contained in the downloaded version.

The main drawback of downloadable media is the storage demand it places on the viewer's computer. Even videos of short duration require many megabytes of temporary storage, which may be a problem if the viewer has a nearly full hard disk. The other problem is that downloadable media does not allow random access. If you want to view only the last few minutes of a long clip you must wait for the entire clip to download. One solution to both problems is to split longer media segments into smaller chunks. This reduces the demands on the client machine and allows users more direct access to the material they want. Splitting longer video segments is much like chunking text content: web users are not expecting to sit through long video programs like television viewers. Most web videos are short, to-the-point segments on a tightly focused topic.

DESIGN AND MULTIMEDIA

The combination of low-bandwidth considerations and limited interface options creates interesting design challenges for incorporating multimedia elements into web sites. The key guidelines for designing for multimedia are to inform users when they are entering a high-bandwidth area and give them the tools they need to control their experience.

INFORM YOUR USERS

One aspect of the web is that you don't always know where you're going or what you'll find there. While the element of surprise is certainly exciting, it can also be annoying, particularly when a long wait is involved. Most frustrating is when you finally receive the requested page only to find that is not what you expected or that it contains materials in a format you are not set up to view. With content that is as technologically demanding as multimedia, it is especially important to give users enough information to make an informed decision before they click, so that they know what to expect and are prepared to receive your materials.

High-demand content such as large multimedia files should not be part of your basic page design (unless, of course, your site's reason for being is delivering high-demand multimedia files). These materials should appear on secondary pages that are described and can be accessed from the main pages of your site. Make the menu page a plain HTML page that loads quickly and does not require special software. Include descriptive information about the materials along with previews, such as still shots from the video. Include the running time for media clips so viewers know what to expect, and include the file size for media that downloads. In addition, fully explain any special software requirements for accessing the materials and provide a download link to any required browser plug-ins. Your users should have a clear idea of your materials before they begin to download. With a menu interface, users can confirm that their systems are properly configured and that they have enough bandwidth, time, and patience to load the materials (fig. 12.4).

PROVIDE CONTROLS

Be sure to give users status information and controls when you are presenting multimedia materials. If you don't include controls, users will hit your page with no way to control their viewing environment. For example, if a visitor is looking at your page at a public computer or in an open office situation

and you have looping birdcalls as a background sound without any control options, the visitor will experience an unsettling (and potentially embarrassing) moment when he or she cannot control interaction with your site. Many users in this situation will simply close the browser window to make the sound stop, which means that they never get to see the page content.

The QuickTime controller bar is an extremely effective interface element that provides both controls and status information. It allows users both to adjust the volume control and to play, stop, and scrub through a movie, and it provides information about the movie's download status.

When designing a media interface, let your viewers choose when and how to listen to your media content. Always include user controls, such as a media controller bar, and make sure that users have a way to turn playback off. Avoid options like auto play or looping that take control away from the user. With auto play, for example, media files begin playing when a web page is loaded. If the page has other elements, such as descriptive text, the user who wants just the text will find the video distracting. Design your media interface so that files play only when the user explicitly elects to initiate playback.

FIGURE 12.4
Give users information about your multimedia content that allows them to judge whether they have the time and technology to enjoy your programming.

SUPPORT KEYBOARD INTERACTION

Not all users can or choose to use a point-and-click device, such as a mouse, to manage interaction, and not all devices offer pointing controls. For example, non-visual users cannot see the screen to point and click, and many portable devices only provide keyboard controls. To design for universal access and usability, make sure your media controllers are operable using the keyboard.

Keyboard interaction is a two-step process of selecting and then activating a control. The tab or arrow keys move the cursor focus from element to element, and the enter key activates the element and triggers its associated function. For basic media playback, make sure users can select and activate the play and pause buttons, and select the volume control and adjust the volume using the arrow keys. For more complex interfaces, make sure all interactive elements, such as menus and buttons, can be selected and activated from the keyboard.

OFFER CHOICE

Although there are certainly favorites, there are no established standards for multimedia formats. There is no single answer to the question: "Which format should I use to ensure that everyone can access my multimedia content?" Instead, the best approach is to offer a range of choices and allow the user to select the one that best suits his or her environment and preferred access method.

For instance, audio and video can be embedded into web pages, presented as a download link, or made available as a podcast. The embedded version has the benefit of being presented within the context of the web site, which means the video can have accompanying text and images that support the video materials. In contrast, downloadable media can be viewed on different devices, including television and portable devices. Podcasts allow users to download media for offline access, with the added benefit of subscription, which results in new media files downloading automatically. Each of these scenarios has its benefits and drawbacks depending on the user context. Providing all options does not require much additional effort on the part of the designer and allows users to choose the option that suits them best (fig. 12.5).

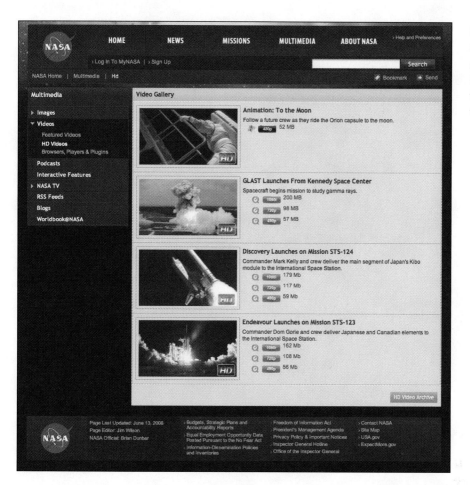

FIGURE 12.5
An excellent presentation of bandwidth and format choices for video content.

Abbreviations

Ajax	Asynchronous JavaScript and XML
ARIA	Accessible Rich Internet Applications
ASP	active server page
CGI	common gateway interface
CMS	content management system
CSS	Cascading Style Sheets
dpi	dots per inch
DSL	digital subscriber line
fps	frames per second
GIF	Graphic Interchange Format
GUI	graphic user interface
HSB	hue, saturation, brightness
HTML	HyperText Markup Language
http	HyperText Transfer Protocol
IE	Internet Explorer
ISDN	integrated services digital network
IIS	Internet information server
ISP	Internet service provider
IT	information technology
JPEG	Joint Photographic Experts Group
JSP	Java server page
kbps	kilobytes per second
LZW	Lempel Zev Welch
MOSS	Microsoft Office SharePoint Server
NTSC	National Television System Committee
PDA	personal digital assistant
PDF	portable document format
PHP	Hypertext preprocessor
PNG	Portable Network Graphic
ppi	pixels per inch

QA	quality assurance
RFP	request for proposal
RGB	red-green-blue
ROI	return on investment
RSS	Really Simple Syndication
SEO	search engine optimization
SMIL	Synchronized Multimedia Integration Language
SVG	scalable vector graphics
UCD	user-centered design
URL	uniform resource locator
W3C	World Wide Web Consortium
WAI	Web Accessibility Initiative
WYSIWYG	what you see is what you get
XHTML	Extensible HyperText Markup Language
XML	Extensible Markup Language
XSLT	Extensible Style Language Transformation

References

CASCADING STYLE SHEETS

Budd, A., C. Moll, and S. Collison. 2006. CSS *Mastery: Advanced Web Standards Solutions*. Berkeley, CA: Apress.

Cederholm, D. 2004. *Web Standards Solutions: The Markup and Style Handbook*. Berkeley, CA: Apress.

———. 2006. *Bulletproof Web Design: Improving Flexibility and Protecting against Worst-Case Scenarios with* XHTML *and* CSS. Berkeley, CA: New Riders.

Meyer, E. 2002. *Eric Meyer on* CSS: *Mastering the Language of Web Design*. Berkeley, CA: New Riders.

———. 2004. *Cascading Style Sheets: The Definitive Guide*. 2nd ed. Sebastopol, CA: O'Reilly.

———. 2004. *More Eric Meyer on* CSS. Berkeley, CA: New Riders.

EDITORIAL STYLE

Adam, P., S. Quinn, and R. Edmonds. 2007. *Eyetracking the News*. St. Petersburg, FL: Poynter Institute.

Franklin Covey. 2000. *Franklin Covey Style Guide for Business and Technical Communication*. Salt Lake City, UT: Franklin Covey.

Goldstein, N., ed. 2007. *The Associated Press Stylebook and Briefing on Media Law*. Cambridge, MA: Perseus.

Harrower, T. 2007. *The Newspaper Designer's Handbook*. 6th ed. Boston: McGraw-Hill.

Krug, S. 2006. *Don't Make Me Think: A Common Sense Approach to Web Usability*. 2nd ed. Berkeley, CA: New Riders.

McGovern, G., R. Norton, and C. O'Dowd. 2002. *The Web Content Style Guide*. New York: Pearson Education.

Microsoft Corporation. 2003. *The Microsoft Manual of Style for Technical Publications*. 3rd ed. Redmond, WA: Microsoft.

Orwell, G. 1946. "Politics and the English Language." *Horizon* (London), April. Reprinted in *The Collected Essays, Journalism, and Letters of George Orwell*. Ed. Sonia Orwell and Ian Angus. New York: Harcourt, Brace, 1968. www.mtholyoke.edu/acad/intrel/orwell46.htm.

Outing, S., and L. Ruel. 2004. *Eyetrack III*. St. Petersburg, FL: Poynter Institute. poynterextra.org/eyetrack2004.

Sabin, W. 2005. *The Gregg Reference Manual*. 10th ed. New York: McGraw-Hill.

Siegal, A., and W. Connolly. 2002. *The New York Times Manual of Style and Usage: The Official Style Guide Used by the Writers and Editors of the World's Most Authoritative Newspaper*. New York: Three Rivers.

Strunk, W., Jr., and E. B. White. 2000. *The Elements of Style*. 4th ed. New York: Macmillan.

Thurow, S. 2008. *Search Engine Visibility*. 2nd ed. Berkeley, CA: New Riders.

University of Chicago Press. 2003. *The Chicago Manual of Style: The Essential Guide for Writers, Editors, and Publishers*. 15th ed. Chicago: University of Chicago Press.

Walker, J., and T. Taylor. 2006. *The Columbia Guide to Online Style*. 2nd ed. New York: Columbia University Press.

Zinsser, W. 2006. *On Writing Well, Thirtieth Anniversary Edition: The Classic Guide to Writing Nonfiction*. New York: Collins.

GRAPHIC DESIGN

Arnheim, R. 2004. *Art and Visual Perception: A Psychology of the Creative Eye*. Berkeley: University of California Press.

Bhaskaran, L. 2004. *Size Matters: Effective Graphic Design for Large Amounts of Information*. Mies, Switzerland: RotoVision.

Bringhurst, R. 2004. *The Elements of Typographic Style*. 3rd ed. Vancouver, BC: Hartley and Marks.

Carter, R., B. Day, and P. Meggs. 2006. *Typographic Design: Form and Communication*. 4th ed. New York: Van Nostrand Reinhold.

Design Observer. www.designobserver.com.

Harrower, T. 2007. *The Newspaper Designer's Handbook*. 6th ed. Boston: McGraw-Hill.

Lidwell, W., K. Holden, and J. Butler. 2003. *Universal Principles of Design*. Gloucester, MA: Rockport.

Lupton, E. 2004. *Thinking with Type: A Critical Guide for Designers, Writers, Editors, and Students*. New York: Princeton Architectural Press.

McCloud, S. 1993. *Understanding Comics: The Invisible Art*. New York: HarperCollins.

Müller-Brockmann, J. 1996. *Grid Systems in Graphic Design*. 4th ed. Basel, Switzerland: Niggli.

Samara, T. 2005. *Making and Breaking the Grid: A Graphic Design Layout Workshop*. Beverly, MA: Rockport.

Spiekermann, E., and E. M. Ginger. 2002. *Stop Stealing Sheep and Find Out How Type Works*. 2nd ed. Mountain View, CA: Adobe.

Tinker, M. 1963. *Legibility of Print*. Ames: Iowa State University Press.

Tufte, E. 1989. *Visual Design of the User Interface*. Armonk, NY: IBM.

———. 1990. *Envisioning Information*. Cheshire, CT: Graphics Press.

———. 1997. *Visual Explanations*. Cheshire, CT: Graphics Press.

———. 2001. *The Visual Display of Quantitative Information*. 2nd ed. Cheshire, CT: Graphics Press.

———. 2006. *Beautiful Evidence*. Cheshire, CT: Graphics Press.

Wheildon, C. 1995. *Type and Layout: How Typography and Design Can Get Your Message Across—Or Get in the Way*. Berkeley, CA: Strathmoor.

Williams, R. 2007. *The Non-Designer's Design and Type Books*. Deluxe ed. Berkeley, CA: Peachpit.

Wilson, A. 1993. *The Design of Books*. San Francisco: Chronicle Books.

HTML

Cohen, J. 2003. *The Unusually Useful Web Book*. Berkeley, CA: New Riders.

MacDonald, M. 2006. *Creating Web Sites: The Missing Manual*. Sebastopol, CA: Pogue Press/O'Reilly.

Musciano, C., and B. Kennedy. 2006. HTML *and* XHTML: *The Definitive Guide*. 6th ed. Sebastopol, CA: O'Reilly.

Niederst, J. 2006. *Web Design in a Nutshell*. 3rd ed. Sebastopol, CA: O'Reilly.

Worldwide Web Consortium (W3C). www.w3.org.

Zeldman, J. 2007. *Designing with Web Standards*. 2nd ed. Berkeley, CA: New Riders.

INFORMATION ARCHITECTURE

Adam, P., S. Quinn, and R. Edmonds. 2007. *Eyetracking the News*. St. Petersburg, FL: Poynter Institute.

Anderson, C. 2006. *The Long Tail: Why the Future of Business Is Selling Less of More*. New York: Hyperion.

Arnheim, R. 2004. *Art and Visual Perception: A Psychology of the Creative Eye*. Berkeley: University of California Press.

Battelle, J. 2005. *The Search: How Google and Its Rivals Rewrote the Rules of Business and Transformed Our Culture*. New York: Penguin-Portfolio.

Bernard, M., and A. Sheshadri. 2004. *Preliminary Examination of Global Expectations of Users' Mental Models for E-Commerce Web Layouts*. psychology.wichita.edu/surl/usabilitynews/62/web_object_international.htm.

Brown, D. 2007. *Communicating Design: Developing Web Site Documentation for Design and Planning*. Berkeley, CA: New Riders.

Brown, J., and P. Duguid. 2000. *The Social Life of Information*. Boston: Harvard Business School Press.

Garrett, J. 2002. *A Visual Vocabulary for Describing Information Architecture and Interaction Design*. www.jjg.net/ia/visvocab.

———. 2003. *The Elements of the User Experience: User-Centered Design for the Web*. Berkeley, CA: New Riders.

Google. 2008. *Webmaster Tools: XML Sitemap Format*. www.google.com/webmasters/tools/docs/en/protocol.html.

Kahn, P., and K. Lenk. 2001. *Mapping Web Sites*. Mies, Switzerland: RotoVision.

Kalbach, J. 2007. *Designing Web Navigation*. Sebastopol, CA: O'Reilly.

Louisrosenfeld.com. www.louisrosenfeld.com/home.

Morville, P. 2005. *Ambient Findability: What We Find Changes Who We Become*. Sebastopol, CA: O'Reilly.

———. Semantic Studios. semanticstudios.com.

Nielsen, J. 1997. *Zipf Curves and Website Popularity*. www.useit.com/alertbox/zipf.html.

Nielsen, J., and H. Loranger. 2006. *Prioritizing Web Usability*. Berkeley, CA: New Riders.

Nielsen, J., and K. Pernice. 2008. *Eyetracking Web Usability*. Berkeley, CA: New Riders.

Rosenfeld, L., and P. Morville. 2002. *Information Architecture for the World Wide Web*. 2nd ed. Sebastopol, CA: O'Reilly.

Shaikh, A., and K. Lenz. 2006. *Where's the Search? Re-Examining User Expectations of Web Objects*. psychology.wichita.edu/surl/usabilitynews/81/webobjects.htm.

Van Dijck, P. 2003. *Information Architecture for Designers: Structuring Websites for Business Success*. Mies, Switzerland: RotoVision.

Wodtke, C. 2003. *Information Architecture: Blueprints for the Web*. Berkeley, CA: New Riders.

INTERFACE DESIGN

Bernard, M., and A. Sheshadri. 2004. *Preliminary Examination of Global Expectations of Users' Mental Models for E-Commerce Web Layouts*. psychology.wichita.edu/surl/usabilitynews/62/web_object_international.htm.

Courage, C., and K. Baxter. 2005. *Understanding Your Users: A Practical Guide to User Requirements, Methods, Tools, and Techniques*. New York: Morgan Kaufmann.

Garrett, J. 2003. *The Elements of the User Experience: User-Centered Design for the Web*. Berkeley, CA: New Riders.

Hoekman, R., Jr. 2007. *Designing the Obvious: A Common Sense Approach to Web Application Design*. Berkeley, CA: New Riders.

Horton, S. 2006. *Access by Design: A Guide to Universal Usability for Web Designers*. Berkeley, CA: New Riders. www.universalusability.com.

Issacs, E., and A. Walendowski. 2002. *Designing from Both Sides of the Screen: How Designers and Engineers Can Collaborate to Build Cooperative Technology*. Berkeley, CA: New Riders.

Kalbach, J. 2007. *Designing Web Navigation*. Sebastopol, CA: O'Reilly.

Koyani, S., R. Bailey, and J. Nall. *Research-based Web Design and Usability Guidelines*. 2006. Washington, DC: Department of Health and Human Services, General Services Administration.

Krug, S. 2006. *Don't Make Me Think: A Common Sense Approach to Web Usability*. 2nd ed. Berkeley, CA: New Riders.

Lazar, J. 2006. *Web Usability: A User-Centered Design Approach*. Boston: Addison-Wesley.

Linderman, M., and J. Fried. 2004. *Defensive Design for the Web: How to Improve Error Messages, Help, Forms, and Other Crisis Points*. Berkeley, CA: New Riders.

McCloud, S. 1993. *Understanding Comics: The Invisible Art*. New York: HarperCollins.

Mullet, K., and D. Sano. 1995. *Designing Visual Interfaces: Communication Oriented Techniques*. Englewood Cliffs, NJ: SunSoft.

Nielsen, J. 2000. *Designing Web Usability*. Berkeley, CA: New Riders.

Nielsen, J., and H. Loranger. 2006. *Prioritizing Web Usability*. Berkeley, CA: New Riders.

Nielsen, J., and M. Tahir. 2002. *Homepage Usability: Fifty Websites Deconstructed*. Berkeley, CA: New Riders.

Norman, D. 2002. *The Design of Everyday Things*. New York: Basic Books.

Pruitt, J., and T. Adlin. 2006. *The Persona Lifecycle: Keeping People in Mind throughout Product Design*. New York: Morgan Kaufmann.

Schwartz, B. 2003. *The Paradox of Choice: Why More Is Less*. New York: Ecco.

Shafer, D. 2007. *Designing for Interaction: Creating Smart Applications and Clever Devices*. Berkeley, CA: New Riders.

Shaikh, A., and K. Lenz. 2006. *Where's the Search? Re-Examining User Expectations of Web Objects*. psychology.wichita.edu/surl/usabilitynews/81/webobjects.htm.

Sharp, H., Y. Rogers, and J. Preece. 2007. *Interaction Design: Beyond Human-Computer Interaction*. Indianapolis, IN: Wiley.

Shneiderman, B., and C. Plaisant. 2004. *Designing the User Interface: Strategies for Effective Human-Computer Interaction*. 4th ed. Boston: Pearson/Addison-Wesley.

Tidwell, J. 2006. *Designing Interfaces*. Sebastopol, CA: O'Reilly.

Zeldman, J. 2007. *Designing with Web Standards*. 2nd ed. Berkeley, CA: New Riders.

MULTIMEDIA

Aronson, I. 2006. DV *Filmmaking: From Start to Finish*. Sebastopol, CA: O'Reilly.

Follansbee, J. 2006. *Hands-On Guide to Streaming Media: An Introduction to Delivering On-Demand Media*. New York: Elsevier/Focal Press.

Geoghegan, M., and D. Klass. 2005. *Podcast Solutions: The Complete Guide to Podcasting.* Berkeley, CA: Apress.

Horton, S. 2006. *Access by Design: A Guide to Universal Usability for Web Designers.* Berkeley, CA: New Riders. www.universalusability.com.

Larson, L., and R. Costantini. 2007. *Flash Video for Professionals: Expert Techniques for Integrating Video on the Web.* New York: Wiley-Sybex.

Richter, S., and J. Ozer. 2007. *Hands-On Guide to Flash Video: Web Video and Flash Media Server.* Boston: Focal Press.

Shyles, L. 2007. *The Art of Video Production.* Thousand Oaks, CA: Sage.

Videomaker. 2004. *Videomaker Guide to Digital Video and DVD Production.* 2nd ed. Boston: Focal Press.

PROJECT MANAGEMENT

Burdman, J. 1999. *Collaborative Web Development: Strategies and Best Practices for Web Teams.* Boston: Addison-Wesley.

Cohen, J. 2003. *The Unusually Useful Web Book.* Berkeley, CA: New Riders.

Duyne, D., J. Landay, and J. Hong. 2006. *The Design of Sites: Patterns, Principles, and Processes for Crafting a Customer-Centered Web Experience.* 2nd ed. Boston: Addison-Wesley.

Friedlein, A. 2001. *Web Project Management: Delivering Successful Commercial Web Sites.* San Francisco: Morgan Kaufmann.

Goto, K., and E. Cotler. 2005. *Web Redesign: Workflow That Works.* Berkeley, CA: New Riders.

Issacs, E., and A. Walendowski. 2002. *Designing from Both Sides of the Screen: How Designers and Engineers Can Collaborate to Build Cooperative Technology.* Berkeley, CA: New Riders.

MacDonald, M. 2006. *Creating Web Sites: The Missing Manual.* Sebastopol, CA: Pogue Press/O'Reilly.

Niederst, J. 2006. *Web Design in a Nutshell.* 3rd ed. Sebastopol, CA: O'Reilly.

Project Management Institute. 2004. *A Guide to the Project Management Body of Knowledge.* 3rd ed. Newtown Square, PA: Project Management Institute.

Shelford, T. 2003. *Real Web Project Management: Case Studies and Best Practices from the Trenches.* Boston: Addison-Wesley.

Sterne, J. 2002. *Web Metrics: Proven Methods for Measuring Web Site Success.* New York: Wiley.

SEARCH ENGINE OPTIMIZATION

Anderson, C. 2006. *The Long Tail: Why the Future of Business Is Selling Less of More*. New York: Hyperion.

Battelle, J. 2005. *The Search: How Google and Its Rivals Rewrote the Rules of Business and Transformed Our Culture*. New York: Penguin-Portfolio.

Kent, P. 2004. *Search Engine Optimization for Dummies*. New York: Wiley.

Morville, P. 2005. *Ambient Findability: What We Find Changes Who We Become*. Sebastopol, CA: O'Reilly.

Thurow, S. 2008. *Search Engine Visibility*. 2nd ed. Berkeley, CA: New Riders.

TYPOGRAPHY

Bringhurst, R. 2004. *The Elements of Typographic Style*. 3rd ed. Vancouver, BC: Hartley and Marks.

Carter, R., B. Day, and P. Meggs. 2006. *Typographic Design: Form and Communication*. 4th ed. New York: Van Nostrand Reinhold.

Chisholm, W., G. Vanderheiden, and I. Jacobs, eds. 1999. *Web Content Accessibility Guidelines* 1.0. www.w3c.org/tr/wai-webcontent/wai-pageauth.html.

Koyani, S. J., R. Bailey, and J. Nall. *Research-Based Web Design and Usability Guidelines*. U.S. Department of Health and Human Services, September 2003. usability.gov/pdfs/guidelines.html.

Lupton, E. 2004. *Thinking with Type: A Critical Guide for Designers, Writers, Editors, and Students*. New York: Princeton Architectural Press.

Spiekermann, E., and E. M. Ginger. 2002. *Stop Stealing Sheep and Find Out How Type Works*. 2nd ed. Mountain View, CA: Adobe.

Tinker, M. 1963. *Legibility of Print*. Ames: Iowa State University Press.

Wheildon, C. 1995. *Type and Layout: How Typography and Design Can Get Your Message Across—Or Get in the Way*. Berkeley, CA: Strathmoor.

Williams, R. 2007. *The Non-Designer's Design and Type Books*. Deluxe ed. Berkeley, CA: Peachpit.

Wilson, A. 1993. *The Design of Books*. San Francisco: Chronicle Books.

UNIVERSAL USABILITY

Adobe. *Adobe: Accessibility*. www.adobe.com/accessibility.

Arditi, A. 2005. *Effective Color Contrast: Designing for People with Partial Sight and Color Deficiencies*. Lighthouse International. www.lighthouse.org/color_contrast.htm.

———. 2005. *Making Text Legible: Designing for People with Partial Sight.*
Lighthouse International. www.lighthouse.org/print_leg.htm.

Brewer, J., ed. 2001. *How People with Disabilities Use the Web.* www.w3.org/
wai/eo/drafts/pwd-use-web/.

Brinck, T., D. Gergle, and S. D. Wood. 2001. *Usability for the Web:
Designing Web Sites That Work.* New York: Morgan Kaufmann.

Cohen, J. 2003. *The Unusually Useful Web Book.* Berkeley, CA: New Riders.

Connell, B. R., et al. 1997. *Universal Design Principles.* North Carolina
State University, Center for Universal Design. www.design.ncsu.edu/
cud/about_ud/udprinciples.htm.

Cooper, A. 2004. *The Inmates Are Running the Asylum.* Indianapolis, IN:
Sams.

Courage, C., and K. Baxter. 2005. *Understanding Your Users: A Practical
Guide to User Requirements, Methods, Tools, and Techniques.* San
Francisco: Morgan Kaufmann.

Henry, S. *Just Ask: Integrating Accessibility throughout Design.*
www.uiaccess.com/accessucd.

Horton, S. 2006. *Access by Design: A Guide to Universal Usability for Web
Designers.* Berkeley, CA: New Riders. www.universalusability.com.

IBM. *Human Ability and Accessibility Center.* www-03.ibm.com/able.

Koyani, S. J., R. Bailey, and J. Nall. *Research-Based Web Design and Usability
Guidelines.* U.S. Department of Health and Human Services, September
2003. usability.gov/pdfs/guidelines.html.

Lazar, J. 2006. *Web Usability: A User-Centered Design Approach.* Boston:
Addison-Wesley.

———. 2007. *Universal Usability: Designing Computer Interfaces for Diverse
User Populations.* New York: Wiley.

Mulder, S., and Z. Yaar. 2006. *The User Is Always Right: A Practical Guide to
Creating and Using Personas for the Web.* Berkeley, CA: New Riders.

Nielsen, J. *Alertbox: Current Issues in Web Usability.* www.useit.com/
alertbox.

Pruitt, J., and T. Adlin. 2006. *The Persona Lifecycle: Keeping People in Mind
throughout Product Design.* New York: Morgan Kaufmann.

Section 508: The Road to Accessibility. www.section508.gov.

Shneiderman, B. 2000. Universal Usability. *Communications of the ACM 43*,
no. 5: 84–91.

———. 2003. *Leonardo's Laptop: Human Needs and the New Computing Technologies*. Cambridge, MA: MIT Press.

Trace Research and Development Center. *General Concepts, Universal Design Principles and Guidelines*. trace.wisc.edu/world/gen_ud.html.

Usability News. psychology.wichita.edu/surl/usabilitynews.

W3C Web Accessibility Initiative (WAI). www.w3.org/WAI.

WebAIM: Web Accessibility in Mind. www.webaim.org.

Worldwide Web Consortium (W3C). www.w3.org.

WEB DESIGN

A List Apart. www.alistapart.com.

Cederholm, D. *SimpleBits*. www.simplebits.com.

Digital Web Magazine. www.digital-web.com.

Harrower, T. 2007. *The Newspaper Designer's Handbook*. 6th ed. Boston: McGraw-Hill.

Issacs, E., and A. Walendowski. 2002. *Designing from Both Sides of the Screen: How Designers and Engineers Can Collaborate to Build Cooperative Technology*. Berkeley, CA: New Riders.

Kalbach, J. 2007. *Designing Web Navigation*. Sebastopol, CA: O'Reilly.

Meyer, E. *meyerweb.com*. meyerweb.com.

Tufte, E. 1989. *Visual Design of the User Interface*. Armonk, NY: IBM.

Web Design Reference Guide. Peachpit. www.peachpit.com/guides/guide.aspx?g=webdesign.

WEB GRAPHICS

MacDonald, M. 2006. *Creating Web Sites: The Missing Manual*. Sebastopol, CA: Pogue Press/O'Reilly.

McClelland, D. 2007. *Adobe Photoshop CS3 One-on-One*. Sebastopol, CA: Deke Press/O'Reilly.

Roelofs, G. 1999. *PNG: the Definitive Guide*. Sebastopol, CA: O'Reilly.

Webster, T. 1997. *Web Designer's Guide to Graphics: PNG, GIF, JPEG*. Indianapolis, IN: Hayden Books.

Weinman, L. 2003. *Designing Web Graphics: How to Prepare Images and Media for the Web*. 4th ed. Berkeley, CA: New Riders.

Illustration Credits

Adaptive Path, www.adaptivepath.com (fig. 4.14)

Amazon, www.amazon.com, © Amazon.com, Inc. or its affiliates, all rights reserved (figs. 6.5, 6.6, 6.13, 8.13, 10.6)

American Memory, memory.loc.gov/ammem (p. 55)

Atlantic, www.theatlantic.com, © 2008 TheAtlantic.com (figs. 6.13, 7.7, 8.13)

The Art Institute of Chicago, www.artic.edu/aic (fig. 6.11)

Bank of America, www.bankofamerica.com, (fig. 6.6)

Capgemini, www.capgemini.com, used with permission © 2008 Capgemini SA (fig. 4.15)

Coastal Field Guides, www.coastalfieldguides.com, © 2008 (figs. 3.6, 7.15)

Creative Commons, creativecommons.org (fig. 7.20)

Dartmouth College, Dartmouth Computing, Dartmouth Daily Updates, www.dartmouth.edu (figs. 4.6, 4.20, 6.14, 8.4); Hood Museum, hoodmuseum.dartmouth.edu, courtesy of Hood Museum of Art (fig. 4.6)

Denver Zoo, www.denverzoo.org, courtesy of Denver Zoo, designed by Malenke | Barnhart (fig. 6.17)

Digg, www.digg.com (figs. 4.18, 10.9)

Digital Web Magazine, www.digital-web.com (figs. 4.11, 9.4)

eBay, PayPal, www.ebay.com, www.paypal.com, these materials have been reproduced with the permission of eBay Inc., © 2008 eBay Inc., all rights reserved (fig. 6.6)

Facebook, www.facebook.com, Facebook is a trademark of Facebook, Inc. (fig. 6.6)

Gartner, www.gartner.com, © 2008 Gartner, Inc., all rights reserved (fig. 10.5)

Google, www.google.com (figs. 1.7, 1.9, 2.3, 4.16, 6.3, 6.13, 6.16, 7.14, 8.3, 8.13, 10.4)

Hiram College, www.hiram.edu (figs. 6.19, 7.8)

Hotwire, www.hotwire.com (fig. 2.4)

IBM, www.ibm.com, © International Business Machines (figs. 4.19, 4.21, 7.21, 8.13)

Jeffrey Zeldman Presents, www.zeldman.com, © 1995–present, L. Jeffrey Zeldman (figs. 1.4, 1.6)

Jesse James Garrett, blog.jjg.net (fig. 3.10, pp. 8–9)

Kayak, www.kayak.com (from March 8, 2008) (fig. 10.3)

Kiva, www.kiva.org (figs. 1.12, 6.15)

Mayo Clinic, www.mayoclinic.org, © Mayo Foundation for Medical Education and Research, all rights reserved, used with permission from MayoClinic.com (figs. 7.3, 7.5, 9.2)

Microsoft, www.microsoft.com, Microsoft product screen shots reprinted with permission from Microsoft Corporation (figs. 6.6, 8.13, 11.1)

NASA, www.nasa.gov (figs. 7.5, 12.3, 12.5)

National Cancer Institute, www.cancer.gov (fig. 8.2)

National Geographic, photography.nationalgeographic.com, James L. Stanfield/National Geographic Image Collection (fig. 11.15)

National Institutes of Health, health.nih.gov (fig. 4.2)

National Park Service, www.nps.gov, the arrowhead symbol is a registered trademark of the National Park Service (figs. 7.24, 8.8, 8.10, 11.1)

Nature, www.pbs.org/wnet/nature, Thirteen/WNET New York, Michael DiMauro (fig. 12.1)

Netflix, www.netflix.com, reproduced by permission of Netflix, Inc., © 2008 Netflix, Inc., all rights reserved (fig. 4.18)

New York Times, www.nytimes.com, from the *New York Times*, January 29, 2008 © 2008, The New York Times, all rights reserved, used by permission and protected by the Copyright Laws of the United States, the printing, copying, redistribution, or retransmission of the Material without express written permission is prohibited (fig. 7.22); © 2007, The New York Times (fig. 11.2)

Ning, www.ning.com, Ning, Inc. (fig. 10.10)

Nothing But Nets, www.nothingbutnets.net, U.N. Foundation's Nothing But Nets Campaign (fig. 12.2)

Nova, www.pbs.org/wgbh/nova, courtesy of NOVA/WGBH Educational Foundation, © 1996–2008 WGBH/Boston (figs. 7.10, 12.4)

Nutrition.gov, www.nutrition.gov (fig. 9.3)

Opera, www.opera.com (figs. 4.13, 4.18, 6.18, 11.16)

Patrick Lynch, www.patricklynch.net, © 2008 (figs. 5.2, 5.6, 7.6, 9.1)

PBS, www.pbs.org (fig. 11.1)

Princeton University, www.princeton.edu, courtesy of Princeton University, Office of Communications (fig. 2.2)

SimpleBits, www.simplebits.com, SimpleBits, LLC (fig. 7.17)

Scientific American, www.sciam.com, reproduced with permission, © 2008 by Scientific American, Inc., all rights reserved (figs. 4.2, 7.21)

Universal Leonardo, www.universalleonardo.org, project created by Artakt, University of the Arts, London, web design by Keepthinking (www.keepthinking.it) and ustwo (www.ustwo.co.uk) (p. 237)

Universal Usability, www.universalusability.com, © 2008 (figs. 7.1, 11.18)

useit.com, www.useit.com, © Jakob Nielsen, reproduced with permission (figs. 4.2, 6.3, 9.4)

U.S. Forest Service, www.fs.fed.us (figs. 8.8, 8.10)

Wikipedia, www.wikipedia.org, licensed under the GNU Free Documentation License, www.gnu.org/copyleft/fdl.html (figs. 1.5, 6.6, 7.4; p. 54)

Wired, www.wired.com (figs. 2.1, 5.1, 10.7)

Yahoo!, www.yahoo.com, reproduced with permission of Yahoo! Inc., © 2008 by Yahoo! Inc., Yahoo! and the Yahoo! logo are trademarks of Yahoo! Inc. (figs. 6.16, 10.4, 10.8)

Yale University, Yale School of Medicine, www.yale.edu, info.med.yale.edu, medicine.yale.edu, © 2008 Yale University (figs. 5.1, 6.4, 6.12, 6.13, 7.25, 10.11, 11.2; p. 269)

Index

above the fold, 166–67, 198
accessibility
    application design for, 256
    development process and, 31
    forms and applications, 252–53
    multimedia and, 302, 305–6
    of navigation, 154
    page templates and, 202
    splash screens and, 169
    universal usability and, 51–52
Accessible Rich Internet Applications
    (ARIA), 253
adaptation, support for, 53–58
adaptive design, 172–73
Adaptive Path site, 107
additive color model, 272, 286
Adobe Photoshop, 229, 273–74, 277, 281,
    287
advertising, 156, 157
Ajax, 124, 126, 251–52
alignment options, 212–14
alphabetical organization of content, 75
alt-text. *See* text alternates
Amazon.com, 156, 164, 258
analytics. *See* web analytics
Anderson, Chris, 138
animation, 304–5
anti-aliasing, 205, 222, 229, 278, 289
application design, 253–62
    controls, 254–56
    design patterns and, 254
    error response, 260–62
    feedback methods, 260–61
    field labels, 257–58
    help and instructions, 258–60
    input fields, 255
    interactive technologies, 249–53
    iterative process, 263
    keyboard accessibility, 256

    menus, 255
    process for, 263–65
    prototypes, 264–65
    restraint in, 253
    simplicity in, 253
    text areas, 255
    wireframes, 263–64
archiving plan, 37–38, 283–84
Arial typeface, 218
art director, 5–6
audiovisual content, 27, 125, 176, 303.
    See also multimedia
auto play of multimedia, 311

backgrounds, 295–98
backup and archive plan, 37–38, 283–84
bandwidth issues, 26, 109–10, 274
banner advertising, 156
bitmap images, 275
blogs, 18
bold emphasis, 224
brainstorming, 74–76
breadcrumb navigation, 155, 158
brightness, 297
browse functionality of site, 79, 100
browser variations, 26, 59, 126–27, 308
budget, 46, 47
bullets, 185–86

canonical form in page design, 90–93
Capgemini site, 107–8
capitals for emphasis, 225–26
card sorting, 76–77
cascade hierarchy, 133
Cascading Style Sheets. *See* CSS
categorical organization of content, 75
cell phone displays, 56, 172, 191
centered text, 213
Center for Universal Design, 54–55

chartjunk, 228
checkboxes, 255
checklist, site production, 26–28
checkout baskets, 156
The Chicago Manual of Style, 114, 151
chunking of information, 77–78, 179, 232
click depth, 86
client-side scripting, 16, 250–51, 260
"cliff of complexity," 229
closure in visual design, 180
CMS. See content management system
codecs, 307
coding of site, 32–34. See also CSS; HTML
coherence in interface design, 118
color
    graphics, 272–73, 294–98
    harmonies, 297
    legibility and, 216–17, 295–98
    RGB additive color model, 272, 286
    terminology of, 296–97
    in typography, 184–85, 224
color-blind users, 184–85, 295. See also
    accessibility
columns, 112–13, 156–57
compression, 276–80, 303, 307
CompuServe Information Service, 275, 281
consistency
    in interface design, 12, 98, 105–7
    in typography, 211
    in visual design, 182
contact information, 157
content
    chunking of, 77–78, 179, 232
    client-side scripting and, 16
    domain experts and, 15
    editorial style and, 238
    front-loading of, 238
    graphics as, 268–72
    on home page, 166–67
    home page and, 163
    inventory of, 15, 72–77
    management, 16–20
    page structure for, 158
    semantic markup of, 121–27, 135–36
    server-side scripting and, 16
    typography and, 206–7

content management system (CMS), 7, 10,
    16–18
contextual help, 258–60
continuity in visual design, 180
continuum organization of content, 75
contrast
    design grids for, 198, 200
    editorial style, 236–38
    gamma, 273–74
    graphics and, 298
    in page design, 182–86
    in typography, 184–85, 224
    variability, 185
controlled vocabularies, 5, 73–74
controls, 254–56, 310–11
copyrights, 29, 158
crawler visibility, 138, 140–42
CSS (Cascading Style Sheets)
    advantages of, 207–9
    background graphics and, 298
    cascade hierarchy, 133
    code validation, 34
    graphics and, 291
    header navigation lists, 112
    HTML document structure and, 123
    leading control in, 216
    maintainable code structure, 32–34
    media style sheets, 134–35, 210
    page templates and, 202
    semantic emphasis, 226
    shared, 133–34
    site production lead and, 10
    site structure, 125, 133–34
    "skin" files, 134
    standards of, 151
    type size in, 221
    typography and, 207–10

Dartmouth College site, 164
database support, 27
data ink, 228
data rate, 306, 307, 309
data security, 46–47
date formats, 259
dead-end pages, 104–5
deliverables, 41

Denver Zoo site, 167
design. *See also* document design; interface
    design; page design; visual design
    canonical form in, 90–93
    critiques, 14–15
    evaluation of, 65–69
    iterative vs. linear process model, 71
    prototypes, 68
    satisficing in, 42
    universal usability in, 58–69
    user-centered, 52
design grids, 198–203
design patterns, 254
development process
    accessibility issues, 31
    backup and archive plan, 37–38
    information architecture, 29
    iterative vs. linear, 61
    maintenance, 36–37
    marketing, 35
    production checklist, 26–28
    site construction, 31–34
    site definition and planning, 26–29
    site design, 30–31
    "waterfall" model, 61
development team, 1–11, 43
diagrams, 270, 282–83, 287–89
dialog in interface design, 109
Digital Web Magazine site, 104
direct access interface design, 105
directory structures, 87–88, 129
displays
    cell phone, 56, 172, 191
    resolution of, 205, 270, 273, 285–86
districts in interface design, 98
dithering, 276–77
divisions, 135–36
document design, 123–24, 126, 171–77
domain experts, 15, 17
downloadable multimedia, 309
downsampling multimedia, 303, 307
down-style text, 225, 242
dropdown menus, 167–68
dynamic web pages, 16

edges in interface design, 98
editorial style, 231–47
    content and, 238
    contrast, 236–38
    front-loading content, 238
    for global audience, 239
    HTML markup and, 243–44
    keywords, 239–41
    links, 243, 244–47
    maintenance of, 47
    online style, 236–43
    page titles, 242–43
    prose structure and style, 231–36, 238
    rhetoric and, 240–41
    SEO and, 239–41
    text formatting, 243–44
    titles and subtitles, 241–42
    uniform connectedness and, 237
    voice and, 239
8-bit color, 276–77, 281
embedded hypertext links, 244–45
embedded multimedia, 312
emphasis of text, 222–27, 236–38
enterprise interface design, 117–19
enterprise web content management
    systems, 16–17
enterprise web identity, 152
Epicurious site, 197
equitable use in universal design, 54
error response, 260–62
Extensible HyperText Markup Language.
    See XHTML
Extensible Markup Language. *See* XML
Extensible Style Language Transformation
    (XSLT), 17
eye physiology, 192
eye-tracking studies, 90–91, 112, 144

Facebook, 23
feedback methods, 109, 260–61
fields, input and text, 255, 257–58
field studies, 64–65
figure-ground relationship, 179, 181
file compression. *See* compression
file formats, 275–81, 284–85
file structures, 87–88, 127–36

fixed width pages, 186, 189–91, 215
Flash format, 126, 140, 251
flexible use in universal design, 55
flexible width, 186–87, 191–92, 215
Flickr, 23
focus groups, 63
folder tabs, 111
"the fold" on home page, 166–67
fonts. *See* typography
footers, 116, 158, 195–97
forms and applications, 249–65. *See also* application design
frameworks in page design, 188–92
Franklin Covey Style Guide for Business and Technical Communications, 114
freestanding pages, 114–16
frequency of keywords, 144
functional stability of interface design, 108

gamma, 273–74
Gantt charts, 3, 4
Garrett, Jesse James, 8, 86
Georgia typeface, 218
Gestalt perception, 177, 180–81, 188, 237
GIF (Graphic Interchange Format) files, 275–78, 281–82, 284
global navigation, 154–55
goals, project, 11–13, 39
Google, 139–40, 143–44, 146, 155, 164, 188
Google Analytics, 14, 36, 109, 110
Google Docs, 21–22, 23
Google Search Appliance, 14
graphics, 267–99
    archiving of, 283–84
    background, 294–98
    bandwidth issues of, 274
    characteristics of, 272–75
    color and, 272–73, 294–98
    compression of, 276, 277, 279–80
    as content, 268–72
    diagrams and illustrations, 270, 282–83, 287–89
    dithering, 276–77
    embedded image links for, 129
    file formats, 275–81, 284–85

gamma and, 273–74
    hiding of, 291
    HTML markup of, 291–98
    integrated visual presentations, 270
    interface elements, 281
    interlaced, 277–78
    photographs, 281–82, 287
    for quantitative data, 270
    resolution and, 273
    role of, 267
    screen vs. print, 285–86
    size of, 197, 290
    strategies for, 281–85
    text as, 220–21, 289–90
    transparent, 278–79
    in typography, 227–29, 289–90
    vector graphics, 282–83
The Gregg Reference Manual, 114
Gutenberg z pattern, 90–91

headers, 104, 107, 111–12, 153–56, 195–97
headings. *See* titles and subtitles
hearing-impaired users, 302, 306. *See also* accessibility
height and width tags, 291–92
help files, 258–60
hierarchies, 73, 82–83
Hiram College site, 182
home link, 154
home page, 163–69
    on marketing materials, 35
    search and, 101
horizontal rules, 185–86
HTML (HyperText Markup Language)
    alt-text for graphics, 292–94
    code validation, 34
    content markup, 124
    document structure, 122–26
    editorial style and, 235–36, 243–44
    graphics and, 291–98
    header navigation lists, 112
    maintainable code structure, 32–34
    semantic approach, 135–36, 226–27
    SEO and, 147
    in site structure, 122–26

hub-and-spoke hierarchy structure, 82
hue, 184, 296
hypertext links, 103–4, 109, 195, 224, 244–45
HyperText Markup Language. *See* HTML
hyphenation, 213, 244

IBM corporate site, 118, 119, 197
icons, 185–86, 287
"id" attribute, 257
identity, web, 74, 152–53
illustrations, 270, 282–83, 287
The Image of the City (Lynch), 95
include files, 131–33
indentation, 216–17, 226
Information Anxiety (Wurman), 75
information architecture, 71–93
    brainstorming and, 74–76
    canonical form in, 90–93
    card sorting and, 76–77
    chunking information, 77–78, 179, 232
    content inventory, 72–77
    design guidelines for, 116–17
    in development process, 29
    directory structures, 87–88
    file structures, 87–88
    freestanding pages, 114–16
    hierarchies, 73, 82–83
    organization of information, 72–78
    site diagrams, 86–88
    site structure and, 78–85
    taxonomies, 73–74
    team role of, 5
    whiteboard sessions, 76–77
    wireframes, 88–93
information graphics, 269
input fields, 255
instructions and help files, 258–60
interactivity, 109–10, 126, 251–52, 257–60, 312
interface design, 95–119
    bandwidth issues, 109–10
    browse users, 100
    coherence, 118
    columns for navigation links, 112–13
    consistency, 105–7

    conventions, 110–13
    dead-end pages, 104–5
    dialog, 109
    direct access, 105
    districts and edges, 98
    enterprise, 117–19
    feedback, 109
    freestanding pages, 114–16
    headers, 111–12
    information design and, 113–17
    integrity of, 108
    interactive, 109–10
    landmarks, 99
    market positioning, 118–19
    navigation and wayfinding, 95–103, 104
    nodes, 98
    organizational context of, 117–19
    orientation, 100–101
    paths, 97
    search users, 100, 102–3
    simplicity of, 105–7
    stability of, 108
    symbolism in, 118
interlaced graphics, 277–78
internal page templates, 159–60
interviews for user research, 62–63
intuitive use in universal design, 55
inverted pyramid journalism style, 234–35
isometric perspective graphics, 287
ISPs (Internet service providers), 36
italics for emphasis, 223–24
iterative design development process, 12, 25, 61, 263

JavaScript, 27, 126, 251–52
JotSpot, 19
journalism style prose, 234–35
JPEG (Joint Photographic Experts Group) files, 279–80, 282, 285
jump-to-top links, 158
justified text, 213

keyboard accessibility, 57, 252–53, 256, 312
keywords, 141, 144, 239–41
Kiva corporate site, 48–49, 165

landing pages, 162
landmarks in interface design, 99
leading, 216
left-justified text, 214
legibility, 211–17, 295–98
Lempel Zev Welch (LZW) compression, 276, 277, 281
linear design development process, 61
line length, 192–98, 214–15
line spacing, 216
links
    descriptive, 246
    editorial style and, 243, 244–47
    embedded hypertext, 244–45
    home link, 154
    on home page, 166
    hypertext, 103–4, 109, 195, 224, 244–45
    jump-to-top, 158
    maintenance of, 47
    SEO and, 142, 146
    underlining of, 246–47
    visited and unvisited, 247
location-based organization of content, 75
long-tail of web search, 137–38
Lynch, Kevin, 95–96
LZW. See Lempel Zev Welch compression

Macintosh operating system, 218–19, 273–74
mailing address, 157
maintenance, 36–37, 47, 130–35
margins, 212. See also white space
marketing, 13, 35, 117–19, 152
markup. See CSS; HTML; semantic content markup
MathML, 124
media style sheets, 134–35, 173, 210
MediaWiki, 19
menus, 107, 162, 167–68, 255
meta tags, 147
Microsoft SharePoint, 22
Microsoft Windows, 218–19, 273–74
multimedia, 301–13
    animation, 304–5
    audio, 303

controls for, 310–11
delivery of, 308–9
design for, 310–12
downloading, 309
format choices, 312
keyboard interaction and, 312
preparation of, 307–9
processing of, 307
slide shows, 303
strategies for, 302–6
streaming, 308–9
text alternates for, 305–6
video, 303–4

naming conventions, 88, 128–30, 143–45
National Geographic, 269, 290
National Park Service, 200–201
navigation, 95–103
    breadcrumbs, 155
    browse functionality of site, 79
    browse users, 100
    districts and edges, 98
    dropdown menus, 167–68
    global, 154–55
    in header, 154–55
    home page and, 163
    interface design for, 104
    keyboard accessibility of, 57
    landmarks, 99
    links in columns, 112–13
    nodes, 98
    orientation, 100–101
    page templates, 162
    paths, 97, 168–69
    search users, 79–80, 100, 102–3
    SEO and, 141, 148
    site search as, 79–80
    tab-based, 111
    topical, 168–69
negative space. See white space
New York Times home page, 198, 199
Nielsen, Jakob, 90, 138, 152
"The Nine Pillars of Successful Web Teams" (Garrett), 8
North Carolina State University College of Design, 54–55

Opera corporate site, 106, 112, 113
operating systems, 26. *See also* Macintosh
    operating system; Microsoft Windows
organizational context of interface design,
    117–19
organization of information, 72–78. *See also*
    information architecture
orientation in interface design, 100–101
Orwell, George, 238

page design, 171–203
    document design and, 171–77
    fixed vs. flexible width pages, 189–92
    footers, 195–97
    frameworks, 188–92
    graphics, 281
    grids for, 198–203
    headers, 195–97
    interface elements, 91–92, 281
    length of pages, 194–95
    line length, 192–98
    SEO and, 142–49
    templates for, 198–203
    vertical stratification in, 198
    visual design and, 177–88
    white space, 186–87
    width of pages, 189–98
page structure, 151–69
    advertising, 156, 157
    breadcrumb navigation, 155
    checkout baskets and shopping carts,
        156
    content area, 158
    enterprise web identity and, 152
    footers, 158
    global navigation, 154–55
    headers, 153–56
    home link, 154
    mailing address, 157
    naming conventions, 129
    prose structure and, 232–36
    scan columns, 156–57
    search, 155
    site design and, 151–58
    templates, 159–69
The Paradox of Choice (Schwartz), 98

paragraphs, 216–17
paths in interface design, 97
path-splitting navigation, 168–69
PBwiki, 19
PDF (Portable Document Format) files, 126,
    141
perceptible information, 55
personas in design evaluation, 65
photographs, 281–82, 287
Photoshop. *See* Adobe Photoshop
Picasa, 23
picture superiority effect, 275
pixels, 273
planning process, 1–49
    advice for, 48–49
    content inventory, 15
    content management, 16–20
    design critiques in, 14–15
    development process, 24–38
    development team, 1–11
    dynamic web pages, 16
    goals, communication of, 11–13
    initial planning, 11–15
    market research, 13
    project charter development, 38–47
    static web pages, 15–16
    types of sites and documents, 15–24
    web analytics in, 14
plug-ins, 27, 250, 283, 310
PNG (Portable Network Graphic) files, 281
podcasts, 312
Portable Document Format (PDF) files, 126,
    141
PostScript graphics, 282–83
Poynter Institute, 90
process manager, 28–29
production issues, 39
project charter development, 38–47
project manager, 3
project stakeholder or sponsor, 2–3
prose structure, 231–36
prototypes, 29, 68, 264–65
proximity in visual design, 179, 180
Pulitzer, Joseph, 269

QuickTime videos, 305, 311

radio buttons, 255
raster format files, 282–83
reading gravity, 90
Really Simple Syndication (RSS), 18, 19–20
redirects, 141
resolution
    diagrams and, 270
    graphics, 273, 285–86
    typography and, 205
RGB additive color model, 272, 286
rhetoric and editorial style, 240–41
right-justified text, 213
RSS (Really Simple Syndication), 18, 19–20
rule of thirds, 90–91

sampling of multimedia, 303, 307
sans-serif typefaces, 218
saturation, 297
scalable text, 220–22
Scalable Vector Graphics (SVG), 124, 283
scan columns, 156–57
Schwartz, Barry, 98
scope and scope creep, 40–41, 43
screens. See displays
search
    editorial style and, 239–41
    interface design, 100, 102–3
    links and, 246
    page structure and, 155
    site editor and, 10
search engine optimization (SEO), 136–49
    basic concepts, 138–42
    crawler visibility and, 140–42
    editorial style and, 10, 238
    external factors, 139–40
    HTML meta tags, 147
    internal factors, 139–40
    keywords, 142–45
    links from other sites, 146
    long-tail of web search, 137–38
    navigation and, 148
    page titles and, 130
    site maps, 148–49
    splash screens and, 169
    submission to search engines, 146
    titles, 142–44

secondary page templates, 160–63
security risks, 24, 46–47
segmented text, 234
selective display, 174–75
semantic content markup, 121–27, 135–36.
    See also CSS; HTML
semantic emphasis, 226
sequential theme for site structure, 81–82
serif typefaces, 217, 218
server-side scripting, 16
Shneiderman, Ben, 53
Shockwave format, 126
shopping carts, 156
signal-to-noise ratio, 228–29
Simon, Herbert, 42
simplicity of design, 55, 105–7, 187–88,
    253
site construction in development process,
    31–34
site definition and planning, 26–29
site diagrams, 86–88
site editor, 10–11
site maps, 148–49
site production checklist, 26–28
site production lead, 7–10
site search, 79–80. See also search
site structure, 121–49
    audiovisual content, 125
    browse functionality of site, 79
    browser variations and, 126–27
    CSS, 125, 133–34
    document formats, 126
    document structure, 123–24
    efficiency of, 130–35
    file structure, 127–36
    hierarchies for, 82–83
    HTML, 122–26, 135–36
    include files, 131–33
    information architecture and, 78–85
    interactive scripting, 126
    maintainability of, 130–35
    navigation of, 79–80
    prose structure and, 232
    semantic content markup, 121–27,
        135–36
    SEO and, 136–49

sequential themes for, 81–82
site search, 79–80
themes for, 81–84
webs for, 83–84
size of type, 220–22
"skin" files, 134
Slate home page, 164
slide shows, 303
SMIL (Synchronized Multimedia
    Integrations Language), 124
spacing of text, 216, 226
spans, 135–36
splash screens, 169. *See also* Flash format
sponsor, project, 2–3
stability of interface design, 108
stakeholder, project, 2–3
star hierarchy structure, 82
statement of work, 41
static web pages, 15–16
streaming multimedia, 308–9
submenu pages, 162
subtitles. *See* titles and subtitles
success metrics, 41–43
Sullivan, Louis, 12
SurveyMonkey, 23
surveys for user research, 62
SVG (Scalable Vector Graphics), 124, 283
symbolism in interface design, 118

tab-based navigation, 111
taglines, 165
taxonomies, 73–74
technical support maintenance, 47
templates, 159–69
    department and program home pages,
        162–63
    enterprise use of, 202–3
    home page, 163–69
    internal page, 159–60
    landing pages, 162
    navigation pages, 162
    page design and, 198–203
    secondary page, 160–63
    site design, 30–31
    submenu pages, 162
    typography in, 203

text alternates
    in document design, 175–76
    for graphics, 292–94
    for multimedia, 125, 302, 305–6
    SEO and, 143
    universal usability and, 57–58
text fields, 255
time-based organization of content, 75
Times New Roman typeface, 217, 218
titles and subtitles
    bold emphasis in, 224
    down-style, 225, 242
    editorial style and, 241–43
    HTML markup and, 123
    justification of, 214
    page structure and, 158
    prose structure in, 234–35
    SEO and, 130, 142–44
topical navigation, 168–69
traditional typefaces, 217
traffic analysis, 36, 109
transparent graphics, 278–79
Tufte, Edward, 228
24-bit color, 272, 282, 285, 287
256-color images, 276–77, 281
typography, 205–29
    bold, 224
    capitals, 225–26
    choosing typefaces, 218–20
    color and contrast in, 184–85, 224
    CSS and, 207–10
    designed for computer screens, 218
    editorial style and, 243–44
    emphasis, 222–27
    graphics as, 227–29, 289–90
    indentation, 226
    italics, 223–24
    legibility, 211–17
    page templates and, 202
    semantic emphasis, 226
    size, 220–22
    spacing, 226
    typefaces, 217–22
    underlined, 224
    visual design and, 184–85
    web characteristics of, 205–11

UCD (user-centered design), 52
Ultraseek Enterprise Search, 14
underlining for emphasis, 224, 246–47
uniform connectedness, 179, 181, 237
uniform resource locator address, 116
Unigrid design system, 200–201
Unisys Corporation, 281
universal design, 52–55
universal usability, 51–69
    accessibility, 51–52
    adaptation, support for, 53–58
    application design and, 256
    color and contrast in, 184–85
    CSS and, 208–9
    design process for, 58–69
    evaluation of, 65–69
    flexibility, 56
    guidelines for, 53–58
    keyboard functionality, 57
    links and, 246–47
    scalable text and, 220–22
    text equivalents, 57–58
    universal design and, 52–53
    user-centered design and, 52
    user control, 56
    user research, 62–65
URL address, 116
usability. See universal usability
usability lead, 4
useit.com site, 155
user-centered design (UCD), 52
users, 62–65, 68–69. See also hearing-
    impaired users; vision-impaired users

vector graphics, 282–83
Verdana typeface, 218
vertical stratification, 198
Vignelli, Massimo, 200–201
vision-impaired users, 52–53, 184–87, 224,
    295, 302. See also accessibility
visited and unvisited links, 247
visual design, 177–88
    consistency in, 182
    contrast in, 182–200
    gestalt perception and, 188
    principles of, 180–82

simplicity in, 187–88
style, 187
typography and, 184–85
white space, 186–85
visual logic and typography, 206–7
voice and editorial style, 239

WAI. See Web Accessibility Initiative
"waterfall" design development process, 61
Web Accessibility Initiative (WAI), 31,
    51–52
web analytics, 14, 58, 63–64
web-based services, 22–24
web crawlers, 138, 140–42
web servers, 14, 27, 109, 308–9
web spiders, 138, 140–42
Web Style Guide site, 292–93
web technology lead, 6–7
web tools, 20–22
West Elm site, 196
whiteboard sessions, 76–77
white space, 182, 186–87, 212
width, page, 189–98
width tags, 291–92
Wikipedia, 18–19
Windows (Microsoft), 218–19, 273–74
wireframes, 68, 88–93, 263–64
World Wide Web Consortium (W3C), 31,
    34, 51–52, 293
Wurman, Richard Saul, 75

XHTML (Extensible HyperText Markup
    Language), 10, 123–24, 151, 202.
    See also HTML
XML (Extensible Markup Language), 17, 19,
    124, 148
XSLT (Extensible Style Language
    Transformation), 17

Yahoo!, 144, 146
Yale University site, 164, 202–3
"you are here" markers, 97, 99
YouTube, 23

Zipf curves, 138